Asphalt and Polit

Asphalt and Politics

A History of the American Highway System

THOMAS L. KARNES

McFarland & Company, Inc., Publishers
Jefferson, North Carolina, and London

LIBRARY OF CONGRESS ONLINE CATALOG DATA

Karnes, Thomas L.
    Asphalt and politics : a history of the American highway
system / Thomas L. Karnes.
        p.   cm.
    Includes bibliographical references and index.

    ISBN 978-0-7864-4282-9
    softcover : 50# alkaline paper

    1. Express highways — United States — History.
    2. Express highways — Government policy — United States — History.
    3. Express highways — United States — Finance — History.   I. Title.
    HE355.3.E94 K37   2009
    388.1' 220973 — dc22   2009036071

British Library cataloguing data are available

Cover image ©2009 Clipart

Manufactured in the United States of America

*McFarland & Company, Inc., Publishers
    Box 611, Jefferson, North Carolina 28640
    www.mcfarlandpub.com*

To Scott, who loves the open road and
has tried to drive them all,
and to Hunter, my new great-grandson,
who so far does not seem to care.

Table of Contents

Preface

Fifty years ago the historian Walter P. Webb composed "An Honest Preface" explaining why academics such as himself wrote books. The simple answers were: promotion, salary increases, peer prestige. Those tyrants once obsessed me, but no more. To explain, I would like to copy Walter and be honest about this book.

I had no dominating reason. I wrote for the fun of it. It turned out that the project was ill-timed, most of the writing being interspersed with several surgeries and more hospital stays than you'd want to count. As a result, many strangers went out of their way to help the manuscript along.

One other simple passion triggered this book. From childhood I have been entranced by the "open road." It leads you to places you have dreamed about and perhaps have seen photos of in the *National Geographic*. With my Dad, I often shared the thrill of watching a new highway ribboning across the Illinois prairie, then he would try to be among the first to spin our Ford's wheels on the sparkling white slab. To a little guy, waiting for the twenty-one-day curing period to pass approximated the agonizingly slow approach of Christmas. (Progress today means that you drive right behind the spreader and growl because he cannot pour asphalt at seventy miles per hour.)

So that's about it.

Have I contributed anything? Still being honest, I offer a firm probably. Some great coffee-table books on highways are available, and two or three good histories of the Lincoln Highway. I have used and cited them, but I do not compete with them.

My contribution resulted from the urge to try something different. That I have. Tempting as it may be to glorify our wonderful highway system, "there be dragons" as the ancient maps warned the early explorers.

The national government and every state in the union faces overwhelming highway problems, and every legislator in the land has heard from his public about the need for new roads and bridges and the maintenance of the old. Overhaul costs will be astronomical and may burden us for decades to come.

I have not written a "how to" manual. That probably cannot be done, given the variety of issues. But I have attempted to provide an historical background to our highway system and its problems, with an examination of the torrent of programs, legislation, and private actions to finance modern highways. I have seen no other work that investigates the failures and occasional successes of so many agencies trying so many ways to pay for so many roads.

I do believe that state departments of transportation could benefit from this book, for roads can still be built, and they will be. My research is as timely and as accurate as I could make it, and could help some DOTs avoid very costly errors. (I must confess that some of the legislation defies understanding, however.)

I am responsible for one smaller contribution to highway literature. Until the Eisenhower era, the United States had no southern counterpart to the Lincoln Highway, and, in fact, lacked much of a system at all. This, too, I have examined and tried to explain. (Military archivists have asked me to help them find sources for the southern convoy.)

For the historical chapters I have relied heavily on dozens of newspapers and magazines cited in the footnotes. Their homes range from Washington, D.C., to San Francisco. They were essential and they were fun to read as each town boasted of its receptions for the troops. (To a twenty-first century observer they almost appear to have been choreographed by the same Broadway company.) Equally indispensable were government documents, mostly from the federal government, but also from a broad variety of local agencies, all cited in the footnotes. Copies of, and discussions about, legislation abounds. Especially helpful to me have been the departments of transportation, national and state, in providing such documentation. The greatest resources for original documentation have been the Transportation Library at the University of Michigan, the Detroit Public Library, and the state archives of Tennessee, Alabama, Arizona, and Nevada. They are especially strong in biographical information

Flooding both federal and e-mail, I have been aided by the yeomen and yeowomen in state and county libraries who have done so much to help me and others in the past. Especially did they provide me with old newspaper accounts of military convoys and attitudes toward highway leg-islation. May the days of such folk never be numbered.

Personal help has come from an unusual group of people. I am tempted to copy the practice of one of my mentors, the prolific, pun-lov-ing Tom Bailey, who appears to have cited everyone who walked by his office while he was writing one of his many bestsellers. (I know that I sneaked into one book with no justification other than that we occasion-ally brown-bagged together.)

But lacking Bailey's prescience, I did not record the names of the many doctors and nurses at the University of North Carolina Hospital who were forced to listen to stories of highway progress day after day after day. You know who you are. Then at the Du Bose Health Center, another, smaller group took over. Here, I must finger a few more personal accom-plices. Some — Amber Bishop, Kristin Murphy, Lou Owens, and Dr. Davis Bingham — recognized feigned or incipient claustrophobia and depression and helped support my need for activity. But the moving agent was admin-istrator Sara Flynn, who said, "Do it," and it was done. Locally, at least, this was a first. I know not how many noses Ms. Flynn broke or how much trouble she incurred, but she saw that my hospital room was single-bed-ded and rewired, making possible the installation of my computer and progress on this manuscript. Perhaps only I understand the value of this attack. Forever, thank you, Sara.

The subject of computers requires a separate paragraph for Joan Bing-ham. I do not like computers or wire coat hangers. We tolerate each other, that's all. Ms. Bingham masters computers. (I have not asked her about the hanger thing.) She may be a genius. I do not know. But regularly my busy fingers apparently did things to the machine that should not be done or even rectified. Not to worry, bless her, she rescued me, often, promptly, usually with only minimal complaining. She installed, corrected, instructed, tolerated. She kept me in business. I still don't like comput-ers, but I like Ms. Bingham.

In the case of my daughter, Michele Bergeron, I would like to be able to invent the declaration that her contributions are too numerous to men-tion. It happens to be true. For one period in my life I considered myself pretty good at understanding and managing red tape, but no more. Ms. Bergeron, a successful businesswoman, has taken over. She brought me into the twenty-first century, translating language, people, machinery, agencies for me. Without her help I would still be cursing the federal gov-ernment and its minions — and getting nowhere. And Cajun though he may be, her husband, Scott, to whom this book is dedicated, was a calming influence on me, never tiring of listening to road talk. All families should have a son-in-law like Scott.

Every writer's "thanks" section, honest or not, bogs down when he reaches the spouse. I have thanked Virginia for other books, and I do that again. But only she (and maybe I) know her role with this manuscript. I not only have an honorary MBA in procrastination, I had plenty of fairly honest reasons for quitting. Virginia said, "You can do it." She nursed, nurtured, almost nagged. The lady spent hundreds (really) of hours visiting my hospitals, sustaining my morale. As the saying goes, she kept showing up. Without her efforts there would be no book. Simple as that. I have loved her for a long time. I still do. Thanks, V.B.

CHAPTER ONE

Good Roads

The roads of the Roman Empire were far better than those of colonial America; in 1756 a swift rider needed three days to go from New York to Philadelphia. The people of South Carolina learned about the Declaration of Independence a month after its signing in Philadelphia. In 1789, the first United States congressmen traveled slower and in less comfort than clerics attending church councils in the Middle Ages. Delegates from Georgia struggled through 800 miles of mud to reach the constitutional convention. Delegates from nearby states waited eleven days before achieving a quorum of seven states. Travelers went hundreds of miles out of the way to use coastal shipping rather than early American roads.

When colonials first began talking about separation from Great Britain in the late eighteenth century, leaders from the North and South were as suspicious of one another as peasants in a Balkan village. The differences came close to preventing a union, and then nearly destroyed it less than a century later. They were all Englishmen, but the religious dissenters who settled New England in the early seventeenth century differed in almost every way from the imprisoned debtors who settled Georgia one hundred years later. Geography and distance were to maintain those distinctions and even exaggerate them as the decades passed. Cultural differences were aggravated by 2,000 miles of wilderness with only trails to lead from one colony to another. With total logic, these people wrote a constitution whose article 1 provided for postal roads.

The transportation system of every nation, great and small, is a major element in the material wealth of that state; transport and growth are always closely related. It is a given that today's third-world countries remain that way, in part, because of inadequate communication and transportation. Conversely, rich nations such as the United States have reasonably mastered these problems and have built huge commercial empires within their boundaries. Domestic American commerce is continental as a result.

The vast American highway system has many ancestors — the paths of animals, Indians, stockmen, pioneers, merchants and the army. Most of these trails grew unplanned, as matters of convenience or custom; many were to leave their permanent mark on the land.[1] In the twentieth century, other forces began operating in more premeditated fashion to design our present network of roads. Technical improvements and the speed of production of the car made the old roads rapidly obsolete in the twenty years after the car's introduction in the mid–1890s. But within a period of less than two decades of the twentieth century, new, powerful groups provided the leadership, grass-roots support, political strength, and money to determine where our roads would go, how they would be built, and how they would be financed.

No one had to promote interest in roads; that spirit was older than the Lewis and Clark expedition. In 1842, rotund old John McLoughlin, chief factor of the Hudson Bay Company, complained to his British bosses that American wagons were moving into Oregon too fast. "They will turn their wagons ... and go over to Japan next. Those Americans will drive to China if the wagons would float." McLoughlin was right, and within the decade Oregon was American.[2] Today, twentieth century technology gives Americans an outlet for their love of the road, to go where few have been before, or to get there faster or more comfortably. The open road fulfills many dreams.

How did our modern road system come about? Who were the planners and the builders? How did they go about creating the modern American system of highways, sometimes to the point of costly excess? This is the story of the love of the American people for their highways and how we have now reached the point of choking on them.

In colonial days, towns and villages provided for their own dirt streets with perhaps a trail or two leading off toward another town. Generally these communities raised their own taxes for this purpose, not relying on any external government for such help. Some local jurisdictions borrowed the European corvee idea, whereby adult males would be required to provide a specified number of days' labor on the road each year. (The tire and rubber executive Harvey Firestone claimed to have done such work near his farm to pay a poll tax in his youth.) But such forced labor was not popular in an America where too many of the able-bodied could move on to the next frontier so effortlessly.

Public demand for better roads, especially for mail delivery and moving product from farm to market, manifested itself from colonial times, and varying schemes were tried to meet the need. The first regular mail was dispatched in January 1673 from New York City via Hartford and Springfield to Boston. With growing use, the trail became the Old Boston Post Road. The earliest scheme for designing and building a proper road was the turnpike, a road opened to passage by the turning of a spiked gate after the traveler had paid the toll. The best known and most successful of these, the Lancaster Turnpike, extended from Philadelphia to Lancaster in Pennsylvania. After four years of construction it opened in 1794, the property of a private corporation. Its nine toll gates proved profitable, sometimes paying as much as a 15 percent dividend. It set the standard for early roads and was emulated in state after state, especially in New England and the Middle West. Building material was cheap and plentiful, the usual choice being crushed rock mined locally — the finer the rock, the smoother the paving. Two engineers improved on this form of construction. John McAdam introduced methods of draining the subsoil to provide for heavy loads, and Thomas Telford added to travelers' comfort by sizing stones and using only small, relatively even ones for the surface. A generation later, both types of road might be tarred to cut the inevitable dust.[3]

By 1810, an estimated 300 turnpikes functioned in New England, New York, and Pennsylvania alone. But the growth of canals and railroads brought an end to the turnpike craze in the 1830s. Even the Lancaster Pike needed help from the state of Pennsylvania to finance an extension to Pittsburgh. The turnpike concept was not adequate for funding a vast highway network. Finding other means of financing was essential.

For much of the nineteenth century, the role of the federal government in meeting the demand for roads was heatedly debated in Washington and hamlets alike. Occasionally the national government permitted states to sequester receipts from the sale of public lands to pay for road construction. The generations of Thomas Jefferson and Henry Clay used the expression "internal improvements" when they referred to road- or canal-building or river clearance at the expense of the *national* government. Few people opposed these works, for adequate transportation could make or break rural societies. But most presidents and congressmen believed that federal expenditures for such work, even interstate roads, were unconstitutional. These strict constructionists could be pragmatic, even selective, in their philosophy, but generally this belief prevailed for a century, the occasional exception being based upon the national government's responsibility for defense and the postal service.

Most days, Thomas Jefferson was a strict constructionist in his attitude toward the constitution, but during his first term a budget surplus accrued, and its distribution became a major issue. In 1806 he rewarded his frontier partisans by approving a bill from congress calling for construction of a national highway. Costs of a survey were set at $30,000. To avoid the inevitable quarrels over which cities would get the highway, Jefferson directed that it travel due west from Cumberland, Maryland, in a beeline through the mountains for the Ohio River. In part the road followed the historic Braddock's Trail, so significant in George Washington's life. But local politics overruled Jefferson, and the National or Cumberland Road or Pike as it variously was called, had to be shifted to include Brownsville, Pennsylvania, on the Monongahela. Wheeling, Virginia

The Cumberland Road near Washington, Pennsylvania, as it appeared in 1910 (Library of Congress).

(which became part of West Virginia during the Civil War), became the terminus.

Plans were grand. The cleared right-of-way would be 66 feet, with drainage ditches bordering both sides. The roadbed itself was usually 20 feet wide, made of small stones packed to a depth of 12 to 18 inches. Cut and fill was the policy, with curves minimized. Bridges were made of stone as well, one single arch span in Maryland stretching 80 feet and pushing the limits of engineering know-how. Construction of the National Road did not commence until 1811, shortages of contractors and labor being common, and only ten miles were completed in the first two years. Immensely popular, the road carried pioneer families west and heavy freight wagons east and west almost as soon as work began. In 1835 the road reached Vandalia, Illinois, but by that time the federal government had shed responsibility, and the states had converted the national road into a series of badly managed local toll roads. The National Road was to have no counterpart.

A near exception was a road provided by the Maysville bill of 1829, for 60 miles of a very indirect extension of the National Road. This element of Henry Clay's American System lay totally within the state of Kentucky, Clay's home state. That alone was reason enough for President Andrew Jackson to veto the measure, but he could also declare it unconstitutional on the grounds that the road was purely a matter of one state's jurisdiction. (Jackson, who used the National Road traveling to and from Washington and The Hermitage, found less problem with that road.)[4]

During most of the remaining nineteenth century, demand for federal highway construction was minimal, the heaviest political pressure being exerted toward the building of railroads and the clearing of the log-and-rock-choked western waters. A revolution in transportation did not occur until the 1890s, bringing enormous insistence for better roads.

The unlikely source of this new demand was the bicycle. Its ancestry lies back in antiquity, most of the early versions requiring that the rider push with his feet on the ground, in a sort of uncomfortable, sliding chair. The first United States patent for a bicycle was dated 1866. Three years later the French developed the first chain drive bike, but it was slow in attaining popularity. Initially and briefly, the "ordinary" was the bike of choice, the front wheel of 40 to 60 inches in diameter providing the best propulsion. But the ordinary was hard to manage and required long legs. Within four years, gears and sprockets had been improved enough so that the ordinary was replaced by the "safety."

Pope began manufacturing these in the U.S. in 1877; within a decade the ordinary was no longer being built. Just as important was Dunlop's innovation of the pneumatic tire, introduced about 1888. More or less modern design of bikes was accomplished by the mid–1890s, and these vast improvements resulted in huge sales. Now that the bike was safe and comfortable, its popularity seemed unlimited. Sales in the late 1890s exceeded $27 million annually in the United States, a figure not reached again until the 1930s.[5]

But everything was not well in the bicycle world. Bikers were most unhappy with their roads. While some asphalt had been utilized on New York streets in the 1870s, and Portland cement was introduced about 1894, most towns had few hard surface roads. Nationally, perhaps 10 percent of streets and highways had any kind of hard surface. Usually confined to a few blocks at home, bikers commenced complaining about dust and worse — mud. As their numbers swept into the millions they sought strength in organization.

Thus the movement for good roads in America curiously pre-dated the auto. In 1892 the American Wheelmen began publishing *Good Roads* magazine, catering to the interests of an alleged 10 million bikers in the country. (This was one year before the Duryea brothers first drove their pioneering car on the streets of Springfield, Massachusetts.) Meanwhile, some states were holding road conventions, and Missouri, in 1891, organized a good roads association, soon to be copied by other states. Three years later, eleven states sent delegates to the first national congress to discuss "good roads." A similar conference in Washington, D.C., prompted the two major political parties to put better roads in their state platforms. By 1915, thirty-nine states had active good roads associations of some kind.[6]

Of course, the entire impetus did not come from bikers. Farmers sought better roads to facilitate wagon travel in and out of town. But farmers were often ambivalent about better roads; few of them owned cars and had little interest in road programs that might raise taxes. More cars racing down the backroads meant more frightened horses or cows that would not give milk. Dogs, chickens, and ducks increasingly became casualties. Farmers particularly hated the young "Barney Oldfields" and show-offs with their mufflers cut out, their skinny tires cutting into the roads and blowing fine dust over farmhouses. A road quite tolerable to the farmer and his horse-drawn wagon became sorely rutted and impossibly muddy after a few automobiles chewed it up.

Urban America felt no ambivalence about the new machines, though. The Wheelmen of America had pointed the way to campaigning for roads, but the automobilist soon took over. The American public had been waiting for the automobile, it appeared. Duryea's first gasoline-driven car showed up in 1893; the first Ford in 1896. The first Madison Square Garden auto show was held in 1900. The following year, Ransom Olds employed the first system of mass production, turning out 1,500 Oldsmobiles. Cadillac and Buick were organized in 1902. Costs were kept in line, largely. A trade journal estimated in 1900 that a horse and buggy would cost nearly $500, and annual expenses would average $180. By comparison, the first Oldsmobiles sold for $650, a small differential. In the next three years, Olds sold 12,500 cars. In 1899, William Allen White had a car shipped by rail to his home in Emporia, allegedly the first auto west of the Mississippi. A powerful valve-in-head engine pulled Buick into first place in sales in 1908, even at $1,200 each. The future seemed so assured that in the same year a group of auto executives led by William Durant put together the giant General Motors, soon to include Buick, Oldsmobile, Oakland and Cadillac. Then Henry Ford, using vanadium and other light alloys plus ever more efficient standardized production methods, moved into the industry's lead. His Model T sales jumped from 1,700 in 1905 to nearly 15,000 two years later. Soon the car sold for less than $600. Nationally, passenger car registrations moved from 8,000 in 1900 to 1.25 million in 1913. New York State began requiring motor vehicle registration in 1901. Counties soon began taxing cars, and states initiated licensing procedures. The American Automobile Association was born in 1902. Cars, cars everywhere, but no roads.[7]

To remedy that was the purpose of the first National Good Roads Association meeting, convening in Chicago in 1900. No permanent secretariat resulted, but the association proved sufficiently powerful to get machinery makers to donate enough equipment and operators to fill nine cars of an Illinois Central train. In 1901 this "Good Roads Train" visited sixteen cities in five states, the free labor building sample stretches of gravel road of one half mile or more. After three months the donated road totaled about twenty miles. Not to be outdone the Southern Railroad, using Alexandria, Virginia, as a base, carried speakers some 4,000 miles to preach the good roads gospel in eighteen meetings or conventions, as they were called. Although many drivers still considered road-building to be outside the purview of the national government, a governmental agency played a significant role in bringing these tours about. This was the tiny Office of Public Road Inquiries, strictly designed by Congress to provide educational programs about roads. Significantly, it had been placed under the Department of Agriculture. Thus, the movement started by bikers to improve the quality of American roads was turning into a farm-to-market movement, taken away from the bikers by the sheer numbers of automobile owners.[8]

The grassroots movement needed only some leadership to pull the many groups together, and that was found in the Deep South in the person of John Hollis Bankhead, Sr. Bankhead was born in 1842 in northwestern Alabama, attended rural school and enlisted in an Alabama infantry regiment at the beginning of the Civil War. Wounded three times, he was promoted to lieutenant, then captain after Shiloh. Following the war he returned to his farm in Marion County and was elected to the state legislature in 1865. From 1881 to 1885 he was warden of the state penitentiary. In 1886 he was elected to the U.S. Congress and served from 1887 until 1907. On the death of Senator John Morgan that summer, Bankhead was appointed his successor. He died in 1920 while still in the Senate. At the time of his death he was the oldest senator and the only remaining Confederate soldier in Congress. In his 34 years in Congress, Bankhead was a popular, respected figure of considerable influence, especially in the areas of his committees' responsibility — rivers, harbors, and, most important, agriculture and post office and postal roads. He led in the establishment of the Rural Free Delivery Service in 1896, and in 1903 he helped engineer the merging of the educational Office of Public Roads Inquiries with the much more active Office of Public Roads. In that same year, 963 delegates, representing 24 states and various good roads movements created the United States Good Roads Association and elected Bankhead its president.[9]

No man was to prove more influential in the early development of an American highway system, but it would seem that his vision grew as time passed. Initially he thought only in terms of the farmers and small-town folks of the district that he represented, meaning improved mail delivery and cheaper hauling of farm produce to market. Perhaps his ideas expanded when he entered the Senate in 1907. Along with the usual free seed, he regularly sent his constituents advice on fixing their own roads. He aimed to send every interested person in the state a bulletin on "dragging," using a team of horses and split logs to level one's road. In one talk he declared that good roads would keep "misled boys from our American farms" from combining with the "scum of Europe" in the cities. Roads were needed to prevent that old devil, urbanization.

In 1906 he addressed the Alabama Good Roads convention at Birmingham, telling the faithful that roads represented the most important issue facing the nation. He revealed the results of his survey of fourteen states, which showed savings of two-thirds in marketing costs when road-building expenses were shared by state and county treasuries, not just the towns alone. And, he concluded, bad roads were costing the nation $600 million a year in spoiled or damaged produce. Almost alone among Southern congressmen, he began advocating some system of federal spending on roads.

Alabama Senator John Bankhead, 1911. In 1903 Bankhead became the first president of the Good Roads Association (Library of Congress).

Although he was clearly the nation's leading spokesman advocating federal aid to highways, Bankhead's two sons thought he should be doing more. The sons, law partners in Jasper, Alabama, criticized him for not taking more credit for the campaign. (The actress, Tallulah Bankhead, was the daughter of his son William, later to be speaker of the House of Representatives.) In January of 1908, John Jr. wrote to his father (now a senator) urging him to keep in front of the road issue while the Birmingham papers were "agitating" the question. "Don't let some body come to be the daddy of your child," he wrote. The old days were gone; his father did not appreciate the value of modern advertising. "Keep your name in the papers as doing something ... advertise!!!"

John Sr. took the advice seriously. He began by studying federal expenditures in the territories compared with those in the states. Bankhead thought that he was on to something. By requesting precise figures from the secretary of the treasury and the secretary of war he could show that the U.S. territories received better treatment from the federal government than did the states. He must have been disappointed in the replies; the U.S. had spent nothing on roads in Cuba during the occupation after Cuban independence and only $243,000 on railroads. The country spent $32,000 in Hawaii, all of that at Ft. Shafter; $800,000 in Alaska, and $230 in Puerto Rico!

Undaunted, Bankhead stumped the state and much of the nation for local roads as well as addressed the U.S. Good Roads Associations. Newspapers and magazines regularly quoted him, and citizens wrote him asking for copies of his speeches. His theme was clear: (1) federal assistance was essential for good roads; (2) such expenditures would only be temporary because significant savings would kick in after a few years; (3) the savings would come from lower production costs for the farmer and lower food prices for the city dweller by drastically cutting the expenses of transportation; (4) federal aid was constitutional so long as the rights of the states were preserved.

Bankhead found authority for this last assumption in article 1, section 8, clause 7 of the U.S. Constitution. The founding fathers had said only that Congress had the power to "establish post offices and post roads." That was enough for Bankhead. He now sought to document the need for better post roads. From the postmaster general he asked for answers to sixteen very specific questions about roads, costs, and rural postal services.

The detailed replies contain abundant material about early twentieth century mail service, but much of it is irrelevant here. Bankhead discovered that in 1908 there were more than 38,000 rural routes in operation; 25,000 of them 24 or more miles in length. Better roads would mean substantial savings because the Post Office had found that on poor roads in rugged country where horses were needed, the carrier's rate of travel averaged 3 miles per hour; on good roads, carriers driving autos averaged 7 miles per hour.[10] (The reader recognizes that in 1903 autos did not achieve excessive speeds!) Nevertheless, Bankhead could now contend that the postal service was being severely handicapped by poor roads, and the nation paid for that in mail costs. Calculating the average pay for a rural carrier as $866 annually, Bankhead estimated that the Postal Department might save as much as $38 million in wages by being able to use good roads exclusively. One can find many weaknesses in the logic of these calculations, but that did not matter to the postmaster general or Senator Bankhead; better roads meant more efficient government, and that meant huge savings. For the remaining twelve years of his life Bankhead continued to hammer on the theme that good roads saved on marketing and food costs, improved schools, and greatly reduced the expenses of rural mail delivery.

Bankhead proved tireless in his campaign. He introduced bills in Congress—bills that rarely left committees. He wrote magazine articles. He made speeches to anyone who would listen. When the Fourth International Good Roads Congress met in Michigan in 1911, its president ordered the printing and distributing of 10,000 copies of a Bankhead good roads speech. Bankhead even advocated the creation of a cabinet post for a federal department of highways. He made a major address to the American Automobile Association at the Willard Hotel in Washington in 1912. The Universal Portland Cement Company congratulated him on one of his bills for federal highway aid and sought permission to distribute copies. He meanwhile consistently continued to serve as an officer in Alabama or national good roads associations.

In 1913 Bankhead led an oblique attack on Congress with his bill for federal aid for highway construction. The bill bowed in the direction of postal matters as well as the preservation of states' rights; considered by the 63rd Congress, it provided for the construction, maintenance, and improvement of *post roads* and rural delivery through the "cooperation and joint action of the National Government and the several states in which such post roads or rural delivery routes may be established." The trick lay in the words "cooperation" and "joint action." To satisfy the many factions concerned, a formula was devised that factored each state's area, population, assessed property evaluation, and road mileage. Then each state was required to match the federal contribution. Months passed. Congress chewed on the bill as representatives argued their states' special circumstances—thin population, low assessment, vast distances, or unusual traffic patterns. The various good roads associations did yeoman work pushing for enactment, and they were given powerful support by concerned manufacturers. Nevertheless the bill rested in Senate committees for three years before final passage.[11]

Meanwhile the House of Representatives was considering the similar Shackelford Bill. In 1916, Congress merged the two bills and brought forth the Federal Highway Act, providing a total of $75 million to be distributed among the states on a matching basis over a five-year period. Bankhead's work was done. After a lengthy illness, he died of influenza in Washington on March 1, 1920, still in the Senate, still preaching the blessings of good roads.[12]

CHAPTER TWO

Where There Is No Road

There is something about the American that loves a road, and even when there is no road, American drivers will make one. At least, that seemed to be the case at the turn of the century. While counties, state legislatures, and Congress debated constitutionality, responsibility, and costs of rural roads, automobiles made their own. Sometimes the drivers represented military or corporate America; often they were freelancers — men, women, and small groups out for the fun of it, or professional drivers trying to get from here to there faster than anyone else.

From the 1890s, the better European roads had been luring professional drivers to take daring tours or compete in cross-country races. Some wealthy Americans participated in those activities and sought similar experiences at home. Credit for introducing the hobby in the United States probably should be given to the remarkable Charles J. Glidden.

Glidden (1857–1927) was born in Massachusetts. He got his start as a boy telegrapher, and by 1873 was manager of the Atlantic-Pacific Telegraph Company. Soon he was assisting Alexander Graham Bell's experiments with the telephone. Glidden claimed that he "was the first subscriber in the world to an exchange system," a private line he operated in Lowell, Massachusetts. He then organized and presided over several phone companies. By about 1900 he had become interested in both the auto and the airplane. He retired from the phone business and turned to organizing public tours and performing feats of spectacular driving. He served as a reserve officer in the aviation section of the Signal Corps during World War I, and made 46 balloon ascensions.[1]

Between 1901 and 1906, Glidden made the first trip around the world by automobile, ultimately covering more than 46,000 miles through 39 nations. In 1903, he and his wife, Lucy Cleworth, drove from Copenhagen across the Arctic Circle. The press claimed that they traveled 17,000 miles in 17 European nations that year. In 1906, the Gliddens drove in such exotic spots as Bombay, the Khyber Pass, Cochin China, Ceylon, China, and Japan before returning home. The attendant publicity sold the American public on what became known as Glidden Tours. At first he and his wife actually drove the cars on the tours, but the trips became so popular that the Gliddens had to develop a staff of drivers and cars. A tour could be composed of a family or a small group with hired drivers, the Gliddens thereby providing exciting experiences for the well-to-do vacationer. From 1905 to 1910, thousands of passengers rode in these tours annually to various scenic parts of the United States and Europe where roads were dangerous or barely existent. Especially popular were their drives in the Rockies.

Better known were the "races" that Glidden sponsored jointly with the American Automobile Association, organized in 1902. In these tours, groups of cars of all types and sizes drove together from one city to another and then back home. Usually they were required to carry 500 pounds worth of passengers or equal ballast. Drivers would be charged points for accidents, repairs, not maintaining the prescribed average speed, and so on. (In a 1907 tour, rough roads caused a contending car to throw the owner's son out of the car, causing him to "land in one of the Thank-you-ma'ams [potholes] and lose points." Frequently going where cars had never driven before, these tours were immensely popular with drivers and the public, and often used by manufacturers to showcase a car model. The scoring method made it possible for a small Maxwell to compete with giant Pierce Arrows, and the controlled conditions encouraged the participation of women drivers.

The first tour was held in 1904, the Gliddens leading a fifteen-car caravan from New York to the St. Louis Fair by way of Cleveland and Chicago. Each year the tour became more complex and difficult; in July 1907, for example, 74 cars — 35 makes with 300 passengers — left Cleveland for New York, chugging through Chicago, South Bend (twice), Philadelphia, and Baltimore. Score was kept on a series of accomplishments and requirements, including the usual four passengers. Twelve daily runs of about 130 miles were maintained for a total of 1,570 miles. Two weeks later, 55 cars arrived in New York, 21 with perfect scores in "the longest and most strenuous test anywhere." There were many accidents. For the third year in a row a Pierce Arrow was the winner. One woman, Mrs. A. Cuneo, evidently driving alone with ballast, finished, but lost points because her tough little Rainier struggled to the finish line with a broken front axle. As a group, the finishers averaged 19 miles an hour.[2]

Through such stunts as these, thousands of Americans learned of the glories of the American landscape and hoped for the days when any car and any driver could enjoy them.

What is believed to be the first attempt to cross the United States by car began in the winter of 1901, but the two men, driving a Winton from California, stalled somewhere in the Arizona desert and accomplished only a few hundred miles.

More successful was the effort two years later by a Vermont physician, Dr. Horatio N. Jackson, and his chauffeur, Sewell Crocker. Driving a two-seater, 20-horsepower Winton, the men left San Francisco on May 23 and reached New York on July 26, driving 6,000 miles over something less than a beeline through Oregon, Idaho, North Platte, Chicago, and Cleveland. The journey was not effortless; Crocker once walked twenty-nine miles for gas, and on one occasion they went thirty-six hours without food until a shepherd fed them.[3]

Reaching New York just a few weeks later was the team of Tom Fetch and M.C. Karrup, editor of an auto magazine. Leaving San Francisco on June 20, Fetch, who was sponsored by a Packard dealer in Ohio, drove his 12-cylinder, Model F Packard an average of 80 miles per day to New York. Fetch reported two flat tires and a broken front spring as his only car troubles. Fetch and Karrup took a much more direct route than had Dr. Jackson, and found the roads of Nevada and Utah especially difficult. Their solution was to place long pieces of canvas over the worst sand and mud traps and count on the big engine to pull them through. Jackson and Fetch each took about two months' total time or about a month and a half in driving days. A third team, L.L. Whitman and E.L. Hammond, also crossed the U.S. in 1903, leaving San Francisco on July 6 and reaching New York on September 17. They claimed that in Nevada's sand they had seen Fetch's and Packard's tracks. The challenge was now down, and other teams attempted to break the time record virtually every year before the United States entered World War I.[4]

Carey Bliss, whose bibliography gives unique information about these pioneer drivers, believes that prior to 1909 there were nine transcontinental trips, all with male drivers and with only one female passenger. But in that year a most remarkable young lady also achieved that goal. The lady was twenty-one-year-old Alice H. Ramsey, daughter of a ship captain, unusually capable as driver and mechanic. She received considerable publicity at the time and later described her accomplishment in detail in *Veil, Duster and Tire Iron*, published in 1961.

Ramsey had much help from support groups, but her trip was nevertheless a great personal achievement. She had established a reputation driving in various races and other contests in the state of New York, when Carl Kelsey, the sales manager of the Maxwell-Briscoe car dealership in Tarrytown, suggested the stunt to advertise the safety and convenience of the Maxwell. Kelsey, who considered Ramsey the greatest woman driver he had ever seen, proposed that his company pay the expenses and provide the Maxwell for her to drive. Various factory representatives supplied tires and parts, and John Murphy, a Boston auto editor, served as publicist and advance man. Murphy rode the trains ahead of Ramsey, handling public relations, hotel arrangements, and hundreds of details. On occasion he even hired locals to help pull her out of the mud, so Alice did not face great dangers of any kind. But she was the driver, and she was the mechanic. She was accompanied by a young girlfriend and two older women, sisters of her husband John Ramsey. None of the three passengers could drive, and they made a needlessly tight fit in the little Maxwell. Ramsey permitted each woman to bring one suitcase only, and these could be accommodated only by putting the luggage in the rolled-down top. Thus exposed to the weather, the women were forced to wear heavy, street-length ponchos and rubber helmets when it rained. Most of the time they were exposed to the sun and the blasts of the wind.

The car weighed 2,100 pounds and operated on four cylinders, developing 30 horsepower. Of course, it had to be cranked to start. The steering wheel was on the right hand side. The car had no bumpers, windshield, or gas gauge. Alice measured her fuel supply by raising the front seat, which covered the tank, and dipping a stick into the gasoline.

The women left New York City on June 9, 1909, and drove 76 miles in the rain to Poughkeepsie, where they spent the first night in a hotel. They drove within the security of the Maxwell Corporation, and John Murphy was never far away to help arrange for parts. But the magnitude of Alice Ramsey's accomplishment must not be overlooked. She changed tires — the work of about an hour, entailing removing the tube from the casing, patching, replacing, pumping. She cleaned and adjusted spark plugs; once she even repaired a broken axle well enough to get to a blacksmith. One purpose of the trip was to show what women could do with cars, and Alice succeeded magnificently. (The other three women did nothing but ride along; on one occasion, however, they yielded up tiny toiletry bottles from their suitcases, using them to haul water to the dry Maxwell.)

In eastern states, navigation could be accomplished by following guides called "Blue Books" which described roads in great detail and even provided information about lodging. The books told which roads to take and turns to make by descriptions of the locale — a large red barn, a bridge, a fallen tree. (Ramsey's party got lost when an autophobic farmer repainted his barn to fool tourists.) But no Blue Books had been written for the western states, and the ladies had no map at all from the Missouri River to California. Ramsey said she often merely followed the telephone poles with the greatest number of wires. In Cleveland they saw their first all-brick road. In the middle west many roads were of limestone, hard in the dry season, but very dusty. The Maxwell hit a peak of 42 miles per hour and covered 198 miles one day. Generally, the farther west the Ramsey party went, the worse the roads became. Then they began to meet heavy rain and mud. They crossed the Mississippi on a bridge of loose planks. In the vicinity of Sioux City and Omaha (they tried to follow a straight line across country but still pass through major cities) they encountered nothing but mud and frequently had to be pulled out by teams of horses. The sand hills of western Nebraska provided even worse conditions. They followed three men in a new Pierce Arrow across the unmarked high plains of Wyoming, then through the Wasatch range into the broad avenues of Salt Lake City. They gave the lake a wide berth, inching through the soft sands to the south toward Ely, Austin, and Reno. They crossed the Sierras at 10 miles per hour then luxuriated in the good roads of California. A ferry carried them from Oakland to San Francisco, where they were greeted by a "cavalcade of Maxwells." They had been gone 41 days. A wonderful accomplishment for Alice Ramsey, the trip did a great deal for incipient feminist movements in America. This was but the first of two dozen cross-country trips for Mrs. Ramsey; in 1960 the American Automobile Association proclaimed her "Woman Motorist of the Century." Pioneer and precursor, her exploits stimulated a new demand for cross-country highways.[5]

In 1910, two more women drove cross-country. Like Ramsey, Blanche Scott had a companion who did no driving, but she was accompanied by men in a pilot car from New York to San Francisco. At almost the same time, Harriet White Fischer toured from California to New York, but with a professional chauffeur. Both Scott and Fischer appear to have had dealer sponsorship, and each stayed fairly close to Ramsey's central route; all three cars, by design as well as accident, were anticipating the route of the Lincoln Highway, first announced in 1913.[6]

Several other women made news by driving cross-country between 1914 and 1916. Effie Gladding, who also appears to have toured Europe, left Stockton over what she called the Lincoln Highway, "a golden road of pleasure and usefulness," finding the Lincoln signs "everywhere." The signs were there, all right, but there was yet no Lincoln Highway. She merely followed a variety of existing roads that local people hoped would become part of the proposed road. Gladding said little about what help she received. She also appears to have been in no hurry, doing little camping but staying in the best western hotels, such as the Hotel Utah in Salt Lake and the Shirley Savoy in Denver, well off her shortest route. In Denver she traded her Studebaker for an air-cooled Franklin, test drove an electric car, then visited Boulder and Greeley before resuming the usual road through Ogallala, Omaha, Clinton and the upper middle west.

Gladding also said little about her drivers or passengers, but had many comments about those she met. She exulted over encountering other tourists every day. Many flew pennants saying, "Excuse my dust," or just boasting of their states' name. They all disliked the mud of the Utah Salt Flats. Many were in wagons. They left trash in the camps. She heard of two women walking cross-country but did not see them. A sign in Kearney, Nebraska, told her she was halfway home to New Jersey. She noted that in western Iowa many farmers already owned Fords. Joliet, Illinois, was fouled by factory smoke. She found the National Road to be in bad shape, but did not explain how she got through the mud or rock roads that everyone else encountered. Drivers were paying 18 to 45 cents a gallon for gas and getting ten or more miles per gallon, but using enormous amounts of oil, as much as two gallons a day in the soft going. Somehow, Effie had a fine time.[7]

Emily Post, deprived of her usual European trip by the war, was driven cross country by her son in a magnificent Mercedes, so long that it frequently had to make several attempts to get around the narrow turns of the Rockies. (The Mercedes' wheel base was 144 inches; the huge, modern Buick station wagon is more than two feet shorter.) At Winslow, Arizona, the two gave up on the car and put it on the train for San Francisco. Post published her experiences in a book the next year, telling, not surprisingly, much about what to bring along and what to wear, but little about the road they followed.[8]

The most venturesome of the women driving across the land in the first decade of such efforts was Maud Younger, who accomplished it with the least help and the least publicity. Younger (1870–1936) was the daughter of a world famous dentist, whose skill made the family wealthy and made it possible for Maud to pursue a number of interests. A small woman of much energy, she was a dynamic speaker who enlisted in such causes as women's suffrage and labor reforms. She was a tough lobbyist, labeled a "perpetual picket of the White House." Upon the passage of the Nineteenth Amendment by Congress, she took up the burden of campaigning for ratification by the states, often making three speeches in three towns in one day. In 1923 she was to help initiate demands for an equal rights amendment for women.

In 1920 she was legislative chairman of the National Women's Party, when her father died. The family had homes in New York as well as California, so Maud went to San Francisco to help settle affairs. The business concluded, she decided to return to Washington by car. A couple planning to accompany her backed out at the last moment, and Maud set out alone, in part at least because people told her she could not do it.

She was not only the first woman to make the journey alone, she accomplished the trip during a season of excessively heavy rainfall. She had no corporate sponsor hovering in the wings with parts, tires, and repairmen; she seems scarcely to have considered it more than another interesting job. She left San Francisco in November without fanfare.

An experienced woman driver had told her that helping one another was the law of the desert; Younger counted on spontaneous, non-institutional help, and she frequently received it — and gave it in return. On her first day she got stuck in the sands of the Mojave Desert. She was released by a young man who urged her to permit him to follow her. At the close of the next evening they had to part company; the man gave her his dog, Sandy, and went off in another direction. Drivers she met now warned her not to travel alone and to watch out for Nelson Canyon in Arizona and the mud of Kansas. She escaped harm in the former, but was delayed eight days by heavy rains in the latter at Osage, Kansas. When her car became stuck she merely sat back and read until someone came along to extricate her. Her longest wait on the road was thirty minutes. She always slept under a roof, but often traveled hundreds of miles without seeing another car. The practice seemed to be that whenever two cars met, the drivers stood and talked awhile before resuming their routes. She met health-seekers, ranchers, tourists, drummers, honeymooners, and a wagon train straight from central casting. She was slightly frightened by a lone Indian who appeared from nowhere and pushed her car from the mud for 50 cents. She even ran into another car, head on, in the New Mexico desert! She found women drivers more patient than men. She had some "trying times," but had fun. She reached Washington, D.C., on December 20, 1920, requiring 38 days to travel 3,500 miles.[9]

With so many people interested in testing the national roadways, fictionalized accounts soon followed. Probably the first of these was Sinclair Lewis's novel, *Free Air*, the romantic adventures of a young woman driving to the Pacific northwest, naturally being assisted in dangerous situations by a handsome young man. The hero drove a Teal, described by Lewis as a "bug of a car" and a "tin beetle," a curious precedent to the nickname for a Volkswagen. As far as the roads are concerned, the young couple found new Lincoln Highway signs, many drummers, bad roads, and bad hotels.

Since coast-to-coast travel was becoming commonplace, drivers soon sought to make the quickest run. Ray Harroun did not set any cross-country records but was one of the nation's first racing drivers, who retired to become an automotive engineer. When the first Indianapolis 500 was held in 1911, his employers at Marmon Automotive persuaded him to come out of retirement and drive in it. Using the first rearview mirror, steel wheels, and heated carburetor, Harroun won with an average speed of 74.5 m.p.h.[10]

The 500 brought many improvements to the industry and the fastest drivers now turned to the coast-to-coast race. In 1916, Bobby Hammond went from San Francisco to New York in a record six days, only to be eclipsed twice that same year by drivers in a Marmon and a Hudson, each using five days and a few hours. The coming of the war brought a halt to these activities, but the public was excited by the speed of the accomplishments and sought better and better roads that would be useful to any driver, no matter what the destination.[11]

In the first decade of the century, private citizens, usually supported by the advertising budget of the auto industry, had sought out the routes and reported on the road conditions of the nation. In 1912 the military made its venture into the use of the motor vehicle. The army wanted to test four makes of trucks by driving them some 1,500 miles over what was assumed to be the kind of roads found in combat. The worst roads the army could find were in the upper south, in late winter. The itinerary meandered from Ft. Meyer to Ft. Benjamin Harrison. The trucks carried military supplies, including mule shoes and sand.

After several equipment delays, the trucks left the District of Columbia on February 7 and encountered bad roads before reaching Alexandria, Virginia. Ice and mud forced the frequent use of block and tackle to pull the trucks out of ditches. Most streams and rivers had to be forded. Within a week one truck was sent home because of its inability to handle the water damage. One day in North Carolina, the drivers accomplished 98 miles, the longest achievement of the tour, but generally the drivers (apparently all of them civilians) concluded that the North Carolina roads were worse than those of Virginia. A "continuous stretch of deep mud and bad holes" meant an average of two miles per hour some days. Near Greensboro the mud was so deep the cars smashed their tail lamps. Much of the drivers' time was spent waiting for parts to replace those damaged by the roads. They spent an hour extricating one vehicle from a hole "right in the main street" of one unnamed town. Often they spent hours operating a block and tackle to keep the trucks moving. Near Lexington, N.C., the road was so bad the drivers left it for the higher ground of a farm, only to be accosted by the owner threatening jail for trespass. "Lawyers arranged to have the matter referred to Washington."

Just south of Lexington they bucked through one three-mile stretch of gumbo only by racing the trucks at full speed for a few feet, shifting gears and backing off, then shifting gears and ramming the muck again. Time consumed — one hour. From Atlanta into Tennessee they occasionally found good roads for brief stretches, but outside Chattanooga they encountered the Tennessee River, twenty-five feet above flood stage. The regular ferry boat service could not function so they hired a tug to get them across. They looked forward to the Nashville-Louisville Pike, an old, well-constructed road, but on driving it concluded that it had not been maintained for a century; most of the old roadbed was not to be seen. All that remained was the largest of the bone-jarring rocks.

After seven such weeks the trucks reached Indianapolis and got some publicity at an auto show, then were driven out to Ft. Benjamin Harrison. For the entire expedition, actual travel time was 37 days, an average of 40 miles per day, twice the time planned. (They had met three cars along the way.) The army learned a great deal about its trucks, but it also demonstrated that in the southeastern United States, at least, the army could not rely upon the roads to help defend the nation. But the time was not yet ripe for the military to ask for any major overhaul of the system.[12]

The value of good roads in combat was forcefully brought to the attention of the United States Army during the Mexican Revolution of 1910. The long-running dictatorship of Porfirio Diaz beginning in 1877 had brought unusual stability to Mexico and a friendly business climate that lured thousands of Americans and probably $1 billion in investment. But most Mexicans benefited little from the boom, and when the weakening general became too old to control all the factions, a combination of generals pushed him out of office. The new strongman, taking control in 1913, was General Victoriano Huerta, who resorted to murder to make himself president. This was too much for the democratic sensibilities of President Woodrow Wilson, who on moral grounds refused to grant Huerta diplomatic recognition. This released a whirlwind, as the many rivals, each supported by large bands of regional followers, moved against Huerta. In October of 1915, Wilson finally recognized General Venustiano Carranza as de facto president. But Carranza failed to implement any of the reforms that the revolution had promised the peasants and workers, and many of his followers split from him.

Mexico now turned into such military and diplomatic chaos that many Americans demanded that Wilson dispatch troops into Mexico to bring about some semblance of order. The most threatening of these episodes to the United States was provoked by a former lieutenant of Carranza, General Pancho Villa, an occasional outlaw and something of a reformer to the peasants of Chihuahua. In January 1916, to demonstrate Carranza's weakness and perhaps to insure United States intervention, Villa's forces slaughtered sixteen young American engineers traveling into Sonora to reopen a mine. Then in March he crossed the border to attack the sleepy little cotton-shipping town of Columbus, New Mexico. Another sixteen or seventeen Americans were killed, and the hotel and several stores were burned. Wilson instantly directed that troops enter Mexico to pursue and chastise Villa.

The next day Brigadier General John J. Pershing was ordered from Ft. Bliss near El Paso to take command of a "punitive expedition" with force "adequate" to rout Villa and punish him for his attacks upon Americans. (Nothing was said in the orders about trying to capture Villa.) Within a day Pershing was in Columbus with the first of what was ultimately a force of about 15,000. More than a year later, in February 1917, an angry, frustrated Pershing was back in Columbus without having done much harm to Villa's cause.

The fault was not Pershing's. The Carranza government, frightened by the huge number of Yankee troops, not only did not cooperate with Pershing against Villa, it placed severe restrictions on Pershing. The Americans were forbidden to use the National Railway and were limited to maneuvering in certain areas of trackless Chihuahua. To cope with the problems of intelligence gathering and an extremely long supply line, Pershing utilized the airplane and the auto for the first time in the nation's military history.

The airplane can be disposed of quickly; eight JN-4s, a single-engine biplane, were used for observation and courier service. The plane was to be used extensively as a trainer in World War I, but in Mexico it failed badly. Its propeller cracked in the dry desert air, and its engine lacked the power to clear the many 12,000-foot mountain ranges. Rather quickly they crashed and were discarded.

The truck story is different. Pershing left Ft. Bliss with a half-dozen Dodge command cars and two small truck companies. Three months later he controlled 588 trucks, 57 tankers, 10 motor machine shop trucks, 6 wreckers, 75 autos, 61 motorcycles, and 8 tractors. On one occasion, Lieutenant George S. Patton, with 15 men and three lightly armored cars, attacked a Villista ranch, killing four supporters of the general, in the first U.S. motorized attack. Most of the time the vehicles were used for supply, troop movement, and reconnaissance, however. As they did with civilian cross-country trips, car manufacturers played a major role. Eager to gain publicity as well as to test the cars, eight different builders provided 13 different types of trucks; the best performers were White, Packard, Jeffrey Quads, and Four Wheel Drives. Civilian and military sales became so great that these companies could not meet the demand for the next few years. Pershing consistently used "Betsy," his Dodge command car, and was reported to have taken it to France the same year. No doubt was left that the motorized vehicle would play a major part in future wars. But it did little to help Pershing in Mexico; Chihuahua's roads were nothing but trails and wagon ruts. Pershing's cars could not follow Villa's cavalry. Again the lesson was abundantly clear — the army had to have good roads.[13]

The lesson was repeated in France, later, in 1917 and 1918. Compared with American highways, the French roads were quite good, generally maintained with pride by local governments. But they were not meant to carry heavy trucks and artillery, and they turned to notorious mud in the heavy rains of the winter of 1917. At first labor battalions and prisoners of war maintained the roads of France, but wartime destruction was beyond their capacity; in the first five months of 1919 American forces repaired some 10,000 kilometers of roads damaged by American traffic.

Pershing, now commanding general of the American Expeditionary Force, originally estimated he would need 50,000 vehicles. Before the

The first Packard truck in a convoy of 28 enters McConnellsburg, Pennsylvania, en route from Detroit to Baltimore for shipment to France, December 1917 (State of Michigan).

The Packard truck convoy enters Baltimore, having traveled 580 miles from Detroit (State of Michigan).

armistice, 118,000 were purchased, provided by 216 different makers. General Motors sent 90 percent of its wartime production to the military — some 8,500 vehicles. Cadillac alone sent 2,350 staff cars. A lack of shipping capacity was to keep thousands of vehicles at ports of embarkation until war's end.[14]

Along with their combat memories, most American doughboys returned home with tales of mud and their efforts to keep vehicles moving when roads failed. And they came home to an America that hungered for the normality that would bring every family its car and good roads to make the car enjoyable. Not by coincidence did GM begin installment plan sales in 1919.

Tire companies also made their contribution to the highway knowledge of the American people. Apparently the first trucks to cross the United States were two Packards, property of Goodyear. In September of 1918 the trucks brought loads of pneumatic tires for airplanes from Boston to San Diego, taking three weeks. They returned almost immediately, bringing Arizona cotton back to Akron. The trip was becoming routine for the well-prepared.

The venturesome, whether woman or man, civilian or military, in search of profit or fun, thoroughly probed the nation's geography by car before 1920. They were but the precursors of millions. But in the first quarter of the twentieth century, every one of our drivers found the roads badly wanting. Could the road builders catch the car makers? Some strong-minded, powerful leadership was needed, and it came along just in time.

CHAPTER THREE

The Lincoln Highway Association

Carl Fisher had too much energy to confine himself to one career. His Prest-o-Lite Company, founded in 1904 to manufacture the first reliable automobile head lamps, was bringing him a fortune. In 1909 he opened and directed the Indianapolis Speedway, in its time the world's finest testing ground, and soon to become the world's ultimate race track. Now the one-time Hoosier newsboy, who dropped out of a one-room school house at age 12, had a new, grand plan. In September of 1912 he persuaded a number of men, leaders in the auto and related industries, to meet with him in Detroit to listen to his design for making them all even richer. Moreover, it would be good for the nation.[1]

He called their attention to the growing numbers of wealthy Americans who traveled to Europe each summer to take one of the automobile tours with professional drivers. Now, at home, the Glidden Tours and others were moving people through regions of America almost totally lacking in decent roads. A new market, tourism, was being discovered in America. He pointed out the volume of cars, tires, and parts that would be sold if only the highways were available. But — he reminded them — states' rights questions, entrenched interests, and the surprising apathy of much of the public meant that great opportunities would be missed if the dealers sat around waiting for the demand to develop.

Initially Fisher planned for a single great highway, passing through or near the major industrial cities from New York to San Francisco. He called it the "Coast-to-Coast Rock Highway." The American Automobile Association had proposed a similar highway back in 1902, but the plan went nowhere because it included no method of funding. Fisher thought that the affected towns and counties would be willing to provide labor and machinery to help with construction if the industry would raise the necessary cash for design and materials. He estimated the highway could be completely built and graveled for $10 million. Fisher suggested to the attentive executives that the answer lay in creating a strong organization of businessmen to appropriate the money and direct its expenditure. Then the road would be built. Would his business friends raise the $10 million?

The response was as prompt as it was gratifying to Fisher. Little Frank Seiberling, president of Goodyear Tire, got the giving underway with a check for $300,000; Henry B. Joy of Packard donated $150,000. Roy Chapin of Hudson and John Willys of Willys Overland joined in comparably. One banquet of Indianapolis (an early automobile manufacturing center) businessmen raised $300,000. Members of the association of Portland Cement manufacturers offered a gift of thousands of barrels of cement. (Evidence is lacking, but this may have been a pleasant surprise to Fisher. He had not proposed a concrete road.) The cement and car industries voted annual assessments on their memberships to build the fund. In one month, $1 million dollars was raised by auto and road men alone.

The only holdout was a serious one. Henry Ford, builder of perhaps three-fourths of the cars in America at that time, gave nothing. It was a difference in philosophy. Ford feared the potential for elitism in the car builders — correctly, it turned out. Since the public would use the roads, the public should choose their location and pay for them. Some years later, his son Edsel made a personal contribution and even served on the board administering the fund, but Henry never participated in Fisher's plan in any manner. Fisher went on without Henry Ford.[2]

Popular support for the road was to be encouraged, and the car builders next began devising methods to get towns and private citizens to pay a share too. But first the organization had to be formed. Several meetings were held in Detroit in early 1913, usually chaired by Fisher and hosted by Henry Joy, who soon made it clear that he had ideas independent from Fisher's. The leaders eliminated Fisher's homely proposed road name and subscribed to Joy's suggestion of honoring Abraham Lincoln, as the person best signifying the national import of the road. So they agreed upon a Lincoln Highway and created a Lincoln Highway Association. It began its official life in Detroit's Dime Savings Bank Building, henceforth the national headquarters of the LHA, on July 1, 1913.

They had a name and an organization with money. How would it be run? That same day they created their first board of directors. The president was Henry B. Joy, president of Packard Motor Company and director of the Federal Reserve Board of Chicago and many other prestigious boards. Vice presidents were Roy Chapin, once sales manager of Olds, then of Chalmers Motor Company and currently president of Hudson, later to be in Herbert Hoover's cabinet, and Arthur Pardington, member of the association that built the Long Island Motor Parkway and superintendent of the Methodist Hospital in Brooklyn. The treasurer was Emory Clark, president of First National Bank of Detroit. Like all the officers, he served on many other boards. Clark remained treasurer for the entire life of the Lincoln Highway Association. Henry Bodman, Joy's personal attorney, was retained as counsel to the board. These men would determine policy, raise money, and work with governments and any other agencies with an interest in roads. Next, someone was needed to carry out these policies, plot the road, and deal with the public.[3]

The officers made a superb find in Henry C. Ostermann, another Hoosier. Evidently an orphan, at age six he sold papers, and at nine was a bell boy. He tried a hitch in the Navy, then held many odd jobs — as stage hand and extra with Buffalo Bill's show, flagman, conductor. In 1906 he invented a grain door for freight cars and went into business manufacturing them. In 1913 he was an auto dealer in Deadwood, S.D., when the LHA found him. He became field secretary, retaining that post until he was killed in a car wreck in 1920. He drove across the country many times, getting pledges for the LHA fund and signing up members. Almost incidentally, he, more than anyone, personally determined where the highway would go, as his many travels taught him the possibilities — and impossibilities of the terrain.[4]

Where in this administration was Carl Fisher, who had conceived the plan? He and Joy were beginning to disagree on policies, the first of which was where the road would go. As we have seen, back in 1903, Tom Fetch had driven to California by way of Kansas and Colorado. He reported to Joy that the Rocky Mountains were virtually impassable for cars, and he would recommend that future drivers take advantage of Wyoming's South Pass, just as our ancestors had done with wagons. But Fisher wanted a national highway that would be as scenic as possible, and he sought to convince Joy that the Rockies were manageable.

On the same day that the LHA created its board, Fisher was organizing a convoy for the coast. Pardington liked the plan, but Joy disapproved. Fisher obtained enough support from a number of Indiana car makers, the AAA, and the Hoosier Motor Club to ignore the LHA. Well-managed, the Hoosier Tour had 17 cars and 2 trucks, carrying 70 men — drivers (including professional racers such as Ray Harroun, inventor of the rearview mirror, chief engineer for Marmon, and winner of the first Indianapolis 500), mechanics, much of the press, representatives of AAA and the Blue Book map makers. And Fisher. Their goal — California, by way of Colorado.

The public became greatly confused. Fisher was considered a spokesman for the Lincoln Highway. That organization had not yet delineated its full route, but it had never indicated a preference for the tough Colorado passes. Joy was annoyed. The picture was made muddier by Fisher, whose caravan not only drove over the 11,000-foot Berthoud Pass west of Denver, but seemed to be wandering aimlessly around the Rockies visiting most of the sizeable cities.

In their eagerness to have the road builders shine upon them, many towns graded and graveled nearby portions of road to insure the convoy's stopping by. In Colorado, the convoy was refueled by citizens driving a horse-drawn gasoline wagon that labored seventy miles to provide the gas and then did not charge for fuel or delivery. The mayor of Price, Utah, urged his whole town to come out with shovels, picks, or food to greet the drivers. Almost everyone complied. Fisher encouraged these enthusiastic receptions, but he made the route even more bewildering by splitting the convoy at Bishop, California, with half going to Los Angeles, and half to San Francisco. The convoys received tumultuous welcomes, 1,200 cars meeting the latter contingent at Oakland.[5]

As a public relations stunt the convoy became an instant success, but it definitively strained the relations between Fisher and Joy. Fisher was not fitting into the harness that this group of businessmen fashioned for him and his free-wheeling ways. (Increasingly, Fisher fell out of step with his colleagues and became an advocate of the construction of many highways, not the single perfect one of the LHA agenda. He retained his board position, but never held office in the LHA again. When the First World War broke out, President Wilson asked Fisher to serve by laying out flight paths and landing fields for military planes.) The route Fisher's convoy had taken did not fit the prescription for the most direct, straight road so often discussed by the LHA. Some sort of demurrer was in order. The young LHA acted promptly and decisively.

No mere announcement came forth; on September 14, 1913, newspapers all over the land received a "proclamation" from the Dime Savings Bank offices, a statement outlining the official Lincoln Highway route.

The great road — mostly just on paper — began in New York City, then moved through Jersey City, Newark, Philadelphia, Gettysburg, Pittsburgh, Canton, Mansfield, Lima, Ft. Wayne, South Bend, Chicago Heights, Joliet, and DeKalb. It crossed the Mississippi at Clinton and proceeded to Omaha, Grand Island, North Platte and Kimball, in far western Nebraska. Here the LHA waffled and caused the route to jog down into Denver (Joy called it a loop), then took it back north to Cheyenne. Obviously designed to give Coloradans lip service, the loop was a sham. Before long, the jog was eliminated and the road was planned to pass directly from Kimball to Cheyenne, skipping Denver and Colorado entirely. It then crossed southern Wyoming through South Pass to Ft. Bridger, Evanston, and Salt Lake City. Another loop caused bitterness in Utah. Ogden was at first one of the anointed cities, but again the LHA changed its mind, moving directly to the state's capital from Evanston. Next, the road went southwest across the Utah desert, through various ranches to Ibapah, then Ely in Nevada. Another problem for the future stemmed from listing both Reno and Carson City — an obvious complication — followed by Sacramento, Oakland, and San Francisco.

The proclamation was signed by the officers and directors, who confidently asked public officials to rename roads and signs with the "official" Lincoln title. Copies were sent to President Woodrow Wilson, the Congress, and all the state legislatures. (Wilson responded with his membership check.) The heavy clerical burden of spreading the news to the world fell upon employees of Packard, who stayed up all night finishing the job at Joy's behest. Pushing their conceit a bit more, the LHA asked the state governors to make October 31 a national holiday in honor of the road.

That did not happen, needless to say. But memberships poured in, at $5 a head. Field secretary Ostermann signed up a dozen or so state consuls who had the power to recruit members, as well as other consuls, all spreading the word, raising money, and demonstrating the association's power. In time, about 250 consuls were active in the United States, many serving the full possible fourteen years.

Although signs — literal and figurative — of a Lincoln Highway could be found in many eastern communities, there was no true highway, only short, local stretches of road and maps. Work had to be done. The LHA sought ways to get additional mileage, graveled or paved, in as many places as possible, as quickly as possible.

The first step was Joy's ingenious idea known as seedling miles. Interested towns could request LHA approval of their plan including location, drainage, sub-surface work, and a promise of future maintenance of one

mile of sixteen-foot (changed to eighteen in 1918) highway. The town —
or county — would perform the labor and provide equipment, frequently
state-owned. The Portland Cement Association, through the LHA, would
supply the cement needed to build the road, free of cost. The wholesale
price varied somewhat during the active years, but it appears that one mile
would use about 3,000 barrels at a cost of some six or seven thousand dollars. The first seedling mile was begun in October 1914, near Malta, Illinois. Several more were built in the next few years, Nebraska seeming to
have received the greatest share. Fremont, Nebraska, got six miles in this
manner, the largest number ever awarded. After 1919, the Portland people declined to give away more cement, and no more seedling miles were
poured, but the example had been set. The public enthused over them,
many folks spending Sunday afternoon driving their Model T back and
forth on their town's lone paved mile. As Joy surmised, the seedlings served
as a prod to county officials, and they set the national standard for thousands of miles to come.

Joy, who bore the rank of colonel for service in Washington during
the war, had another plan; he proposed that German prisoners of war be
put to work building the Lincoln Highway. Although he received the support of influential Senator Warren Harding, Joy's plan went nowhere.

The LHA also conceived of an "Ideal Section," a consequence of the
building boom following the World War I armistice. Desiring to take a
further lead in setting road standards, the LHA convoked a consultation
of engineers in December 1920. After days of discussion they recommended
a 110-foot right-of-way and a four-lane road, 40 feet wide plus shoulders.
The concrete would be 10 inches thick, steel reinforced, able to carry 15,000
cars and 5,000 trucks every day at speeds of 35 and 10 miles per hour,
respectively. There would be road signs and rest stops but no advertising.
Such a section was actually built, opening for traffic in December 1922. It
began at Dyer in western Indiana and stretched eastward a distance of
some 7,161 feet toward Schererville. Briefly, the road was even illuminated.
No American road had ever been built to such specifications before. (In
time it was merged into U.S. 30.) Its cost of $166,665 was met by a gift
of $110,000 from U.S. Rubber and an Indiana state contribution of
$33,000, and the balance came from Lake County, Indiana. No other
"ideal section" seems to have been built.[6]

The LHA had told the nation where its major national highway would
go; now was the time to mark it out. Gulf Oil Company had introduced
something like a modern highway map in 1913 for the eastern states. That

system was gradually expanded, but the men at Dime Bank wanted something more substantial that all could see. Beginning in 1917, the association published Lincoln Highway Forum, distributed to consuls and members, describing local road conditions, but not providing a true map of the road.

Several major campaigns were sponsored to delineate the road coast to coast. For the first few years, signs painted on rocks and poles sufficed. The LHA provided stencils, and in typical fashion, persuaded Patton Sun Proof to donate the paint and Wooster Brush the brushes. Consuls and volunteers painted the red, white, and blue stripes with a large "L" in the middle. Sometimes "Lincoln Highway" would be printed above and below the "L." But the paint was not always sun proof, and often faded away. Metal signs were tried; utility companies objected to these on their poles, especially since they encouraged target practice among farm youths. By the fall of 1916, eight thousand small wooden markers had been placed to the Wyoming line, and by 1921, coast to coast. But where the roads were poor, drivers tended to dig up the poles to use as levers for stuck cars, and local citizens found the poles excellent firewood. The last effort came in 1928. By stressing the Lincoln theme, the LHA secured federal approval to put concrete and bronze busts of Honest Abe — and a pointing arrow — across the land. Most of the work was accomplished by the Boy Scouts of America. On one day — September 1— they placed 3,000 markers, an average of one per mile from coast to coast. The road was set. But not quite.[7]

The Lincoln Highway was one road and only one road. It purported to cross the land and to be the official as well as the popular road, designed to meet the nation's needs for years to come. But as the LHA's singleness of purpose and proprietary attitude became clearer to the public, objections arose to its methods and in specific instances, to the exact route.

Several were minor. Woodrow Wilson thought that a truly national road should start at the District of Columbia and include some southern cities, such as Baltimore or Frederick in Maryland.[8] Ohio Senator Warren Harding, speaking for his bitter neighbors in Marion, wanted to know why that town had been bypassed. (After he became president, a stretch of road from Mansfield to Lima suddenly became the Harding Highway to some folks in Washington.) Ogden, Utah, citizens wanted to know why they were being bypassed. Ostermann claimed that Harvey Firestone offered the association $50,000 for a minor change in the route near his farm in Ohio. All alterations were rejected out of hand by the LHA, which offered little rationale but declared that the best route had been "painstakingly selected" and no changes could be made. The officers also liked to point out that they were all from the Detroit area, and even that city was not on the highway.

But out in the salt flats of Utah and the deserts of Nevada the LHA ran into a tougher bunch of citizenry. Neither state had anything resembling a highway system in 1913. Any route would require major and expensive construction, and the two thinly populated states lacked the tax base to build roads in the desert. The usual LHA preference would have been to travel due west from Salt Lake City to Wendover on the state line, thence to Elko, Reno, and California. This would entail driving across the southern portion of the Great Salt Lake, almost dry part of the year, under water the rest of the time. Ostermann, and later Seiberling himself, attempted the route and declared it impassable, not even a road. (This is the region where in later years race cars set outstanding speed records.) Actually, the Wendover route was official Utah's second choice; during World War I, state officials wanted a Lincoln Highway south from Salt Lake City into Arizona. Pressure from Nevada businessmen and the charge of the LHA that Utah was "selfish" in trying to keep people in the state as long as possible forced most Utahans to drop the Arizona plan for the Wendover road.

In 1915, Ostermann pioneered a different road that angled off southwest from Grantsville, over Johnson's Pass through desert ranches to Ibapah in western Utah and Ely and Austin in Nevada. It seemed a minor change, but it aroused the wrath of numerous business and commercial interests from Wendover to Reno. They demanded that the LHA reconsider its choice.

But in 1916, floods washed out the Wendover road, persuading Utah Governor Simon Bamberger to meet with Henry Seiberling, president of LHA. Bamberger agreed to accept the desert or LHA route if the association would pay the costs of improving that road. Seiberling paid about $110,000, and the state began gravelling portions, in particular Johnson Pass, now known to the LHA as the Seiberling cut-off. Before the work was complete, the Utah state highway department halted the job, taking both men and equipment off the site. A very angry LHA was told variously that the work was finished or the money had run out. When the LHA attempted a lawsuit to recover its funds, its members found themselves unable to get a hearing in a Utah court.

A standoff had been reached when in June 1919, the War Department notified all the interested states that the army was preparing to send a convoy of trucks across the Lincoln Highway from Washington to San Francisco. Most states were delighted to have the recognition and presumably increased business as well. But in Utah and Nevada, great opposition arose when businesses learned that the army would use the Seiberling cut-off, ready or not.

Deeply concerned citizens turned in rage to their government officials, demanding to know why the Wendover road had been abandoned. Leading this drive were merchants from northern Nevada in Wells, Elko, Winnemucca, and Reno, who seemed better organized and more numerous than their central Nevada counterparts. (Wendover's tiny population would normally have had little clout, but the town straddles the state line, and the legalized gambling and liquor on the Nevada side of town drew substantial business from venturesome Utahans. Technically, gambling was legalized in Nevada in 1869, outlawed in 1910, and legalized again in 1931, but the availability of easy divorce from 1915 and the frequency of big money prize fights in the state from the 1890s meant lax enforcement of "sin laws.")

Initially the strategy was to have their national representation persuade the army to come through Wendover. Deaf military ears caused a change in plan. Governor Emmet D. Boyle next urged Nevada's congressional delegation to ask for an inspection team to drive to Wendover and judge the conditions. All the men—Senators Key Pittman and Charles Henderson and Representative Charles R. Evans—replied that they were "working on" the plan but getting nowhere. The army even claimed briefly and lamely that the general responsible for the plan was out of town. The next suggestion came from commercial interests in San Francisco, who, fearing that the Seiberling route might mean a terminus in Los Angeles, had joined forces with northern Nevada. (Salt Lake City businessmen suffered occasional boycotts from each side of the controversy when they appeared to be too lukewarm.) The politicians and Wendover partisans thought the San Francisco plan fair and sensible; they asked that the army divide its convoy when it reached Salt Lake, half the trucks taking each road to San Francisco. At the trip's conclusion the presumably unbiased military would decide which was the better way, and they were sure what that decision would be. Turning up the heat, the garage men, mine owners, and hotel men quickly created an organization called the Overland Trail Club, claiming affiliation with a national Pike's Peak association. The Nevada headquarters was in Lovelock. The secretary was W.H. Goodin of Lovelock. Goodin blamed Ostermann and Seiberling personally for abandoning Wendover and waged a strong telegraph campaign to Washington and Carson City. The issue ultimately landed on the desk of Secretary of War Newton D. Baker, who quickly declared that the convoy was a tactical experiment that would be nullified by division. And as for returning by a different route, that was manifestly impossible because the convoy would be broken up at the Presidio in San Francisco.

The Nevada officials who were elected statewide had to be cautious about taking a stand in favor of one road or the other, and none of them seems to have expressed a choice. The representatives in Washington were protected by distance and time and could assure Goodin's group that they were trying to arrange a compromise. But Governor Boyle had a more serious conflict on his hands; he could not hide, and his voters lived along both routes and wanted to know where he stood. He kept himself as lofty as possible, speaking always in vague terms of the good of the whole state, whatever that might be.

Demanding that the army change its plans was a tactic bound to fail, we can see in retrospect. The idea for the convoy came from the LHA, the route came from the LHA, and any changes would have to be approved by the LHA. That organization did not cave in to public opinion. One letter might serve to demonstrate.

The writer was Gael S. Hoag, state LHA consul for Nevada and later field secretary upon the death of Henry Ostermann. Even the very stationery used by Hoag was designed to intimidate. His letterhead included two small maps of the road and a strong, black banner reading LINCOLN HIGHWAY, linking sketches of New York and San Francisco. The left margin included the names of the officers and directors, a who's who of automotive executives. As overkill, the stationery listed a powerful roster of "some contributors," brandishing such names President Wilson, Astor, Colt, DuPont, Ford, Guggenheim, Hearst, Luke Lea (a war hero), Schwab, Studebaker, Swift, Tiffany, and Wanamaker. At the very top were the words, "A continuous connecting improved highway from the Atlantic to the Pacific."

The letter was a reply to a wire from Governor Boyle that spoke of "an avalanche of telegrams" seeking a divided convoy. On July 17, 1919, Hoag wrote Boyle that the Lincoln Highway had been conceived by Ostermann and carefully crafted by the officers. They believed that the "true method is not to scatter our ammunition but to select an objective and then attain it." The itinerary had been worked out in great detail. "It would be quite impossible to make a change at this late date." Then he went on the attack: "In securing this convoy trip the Lincoln Highway Assn. has accomplished such a coup as a mining man would in closing a valuable deal in his line … it would take a gall equal to that of the promoters of the Overland-alias Pikes Peak-alias Pershing-Highway-or whatever its newest name may be — to ask a division of profits by a plain outsider." This was not, he said, as some thought, a government circus on parade, but a true military maneuver. The real reason for the attack on LHA was Reno's failure to be included in the road plans. He went on, "The Reno crowd must furnish its own brains and not try to steal the fruits of the enterprises of others." (The Reno reference is to a running battle between that town and the LHA over whether or not it would be on the Lincoln road.) Hoag concluded, "You want as much as I do to see the Government take upon itself the work of building a Highway across Nevada; you can best further that by assisting in the execution of the present plans." The governor had no response, but, never at a loss for knowing how to save political capital, Boyle hosted a barbeque for the convoy near Lake Tahoe and made a welcoming talk to the troops at Carson City.[9]

The army had been moving across country while the "avalanche" of wires and letters was being delivered, and the trucks were clanking into Illinois when Hoag wrote that reply. The numerous and thorough records kept by the convoy's commanders show no evidence that they had any knowledge of the controversy surrounding their itinerary.

Surprisingly, the LHA ultimately lost its battle for Nevada, which was its only setback. At the close of World War I, the federal government increasingly played a role in highway development. By 1921 it was clear that the LHA could cling to its Seiberling cut-off, but the association would not get any help from the federal government. The Bureau of Public Roads (within the Department of Agriculture) made its own investigation of the Nevada alternatives, and its engineers recommended the Wendover road. In May of 1923, Secretary of Agriculture Henry C. Wallace issued the definitive order that the Wendover–Elko route would get federal aid, and the Seiberling cut-off would not. The LHA protested mildly, but the matter was ended. The strip alongside the salt flats required a lot of funding, because the mushy roadbed had to be built up to escape the brackish water. But at great cost and time the job was done. Today the main highway still passes from Salt Lake City through Wendover and on to Reno, while the Seiberling cut-off is a scarcely traveled back road. In highway matters, the federal government was finally becoming almost as powerful as the LHA.

Major change was coming to the LHA in several ways. In 1920, with his bride of seven months, Henry Ostermann undertook his twenty-first crossing of the United States. On June 7, they were in Tama, Iowa; after dinner he left for business in Marshalltown, his wife staying behind. Perhaps in a hurry to get back to Tama, Ostermann was driving a white Packard Twin Six at 50 miles an hour in a 30-mile zone. He attempted to pass a Ford when his left wheels slipped off the hard surface, hit wet grass and provoked a skid of some 200 feet. The Packard turned over twice, Ostermann being killed instantly when his body crashed into the huge steering wheel. The loss to his family was mirrored in the loss to the LHA, for though he was never its chief executive, he for years was its driving force. He was 43. Gael Hoag, first consul of Nevada, succeeded him as field secretary.[10]

The LHA suffered another, if less personal, loss with the federal highway legislation of 1921, a permanent indication that the power of the association was on the decline. No longer could the LHA dictate road routes and standards to presidents and governors. To press the matter home more firmly, the federal government ruled in 1925 that it would number all highways; no private names like Lincoln would be used.

The directors had been scaling back activities after the army convoy had completed its maneuvers, and the leadership returned to other matters. LHA president Frank Seiberling, whose father helped develop Goodrich Company, had founded Goodyear Tire and Rubber. Internal troubles at Goodyear forced Seiberling out in 1920, seriously interfering with his attention to LHA management. Seiberling retaliated against Goodyear by opening Seiberling Rubber Company six months later. While these matters were boiling, Seiberling asked Henry Joy to replace him as president of LHA. Unwell, Joy served only six months and more or less retired. Seiberling came back for a few more months until replaced by J. Newton Gunn, president of U.S. Rubber. Carl Fisher made a vast fortune creating Miami Beach, lost much of it, then recovered, and was still a wealthy man when he died in 1939 in Miami. Henry Joy died in Michigan in 1936. His family dedicated a marker to him on the Lincoln Highway on the continental divide in Wyoming.[11]

The Lincoln Highway Association began to go out of business by 1925. Seiberling was president again when it closed offices December 31, 1927. The active agent in the last few years was Hoag, who supervised the setting of the 3,000 monuments and evidently introduced the idea of requiring pedestrians to walk facing traffic on rural highways.

From 1912 until 1927, the Lincoln Highway Association was one of the nation's most powerful agencies. During the first ten years of its life it dominated the planning, construction, and use of America's main highways. It told the states how to design and where to build their roads, and what materials to use. It ignored requests for changes, irrespective of their reasonableness. It told governors they were wrong and told a president that his ideas for national roads did not matter. It prevailed upon the army to maneuver along its northern highway, and when the army wanted to duplicate the stunt in the south, the LHA ignored the request, dashing southern dreams of a parallel, national road. Its leaders were rich, powerful, arrogant, accustomed to leading; they were also bright and able and had tremendous vision.

The men of the LHA left an enormous heritage to the American people. Their methods bordered on the strong-arm, but they overcame local apathy, destructive states' rights tendencies, and the reluctance of federal government representatives to spend money on infrastructure within states. Some highway system would, of course, have been built some day. But the men of the LHA saw that a system would be started in their lifetime, and that it would be a vast, national system. Without the work of these men, the American highway network would have been a collection of mismatched roads, totally at the mercy of local politics, farm markets or the postal system. The nation should be eternally grateful.[12]

CHAPTER FOUR

The Military Complex

In the summer of 1919, the United States Army, fresh from its mighty victories in Europe, fell rapidly into sad shape, somewhere below the level of the "normalcy" Senator Warren Harding sought. Too many boys were mustering out too fast; enlistments and re-enlistments were meager; military supply and transportation, which had nearly collapsed in 1918 and with them the entire assault on the German front, needed total overhaul; new motorized equipment had not been tested; and worst of all, the army had concluded it could not have defended the West Coast had the Japanese and another nation attacked it. (The Germans had sought a Japanese-Mexican alliance.) Drastic, dramatic action was needed to attract the attention of Congress and the public to the usual post-war state of military affairs. Besides, "normalcy" was proving to be distracting and exciting.

A little known western bar fighter called Jack Dempsey took on the heavyweight champion of the world, huge Jess Willard, and beat him to the floor five times in the first three minutes. A two-year-old named Man O' War was defining invincibility (for $19 you could win $1 betting on him). The Chicago White Sox moved easily and gracefully toward a pennant and infamy. For four days the Anglo-Saxon world's attention was absorbed by the R-34, a British dirigible making the first lighter-than-air crossing of the Atlantic. And at the same time Woodrow Wilson, his political capital and physical strength spent preaching the League of Nations, steamed home aboard the *George Washington*, preparatory to taking on his own Congress in a losing battle with "normalcy."

To cope with all these distractions, the Lincoln Highway Association had a suggestion, which, not surprisingly, might help it as well: an elaborate, highly publicized, military convoy, crossing the country on the Lincoln Highway.

The father of this plan for a transcontinental military expedition was the one-time circus roustabout, rancher, and automobile dealer Henry C. Ostermann, field secretary and vice president of the Lincoln Highway Association. Labeled a "genius in several ways" by the association's own history, Ostermann was also consul-at-large, chief contact between the association and the public. Unlike the better-known car executives promoting the Lincoln Highway, Ostermann lacked high-profile business experience and was not called to Washington to serve in an executive capacity during the war years. Thus Ostermann became the spokesman and virtual chief operating officer of the LHA in a period when its survival could have been in question. Discovering a gem, the War Department used Ostermann to do what he could accomplish better than any person in the country—find roads to help solve the overwhelming problem of getting trucks and parts from the middle west to ports of embarkation on the East Coast. In the winter of 1917, when road conditions were miserable and rail freight demands could not be met, Ostermann was asked to guide long convoys of government trucks from Akron and Detroit through the mud and snow of the Alleghenies to Boston, Baltimore, and New York. His own testimony is that on one of these trips, he conceived of the plan for a military expedition, coast to coast, along a Lincoln Highway.

Before the war ended, Ostermann had suggested to the War Department that it conduct a highly publicized, combat-ready, cross-country procession of military vehicles of all types, from tanks to mess kitchens and hospitals, traveling under simulated wartime conditions. The men would gain military and mechanical experience. The army could test all its new vehicles, tires, and parts, aided by technical representatives of the manufacturers who would accompany the detachment. Recruiting officers could exhort young men along the way. As the detachments moved across the land, each nightly bivouac in another small town would provide a public relations bonanza. Implicit in all this were the enormous gains to be made by the Lincoln Highway Association and its program for better roads. The convoy would use the Lincoln Highway for its route.

The project would require a combination of efforts. The LHA would lend its considerable convoy experience, and the military would provide the manpower and some of the vehicles. The auto industry and its suppliers were welcome to contribute trucks, tires, and parts for testing and could take whatever advertising gains they could. In short, there was something for everyone — once the war was over. Ostermann wasted no time after the armistice of November 11, 1918, and recommended the expedition be accomplished during the summer of 1919.[1]

Unknown to the public, the army had other reasons for giving strong support to Ostermann. In 1917 and 1918 the American Expeditionary Force under Pershing in Europe frequently suffered from a critical lack of supplies. The failure did not lie with the shipping industry. In time the building program became an enormous success, but the thirty-some rail lines could not work together within the United States. They failed to move freight promptly to the docks and in large cities unmanageable loads stacked up in warehouses awaiting delivery. In December of 1917, President Wilson brought the rail lines under government control, with Secretary of the Treasury (his son-in-law) William G. McAdoo as director general of railroads.

As we have seen, shipping fell to truckers. Pershing and his staff concluded that in future wars the railroads would not be sufficient to meet a national emergency, and therefore America needed a nationwide auto (meaning truck) network for security. The fear of Japan was great. In addition, the army was concerned about its lagging recruitment program. The LHA convoy plan, then, fell upon most receptive ears.[2]

The LHA had to concede but one point; President Wilson correctly concluded that the route would prove very beneficial to northern cities and states only and would not be what he called a "national road." In June 1919, he wrote to Henry Joy, first president of the LHA, that he thought the nation would welcome dissolution of the Mason-Dixon Line. (Wilson was a small boy in Virginia during the Civil War.) Could not the highway include some southern cities? The directors of the LHA yielded on a portion of this point alone. The convoy would depart from Washington, D.C., rather than New York City. Then Wilson endorsed Ostermann's scheme.[3]

The astonishingly quick date of departure — July 7 — badly strained a bureaucracy coping with demobilization and all its attendant problems, and the convoy was to suffer for the haste. But the excitement of selecting the leaders, the men, and the equipment concealed those problems in June of 1919. The first matter was to put an organization together. As commanding officer the army selected a veteran of both the Mexican expedition and the Great War, Charles W. McClure, Quartermaster Corps, recently returned from France. Using Camp Meigs in the District of Columbia as his staging area, McClure assembled two motor transport companies and a service park unit to provide the drivers and repairmen, filling out his expedition with a variety of men with supportive experience. The army combed its ranks for men with automotive skills, even clutching at veterans just disembarking from France and persuading them to re-enlist for the excitement of the venture. A special MTC recruiting team was dispatched to New York City to find interested drivers. Only the best qualified were to be accepted, was the army's optimistic order.

Various official and unofficial reports fail to agree upon the precise number of men and vehicles reporting into Camp Meigs by late June 1919. (So much haste was involved that special orders and other official records often lacked serial numbers and even first names of the members.) McClure's own figures reported 258 enlisted men, 24 expeditionary officers with transport experience, and 15 War Department observers of various backgrounds. The 79 vehicles included 11 passenger cars, 37 cargo trucks, 22 special purpose trucks, and 9 motorcycles.

Two of the observers were volunteers from the Tank Corps, Major Sereno Brett and Lt. Col. Dwight D. Eisenhower. Restless and lonesome for his family in Denver, Ike thought the convoy would be fun and provide him a chance to see his wife and new — and sickly — baby boy. Ike had not served overseas during World War I; at war's end he was in the Tank Corps at Ft. Benning, then was transferred to Ft. Meade for desk duty in the demobilization process. Unhappy with the job and the lack of housing at Meade for Mamie, Ike jumped at the chance to join the convoy. He and Brett caught up with the convoy the first night. They played bridge, took snapshots, showed off a little French tank, and observed. The trip was to make a permanent impression upon Ike. The toddler, Doud Dwight Eisenhower, known as "Icky," was born in 1917. Never robust, he died in January 1921 of scarlet fever.

On July 7, more or less on schedule, the convoy assembled at Meigs and drove over to the Ellipse in Washington. There, within sight of the White House — the LHA never lacked for public relations skills — drivers stilled their roaring engines while formalities took place.

The leaders of the convoy wanted President Wilson to grace the send-off and wish the troops Godspeed, but the president, homeward bound from Paris, did not reach New York and Washington until July 8. Had he been home a day earlier he could have glanced out his windows and seen a most unusual sight. Leaving their trucks scattered on the ellipse road in order of departure, scores of young men clustered around the newly dedicated "Zero Milestone" marker. In the center stood — and sat — a group of well-dressed civilians and officers, seeking the most publicity possible out of this production. Heading the group were Secretary of War Newton D. Baker and Chief of Staff Peyton March. Various congressmen helped dedicate the marker. (The speakers went unrecorded, but Dr. S.M. Johnson spoke for the LHA. General Pershing was still in France. Also unavailable is a list of distinguished persons present, although a small group photograph exists.)

The sweating young soldiers were forced to listen to the formalities for a little more than an hour. At 11:15 A.M., Secretary Baker accepted the milestone on behalf of President Wilson and ordered the convoy to proceed to San Francisco. Unit commanders repeated the order, and the nearly 300 men climbed into their vehicles and started their engines. History does not report the nature of the command to get the trucks moving. Was it a prosaic "Forward March?" or a cinematic "Wagons Ho?" Some reporters claimed that a number of youths shouted, "Giddap," a likely possibility given the backgrounds of most of the men.

On this first day, the caravan paraded out of Washington behind Henry Ostermann and his long, white Packard. Time and circumstances were to dictate the order of the remaining cars on subsequent days. Most of the 39 officers, manufacturers' representatives ("tech. reps."), and local reporters distributed themselves among 11 passenger cars of various types, plus three Willys-Overlands on loan from the manufacturer. (John N. Willys piqued the public's curiosity by calling them "mystery cars" while testing them on the long run. For unstated reasons these three cars were the only vehicles not evaluated by Lt. Col. McClure at the conclusion of the trip, and Willys made no effort to boast of the cars' performance.) McClure drove one of the two Cadillac seven-passenger cars, his being a monster of nearly three tons.

For the next two months the expedition would be led by Ostermann in his Twin Six. After all, the route to be used "belonged" to the Lincoln Highway Association, and had been laid out by him almost in its entirety. In addition, he was the only member of the convoy to have been over the route, not a single military man having had any experience at all with the road. At times Ostermann was as much as a day or two ahead of the convoy, scouting for problems and selling the Lincoln road to every community along the way. Linking him with the convoy were two officers, a captain and a first lieutenant, astride their Harley-Davidsons. Called pilots, the two officers left a half-hour ahead of the troops each morning to determine the condition of the road and to mark the route.

For several years the LHA had been attempting to place identifying signs on the road from coast to coast, but many gaps still existed, and the army could not afford the publicity of being even briefly lost in what Eisenhower was to call "Darkest America." Under Ostermann's instructions, then, the pilots tacked salmon-colored paper triangles on conspicuous posts or fences at each turn of the route. The papers were 5 and one-half inches high and 11 across the base, and the apex of the triangle indicated the direction the convoy should take. Two placed together to form a square meant the location of the night's camp. No maps were available until the men reached California.

Just about half the officers on the convoy had no duties other than observing. Eisenhower said he spent a lot of time pulling pranks on young recruits and playing bridge. (Ike's idea of good fun was placing rubber snakes in the tents of young drivers.) But one E.R. Jackson, a first lieutenant in the Ordnance Department, kept an official record in the form of a daily log and sent telegrams to the War Department each evening. Commander McClure wrote a summary of the expedition, and Eisenhower left us his critique of the whole expedition, incidentally complaining that the War Department had not bothered to tell him what the form should be. From these documents as well as a mass of local newspaper articles, a rather clear picture of the journey emerges.[4]

Except for Sundays, which were devoted to rest and vehicle repair, reveille came at 0450. At 0600 every vehicle was inspected by three officers checking oil, water, gas, and brakes. The troops were on the road from 0630 until approximately noon, resuming travel an hour later. The time to call the evening's halt depended upon Ostermann's planning and his finding a satisfactory bivouac area. Drivers then serviced their vehicles, subject to another inspection before supper. Taps was played at 1100.

Adjustments were made constantly. McClure had planned a light noon lunch and a heavy evening dinner, but all too frequently wrecks and stalled cars meant that some or all of the convoy might arrive at camp as late as midnight, making orderly meals impossible and creating serious morale problems among very hungry men. So the heavy meal was moved up to noon. Totally unexpected was another solution. On the third day the convoy drove from Gettysburg and Chambersburg to tiny Bedford, Pa., where the public adopted the convoy. The army was generously greeted by 2,000 enthusiastic people from Bedford; the ladies of the town had prepared supper for all 300 men. The food was followed by speeches from several officers, the mayor, and Dr. Johnson, representing the LHA. The local band played, and most of the men got a chance to street dance until

The Caterpillar tractor aboard one of the Mack trucks in Pennsylvania (National Archives).

tattoo. There are no indications that Ostermann planned this reception or the dozens of others to follow across the nation. He merely informed the appropriate town each night when the convoy would arrive and where it planned to camp. He left the rest to community spirit. America was saying "welcome to our town" and thanks for a job well done in France — and for bringing the Lincoln Highway through our streets.

The relatively good roads of Maryland and Pennsylvania brought other shakedown changes as well. Mechanical problems were ceaseless. McClure concluded early that the convoy could not wait for repairs to one or two vehicles every few hours. His order — "Cut out the cripples, keep them rolling" (a semi-official slogan of World War II, incidentally) — meant an ordnance crew would remain with the injured truck or car until it was repaired and able to join the rest of the convoy in its slow procession cross-country. If the repairs were too serious for immediate service, the vehicle might be towed the rest of the day to that night's repair shop. It was not unusual for mechanics to work all night on the more pressing jobs.

The importance and magnitude of the towing problem became apparent the first few days out of Washington. Quoting Jackson, "Militor towed Class B with broken magneto coupling one mile into camp at Frederick Fairgrounds." And the next day, "Militor towed Class B machine shop [10 tons] out of mud on bad detour near Emmitsburg, after two Macks in tandem had failed."[5]

What was a Militor? Its history is obscure and almost mysterious. (The Department of Defense has been unable to provide much information about the truck.) Its official title was Military Artillery Wheeled Tractor, corrupted by doughboys to Militor. Basically it was an 11,000-pound wrecker, carrying a winch and a large, ugly sprag which could anchor the Militor when pulling some great weight out of the mud. West of the Mississippi, that was a constant task. The convoy was also provided with a Caterpillar tractor for that, but the tractor had to ride on a Mack truck, and merely taking it off and on proved a serious nuisance. Furthermore the Militor soon demonstrated that its power was significantly greater than that of the Cat. One August day in western Nebraska nine trucks chained together could not extricate themselves from a mess of quicksand; the Militor pulled all nine out, then on the same day towed twelve others in tandem for 13 hours. On another occasion, Sgt. T.E. Wood, Jr. drove the wrecker without rest more than 23 hours, towing three badly needed vehicles. Another driver then drove the Militor 55 miles all night over mountainous roads, towing three more cars. The practice became to put the Militor at the end of the train to pick up the stragglers.

McClure concluded that the unit would never have reached California without the Militor, and Jackson wrote that it "unquestionably was

The invaluable Militor at work on the Lincoln Highway in Nebraska (National Archives).

the most valuable vehicle in the entire Convoy." In Utah it ran into some fairly minor mechanical problems; according to Jackson these were easily fixed, but "the expeditionary commander ordered the Militor returned to Salt Lake City there to be shipped to San Francisco by rail." With that, the wrecker disappears from history, Jackson adding mysteriously that the action was totally unnecessary and "had been made the subject of a spe-

Top— The Militor tows three trucks in Ohio; *bottom*— The Militor at work in Nebraska (National Archives).

cial report." The report appears to be lost. With Nevada deserts and the Sierras still to be negotiated, one wonders with Lt. Jackson; but McClure never explained himself.

Every observer had some acid comments about the roads. No cross-country highway existed in 1919. The Lincoln road was essentially a marked trail, as straight as possible, following a route utilizing existing roads, and sometimes no road, avoiding large cities, and linking communities that had cooperated with the LHA.

The report of Captain William C. Greany of the Motor Transport Corps measured the total distance covered as 3,251 miles. He estimated that about 45 percent of that was hard surface, meaning concrete, macadam, gravel, or rock. He reported that 55 percent, or 1,788 miles, was over dirt roads, wheel paths, mountain trails, desert sands, and alkali flats. Often, so-called roads were so bad that trucks abandoned them for farmers' fields, at best cutting the fields up badly, at worst destroying a crop. (Efforts were made to settle claims on the spot — more often than not the farmer asking for soldier labor to rebuild a fence or repair a culvert.) Greany said that more than 500 miles were impassable for the heavy trucks and negotiated only through "the combined efforts of the most extraordinary character on the part of the personnel." Eisenhower separately concluded that no more truck convoys should be attempted west of the Mississippi until the roads were improved. In Iowa, the roads were normally packed dirt, but the rain and the heavy usage by the army turned the highway into gumbo. Trucks became immersed two feet or more, even up to their floor boards. The Militor once recovered a vehicle in four feet of mud; the sprag held the rescuer in place as the winch screamed, and soldiers pushed and fell cursing into the mud. With the front wheels five feet off the ground pawing like some wild stallion, the wrecker spent more than six hours making the save. Greany said that it was not unusual to spend twenty-four hours getting the 79 vehicles through one mass of gumbo, all the manpower, regardless of rank, pushing, pulling, or placing timber, canvas, grass, even sagebrush under the wheels for traction.

In later years Eisenhower joked that the convoy traveled some 3,000 miles and had an accident for each mile. The truth was bad enough. The official figure was 230 accidents — on the road, that is. (Personal or in-camp accidents largely went unrecorded.) For example:

• The mobile machine shop lost its top in an encounter with a low bridge near Emmitsburg, Pa.

• A light Dodge delivery truck burned out its brakes on a steep Allegheny grade and destroyed its radiator ramming into an ambulance.

• A GMC truck skidded off the road in the Pennsylvania mountains — "damaged beyond hope of repair."

• In South Bend, Indiana, four bolts sheared off and the range fell off the kitchen trailer onto the highway.

• In Valparaiso, a Dodge ran over a civilian, breaking his collar bone. The cause of the accident — unspecified.

• The same day a careless driver ran the ambulance into a ditch, and a plank bridge gave way, dumping truck and driver into stream, neither badly hurt.

• In Joliet a second stove fell into the street.

• Near Council Bluffs, the 6-ton Mack blacksmith shop ran into a 2-ton Packard truck. Both survived.

• Near Gothenburg, Neb., gumbo roads caused 25 cars to spill into ditches one day. "Very apparent all trucks should be equipped with chains," was the laconic report to the War Department.

One day in Wyoming so many accidents took place — a wrecked motorcycle, trucks stuck in culverts causing detours, trucks crashing through bridges, etc., that Jackson was moved to write, "The intensely dry air, absence of trees and green vegetation, and parched appearance of the landscape exerted depressing influence on personnel." In all, the army rebuilt 88 bridges.

And what of the personnel? Ike complained that no "march discipline" existed the first ten days, a remark seconded but never clarified by him or others. But as he and Major Brett had joined the convoy late, they might have been more shocked than other officers about the lack of training of the enlisted men. All of the men claimed to be able to drive, but the majority had driven nothing but Henry Ford's Model T or even some relatively simple tractor. Almost none had been checked out on the particular vehicle they were assigned. Some of the officers complained that their men were raw recruits with no training at all, and Eisenhower added that much of the problem lay with some officers who were "of poor type."

A second lieutenant in supply was among those singled out for being too friendly and lax with his men. A lieutenant colonel who joined the unit in Nebraska brought about a great change in military discipline and was cited for that. The medical and engineering personnel were highly praised; the mess officers, not surprisingly, were chastised in most reports.

The convoy left the pink monument at the ellipse on July 7, 1919, and halted for the last time in Lincoln Park in San Francisco on September 6, two days behind schedule. It had driven as many as 90 miles in one day and as few as five. The average was just under 60 miles driven at average speeds of 5 to 15 miles per hour.[6]

The daily reports to the War Department vividly describe the conditions of America's best road in 1919. For the first two weeks, the drivers praised the hard-surfaced roads leading to Frederick, Maryland, and on into Pennsylvania. The next day the men lunched on the Gettysburg battlefield, repairing and strengthening old covered bridges along the way. Heavy rain in the mountains resulted in a GM truck skidding off the descending slope, then barrel rolling down Laurel Hill, destroying the truck but not injuring the driver. The convoy was making good driving time but still having trouble keeping to schedule because no one had calculated the impact of the daily receptions on the itinerary. Pittsburgh gave the men a "great ovation." Magnetos, transmissions, and clutches began to give out, the first two because they were not sturdy enough for the use, the clutches because unskilled drivers "rode" them for hours at a time. The Militor towed three trucks uphill all night without heating up. A young driver frightened by a steep grade attempted to jam his vehicle into reverse and destroyed his drive shaft. The Pennsylvania mountains proved to be harsh schoolrooms.

The first Sunday was enjoyed in East Palestine, Ohio. Lt. Col. McClure convened a meeting of all officers to discuss the poor driving and other matters of moment, then the entire command was taken in private automobiles to Columbiana, six miles distant, the home of Harvey Firestone, the tire magnate. More than 400 people were served a "fine chicken dinner" in a large tent. The host, several officers, the mayor, and others spoke.[7] A technical movie was shown to the command and the many visitors. A local band played, according to the newspapers, but the army record fails to mention whether or not the convoy's own "Rubber Band," sponsored by Goodyear, was allowed to participate. (The official record almost totally ignored the Goodyear sponsorship, perhaps out of deference to Firestone.)

Harvey Firestone and Frank Seiberling, organizer and president of Goodyear Tire and Rubber Company, both "founders" of the LHA, friends, and sharp business rivals, were involved in endless patent suits. In the years before the convoy, Firestone's sales grossed perhaps two-thirds those of Goodyear.[8] And Firestone's sales would have been minor in com-

**Major Sereno Brett, Harvey S. Firestone, Jr. (center), and Lieutenant Colo-
nel Dwight D. Eisenhower (right) at lunch in Ohio, July 13, 1919 (National
Archives).**

parison had it not been for Henry Ford, who often gave Firestone 60 percent or more of his business. But Firestone was winning the public relations war.

During World War I, Firestone attributed the victory at the Marne
to the French use of trucks; he was among the first to anticipate the failure of the freight railroad system and was a staunch and vocal supporter
of the Good Roads movement. By 1919 he linked in his own mind the
demand for trucks, paved highways and his tires. He hurled his slogan
"Ship by Truck" at manufacturers and the public in addresses all across
the nation. When the military convoy was formed, Firestone supplied two
truckloads of tires to accompany the troops. In his speech to the convoy
at Columbiana he trotted out the past and told how as a young man he
had fulfilled his poll tax duties maintaining the same red brick road that
still bordered his estate. And just before the arrival of the convoy, a group
of his own trucks had been driven from Akron to New Orleans, demon-

strating his new "demountable rims." Perhaps Firestone's major contribution to the convoy was what a Wooster paper called his mobile service station. At Firestone's expense and supervised by a company representative, this truck carried casings and tubes of every size. In this manner the army drivers were freed from carrying spares and had help from tire specialists in repairing tires and rims. The hospitality of the rubber industry to the army was guaranteed to pay dividends. A Firestone truck stopped in Chicago to deliver 800 tires to the Yellow Cab company.

Between South Bend and Chicago Heights, Lt. Jackson recorded the first "perfect score," as he called it: no vehicle had to be towed that day. He celebrated by riding into Chicago in civilian custody. The Four Wheel Drive Auto Club fed him, and the Chicago Auto Club gave him a bed and a drive around the city. It was the perfect holiday for the reporter of the army convoy.

As the troops moved westward, the celebrations became more elaborate, and night after night the enlisted men found themselves playing baseball against the local team (invariably losing), and eating fried chicken, ice cream, and watermelon, washed down with lemonade. Since the stops were usually only forty or fifty miles apart, the towns were often rivals in many ways, and throwing a party with more food and more fun than the neighbor's became the competition of the summer of 1919. Every village on the highway seemed to have a bandstand in its park, where the boys could meet the girls and street dance after dinner. Most popular were those little places with a community swimming pool. Officers generally were segregated off to the YMCA for a dinner-dance with a select group of girls, followed by the inevitable speeches about the glories of the Lincoln Highway. It was small town America at its post-war best. Reports of doughboy misconduct were few; a handful went AWOL, but to go home, not to stay in the latest hamlet with some new-found love.

The ladies of La Porte, Indiana, learned at the last moment that the convoy would pass through town at eight one morning. They met the cars, anyhow, but the convoy did not stop for the ladies and their hot doughnuts.

In central Illinois, the roads, although still hard, turned extremely dusty in the July heat. Motorcycles became almost unmanageable in the deep dust, and the truck drivers ceased tailgating, the convoy now stretching out three miles or more to escape the awful dust.

Late on the night of July 22 a totally exhausted Henry Ostermann crossed the high railroad bridge over the Mississippi into Clinton, Iowa.

The convoy at the Mississippi River crossing, July 23, 1919 (National Archives).

His red, white, and blue Packard looked as dirty and tired as he; he had spent the entire day on the road from Aurora. He complained that there was so much road construction that he had to stop at every cross-road to erect detour signs for the convoy. But he boasted that when the work was done, every mile of the Lincoln Highway from Chicago to Clinton would be paved. Late the next afternoon, the convoy also crossed the river, the excitement of crossing on a high railroad bridge, forcing some of the cars to wait for freight trains, was enhanced by the feeling that the men had now left the east behind and would face a new world in the Wild West.

Celebration was in order. A reported 20,000 Iowans turned out to greet the men, play with the unit's pet raccoon, and "ooh" at the giant searchlight, its 3-million candle power bouncing off the clear Iowa sky. The convoy encamped at River Front Park, where drivers washed their clothes and ate watermelon. They serviced their vehicles, swam at the Y, enjoyed a Red Cross dinner. No official record mentions it, but *The Clinton Herald* reported that the Goodyear Rubber Band had been recalled by the government because the convoy was not supposed to advertise any product, so the boys danced instead to the rhythms of Shean's Jazz Orchestra. (Someone reversed the decision, and the Rubber Band stayed on to San Francisco.) "Best reception yet, all agreed."

Crossing Iowa provoked a few new problems as the summer got hotter. Drivers, unaccustomed to the heat, often failed to service batteries and

A typical mishap in Iowa along the route of the coast-to-coast 1919 convoy (National Archives).

Trucks being towed by tractor over a difficult stretch in Iowa (National Archives).

A truck stuck in mud in Iowa during the 1919 convoy (National Archives).

The convoy found a typical reception in Cedar Rapids, Iowa (National Archives).

fan belts; every Mack ran hot at least once on July 26 from the heavy pulling in the dust. But the convoy moved along on schedule. The Cedar Rapids' consul arranged a chicken dinner in the town square, the huge table being a wheel, with enlisted men sitting on the rim, officers and dignitaries such as the mayor and lieutenant governor on the spokes. A squadron of local airplanes pretended to attack the bivouac, but were turned away by the powerful searchlight. So many folks came to honor the men that one corporal said they traveled coast to coast between two lines of cameras. The Goodyear Rubber Band surfaced again, to play in Marshalltown. Ostermann told the people of Ames the convoy would use the main street; McClure did not know that and stayed as planned on the city's outskirts, seriously miffing a few thousand people. Another slight detour to Glidden, to honor the first member of the A.E.F. killed in France, improved relations.

Omaha's mayor wanted the convoy to spend Sunday with him, but McClure preferred to stay at Denison, where the largest crowd in the little town's history greeted the men. For two nights and one day they camped in Washington Park; the free movie was *The Unpardonable Sin*. Local men were instructed to bring two girls to Saturday's dance, and the next morning everyone who wished had a ride to one of the town's churches. In searing heat, the convoy men lost another baseball game, called after six innings for lack of interest. Orders from Washington required the men to replace the Dixon grease on every vehicle because of an "account argument with Timken." (The bearing company.) Jackson's urgent — and unexplained — request got permission for the Militor only to continue to use the Dixon product. The town constable arrested a wayward teen-age farm girl for having intimate relations with an enlisted man. She was sent home. He stayed on.

The Missouri was crossed on the main Council Bluffs-Omaha bridge after some publicity talk of using a ferry. In Omaha, the remaining Dixon lubricants were removed before the inevitable entertainment. The army announced the completion of fifty enlistments thus far. Rains turned the dust into mud, and roads disintegrated rapidly. Cars stuck in something resembling quicksand; pulling one big Mack out, the Militor's sprag tore a trench in the road several feet long, to a depth of more than two feet, before it recovered the Mack. Near Ogallala the deep sand roads were described as the worst yet. At Lexington men declared their need for a rest from all the entertaining. Ironically, during all the chicken dinners from local ladies, Jackson was complaining to the War Department that the

The Militor at work in Nebraska (National Archives).

poor convoy mess was destroying morale. A new mess officer joined them a few days later. A nineteen-year-old private stole a local car and deserted. He was caught at Council Bluffs and turned over to Ft. Omaha.

In western Nebraska, the roads bordered on the impassable. Ten miles outside North Platte the unit bogged down in one hundred yards (the local press said 200 feet) of quicksand. The first heavy truck through sank almost to the floorboard, the sandy ooze totally hiding the differential. The Militor extracted 16 trucks, the tractor 10, and the two combined to extricate 8 more. Nearly eight hours were required to get all the vehicles through that one morass. Five bridges were rebuilt that day, and 60 feet of corduroy road were constructed. Lunch was a jam sandwich served at four in the afternoon. The 11 P.M. arrival in Ogallala — six hours behind the announced arrival — annoyed hundreds of well-wishers who had driven their buggies and Fords and Saxons in from all over the county to greet the men and gawk at the machines. But the Ogallala Symphony Club nevertheless managed to work in a concert for the boys. When the convoy was a day late reaching Kimball, the sheriff wrote in his diary that he combined various arrests with driving a number of his constituents to town a second time. "Worst road we have yet encountered," wired Jackson.

Major Dwight D. Eisenhower had a pleasant interlude beginning in North Platte. At the close of the war Ike had been assigned to administrative chores at Camp Meade, Md. His wife, Mamie, had wanted to find a house in Baltimore or Washington so that he could be close to her and their infant, Doud Dwight ("Icky") less than two years old, but Ike refused to let her, and she went back to Denver to stay with her parents, the John S. Douds. During the trip west, Ike wrote Mamie, suggesting she take the train and meet him at North Platte, Neb. They would see each other for just one night, but he considered it worthwhile. Ike did not take into consideration his father-in-law's infatuation with his new Packard and his desire to test the car, however.

The upshot was that Mr. Doud drove Mamie across more or less roadless northeastern Colorado some 200 miles to North Platte. The trip, not carefully reported, must have been similar to the daily routine of the convoy. The Packard was an open touring car; carrying their food and water as well as gas, oil and tools for the car, they set off early in the morning along the foothills of the Rockies. They had little trouble except once in starting the engine. Averaging 15 miles an hour, they generally followed wagon tracks, usually in second gear. They reached North Platte in the early evening and took rooms in a hotel. Ike and the convoy arrived at sunset the next day, a grinning Ike yelling to Mamie from the back of a truck. They spent a few days together, and father and daughter drove back to Denver.

Some pertinent facts about the trip are disputed. Dorothy Brandon's biography of Mamie (1954) states that only Mamie and Mr. Doud made the trip, Mrs. Doud and Mamie's sister staying in Denver with little Icky.[9] (A little more than a year later Icky was to contract scarlet fever and die on January 2, 1922.) But in *At Ease,* Ike wrote that "Mamie and all the Douds met the truck train at South [*sic*] Platte and went along with us for the next three or four days, as far, I think, as Laramie, Wyoming." Then, in a 1974 interview with Dianne Fox of the State Historical Society of Iowa, Mamie remembered differently: "With my father, mother and little boy we went to meet him at North Platte and drove up through Wyoming." My inclination is to go along with Mamie's first recollection because it was the first and because one would not expect her to expose a small child to the rigors of the drive; furthermore in her biography she says nothing of bringing along the paraphernalia needed to care for a lad so young. At any rate, Mamie returned home with her dad and Ike continued west.

Looking for someone to blame, the *Chappell Register* discovered that no one in Chappell belonged to the LHA; did that explain why the roads were so bad? It concluded editorially that several city fathers had better join. Somewhere near the Wyoming line a heavy rainstorm hit the convoy for an hour. Then the weather cleared dramatically and turned so much cooler that the boys donned their overcoats — on August 8. The roads were better, too, away from the sand hills of Nebraska, with more gravel and less mud. But the 8,000-foot altitude was something none of the drivers except Ostermann had experienced. They learned to cope with sluggish performance and how to adjust carburetors.

Outside Cheyenne the unit acquired an escort including the governor, the mayor, the 15th Cavalry and its band. They stayed at Ft. Russell and got to see a rodeo. They also saw popular film stars Viola Dana and Fred Stone making an untitled western. They crossed the Continental Divide at 8,247 feet and everyone felt refreshed by the dry, cool weather. They rested and performed repairs in Laramie and enjoyed a barbecue at Medicine Bow's Virginian Hotel. The wind blew all day. Frequently now, the men built corduroy roads to escape soft sand, and near Rawlins they followed an abandoned Union Pacific right-of-way. Some of the trail was winding and even dangerous, the men thought, but they did not get stuck for a change. McClure concluded that the very dry air caused timber to

A rancher's daughter in Wyoming who was thrown from her horse along the convoy route (National Archives).

lose its elasticity, accounting for the many bridges collapsing under the weight of the heavy trucks. The countryside seemed totally deserted, yet every night local folk put on entertainment and meals, coming from miles around to greet the boys. And the menu changed; trout generally replaced chicken. Water was scarce.

The Lincoln Highway now dipped down into Utah, and at Morgan the troops were made welcome by Bishop Anderson of the Church of Latter Day Saints. (Interestingly, it was a church official, not a civil official, acting as state host.) He gave McClure four-foot keys to the state and the town and presented the troops' mess with six cases of "famous" Morgan peas. Flag-waving children lined the highway, the school band played, and many church and city officials escorted the convoy into Ogden. But less friendly was the person who burgled the tent of Ike's Tank Corps friend, Major Sereno Brett, and took off with cash, a Colt automatic, papers and a camera. Lt. Jackson lost a Brownie at the same time.

Between Ogden and Salt Lake City the trucks were forced to take a bad detour. In trying to haul a truck out of some mud, the Militor also sank to a depth of four feet. The big wrecker got out under its own power when the men spent hours putting a road bed of planks under the wheels, but only after a cable broke, spinning a pulley thirty feet into the air with such speed that it severed tree limbs. No one was hurt.

A Red Cross greeting for the convoy in Salt Lake City (National Archives).

By coincidence, a national conference of governors was convening in Salt Lake City just as the convoy arrived. The governors were discussing ways to reduce the high cost of living without cutting the budgets for schools and roads. (Predictably, they wanted the federal government to do more.) Ostermann took advantage of their presence to advertise the good roads movement. He invited local merchants to parade with the army, but restricted their advertising to 40 percent of the possible ad space on the side of each truck. The remaining 60 percent would have to be devoted to stressing the importance of the convoy's goals.

The procession was greeted by piercing whistles, two bands, and thirty governors. The trucks were parked on Main and South Temple in downtown Salt Lake City, and the governors were invited to inspect them. A number of "comely maidens" presented McClure with a huge floral display resembling a truck. Officers, governors, and local officials enjoyed a dinner dance atop the Hotel Utah. The enlisted men had an outing at Saltaire on the Great Salt Lake. The War Department took this day to acknowledge that the convoy's 2,499 miles had broken all convoy records, the longest previous tour (unspecified) being 900 miles.

Leaving the warm acceptance and comfort of the Utah capital, the convoy ran into its severest tests — mechanical, personal, and political.

The Utah desert had not seen rain for 18 weeks. West of Tooele the road became a trail of alkali dust and fine sand, often to a depth of two

Sergeant Theodore Wood drove the Militor 19 hours without rest (National Archives).

feet, peppered with chuckholes. In spite of some minor problems of its own, the Militor continued to keep most of the convoy rolling—until it struck the Utah desert. On one day—August 20—the truck had to quit because of a broken radiator support, a cracked fan belt coupling, a malfunctioning carburetor, and a loose connecting rod bearing. Most of the repair work on the Militor was quickly accomplished except for replacing the rod, when, much to Lt. Jackson's displeasure, McClure ordered the vehicle back to Salt Lake City. There it was to be placed aboard a train for Eureka, Nevada, presumably to rejoin the convoy. Jackson and other officers, vaguely aware of the test the desert would give their equipment, felt the presence of the Militor was essential. But the Militor did not detrain at Eureka; amid rumors of political deals and prejudice on the part of unknown persons, the Militor went home by train and never operated with the convoy again.

The departure of the Militor greatly exaggerated the already low morale of the men. The same desert that had destroyed the Donner party seventy-two years before now grabbed hold of the convoy and nearly broke the spirit of the soldiers. Heavily weighted wheels spun into the soft salt and sand mixture, digging such ruts that even the lighter class "B" trucks got hung up on their chassis. Wheels whirled wildly in the air without any timber and brush for traction. All that could be found after wide searching were small patches of sage brush. Red Cross ladies from Tooele brought lunch to the diggers, but the troops got no dinner until nearly midnight.

They had gone scarcely ten miles the next morning when they encountered a sand drift completely concealing the road. More than an hour was spent shoveling out a road bed. Portions of the so-called Seiberling cut off—explored by Ostermann—proved impassable, necessitating a detour across salt flats that broke with the weight of every truck and even some of the passenger cars. Freeing the vehicles took "almost superhuman effort," in Jackson's report. The unit covered 15 miles between 6:15 in the morning and 2 P.M. when it reached Granite Rock. This was an unscheduled stop; using the Rock as a base they worked until after midnight freeing their trucks from the salt. The next night they ate cold baked beans and hard bread, the fuel truck being stuck in the desert. Water and gasoline were in such short supply that McClure ordered rationing of the water.

For the only time on the entire trip morale was so bad that McClure was unsure of his men; that night he placed armed guards on the water tanks. Bedding was unavailable, and the men slept wherever they could on the desert. The next morning the Utah state superintendent of road construction personally drove a team of horses hauling two tanks of water to the men. They now had sufficient water, but the kitchen trailers remained out of order as often as not. Motorcycles could not negotiate the soft going and had to be put on trucks, bringing a temporary halt to communication with awaiting towns. Several vehicles were shipped by train back to Ft. Douglas in Salt Lake City for "retirement." Scattered across miles of desert were disabled trucks, mechanics feverishly struggling to get them back into service and rejoin the convoy. One soldier commented that desertion would have been common except that there was no place to go. (Stationed at Wendover Field in 1944, the writer often heard the same complaint from eastern GIs.) The convoy even had to travel on Sunday to keep reasonably close to schedule.

The breakdown of vehicles and even the declining morale were probably to be expected. The men had convinced themselves that once they crossed the Rockies or the continental divide — wherever that was — they would be going more or less downhill, the cars would face fewer problems, and the driving would be easier. The great American desert was proving a destructive surprise, just as it had to so many pioneers in the nineteenth century.

The third problem was totally unexpected; it was political and it was aimed directly at the power and prestige of the LHA. That, at least, was the posture taken by its leaders when someone first strongly objected to the convoy's route.

At issue was the LHA's plan to cross the Utah-Nevada deserts by going south and west from Salt Lake City to Tooele and Ibapah in Utah, then into Nevada through Ely, Austin, Fallon, and Carson City, then south of Lake Tahoe to Meyers, Sacramento and Oakland. Strong opposition to this route had been building all that summer from business and other interests in Elko and Reno, who wanted the convoy to travel straight west of Salt Lake to Wendover, then to Elko, Reno, and Auburn, California. Governor Emmet Boyle of Nevada, seeking a compromise, urged the army to split the convoy to soothe what he called "regional feelings." Much illwill resulted, and the LHA lost many friends, but it stuck to Ostermann's route. (See chapter three for details and the outcome of this battle.)

The convoy left the salt flats and most of the alkali behind when it entered Nevada, but the roads were little better. Lt. Jackson told his journal, "Remarkable that all equipment remains serviceable with abuse given ... country of most desolate character ... Poor gravel roads." Now the dryness took its toll on tired machinery. Bearings continued to burn out, clutches gave up, and wooden wheels simply dried up and fell apart. Embarrassingly, if not ominously for the LHA, when a number of tires needed major patchwork, they were shipped to Reno, which was not on the Lincoln Highway, for service. In his report from Fallon, Jackson concluded that the conditions crossing Carson Sink were similar to those on the Great Salt Lake Desert.

Grateful for being on the route, the people of Ely gave the men a grand banquet, with eight cakes and "barrels" of lemonade. Then everyone was invited to a sing on the courthouse lawn. Dusty throats lubricated with lemonade sang "KKKATY," "Keep the Home Fires Burning," "Keep Your Head Down Fritzy Boy," and, for nostalgia's sake, "Beautiful Ohio." The folks at Fallon and Carson City gave the boys more food, and at the capital, preceding the inevitable dance, Governor Boyle spoke — with no hard feelings.

That night, August 31, 1919, the officers spent hours discussing strategies for the great climb over the Sierras. The next morning a check point was established at the base of King's Grade for inspection of brakes, steering, tow chains, and wheel blocks. Supplies of water and gas were verified. Only the most experienced men were to drive, and one passenger per truck was assigned the duty of blocking the wheels at each stop, emergency or otherwise. Vehicles were spaced 100 yards apart, and motorcycle riders assigned to enforce the decree and inspect wheel bearings every four minutes. All eastbound traffic was suspended by the Nevada State Highway Department until the convoy crossed the Sierras.

The precautions paid off. Although grades ranged from 8 percent to 14 percent in the 14-mile drive and the narrow road forgave no error, the passage was achieved without accident. Elapsed time, six hours. The unit was met at the California state line by representatives of the governor and the mayor of San Francisco. The men marveled at the scenery, especially around Lake Tahoe. The temperature was 30 degrees at dawn the next day. Roads were often graveled and the route was truly downhill now. They passed through sparkling American River canyon and overnighted at Placerville.

The remainder of the trip was a victory parade. From Placerville "concrete roads were lined with palm trees;" everywhere the men saw their first orange, almond, and olive ranches. "Populace showered convoy with fruit," Jackson summarized. The soldiers attended the State Fair and a huge dinner courtesy of John Willys at the Willys-Overland showroom in Sacramento. The trucks still broke through bridges, but passed through the "most productive fruit ranches and vineyards in the world." In Stockton the convoy was met by the mayor, the Red Cross, and a parade, and when fire whistles alerted the populace, the town came forth in trucks and cars to escort the men to their camp at Oak Park. The men were described as exhausted, but summoned up the strength to enjoy another dinner dance.

The next day the enlisted men were issued new uniforms to keep up appearances; the Oakland parade met them ten miles outside the city limits and escorted them on "unexcelled roads." Whistles blew without cease for an hour. Brilliant sun whipped at flags honoring them throughout the bay area, and that night a big fireworks show took place while the men luxuriated at the Hotel Oakland.

Next day they crossed San Francisco Bay on two ferries, drove on paved streets to "The End of the Trail" at Lincoln Park, received medals from the LHA, and listened to generals and Mayor James Rolph. Another milestone was dedicated, this one marking the terminus of the Lincoln Highway. The Red Cross served lunch. The trucks made their last stop at the Presidio of San Francisco. Jackson's last wire concluded, "We begin thoro inspection of trucks tomorrow period Militor not yet here period address me care Hotel Victoria." It was September 6, 1919, 11:30 A.M. The LHA and the MTC had linked the Atlantic and the Pacific.

CHAPTER FIVE

The Consequences

Even before the army completed its cross-country journey, publicists at the War Department as well as civilian journalists commenced boasting of the convoy's achievements. Dozens of newspapers heralded the trip, those papers whose city was blessed by a visit doing the greatest amount of trumpeting. Twenty years later the editor of *Motor Transportation* declared that the convoy was "the most important single decision affecting transportation that has ever been made in the twentieth century."[1] Three hundred self-sufficient men with four-score vehicles had pioneered a route across the nation, pretending to endure combat conditions, arriving only two days behind schedule. No soldier was killed or seriously injured, and only three vehicles were lost. Interspersed with a vast amount of boredom, the workload at times had been enormous. Nothing approaching the scope of the expedition had ever been attempted before. How can we assess it?[2]

One is tempted to blunt the accolades with the reminder that the expedition was conducted in very friendly territory in peacetime. True, the men were at times exhausted, but these were soldiers and they were young. The mess was poor, occasionally non-existent, but hardly a day passed without a sumptuous lunch or dinner put on by local folk; the variety and quality of baked goods alone would make the trip worthwhile, it seems to the reader today. This was not Lewis and Clark updated, as some writers suggested. Nor did it in any way compare with a wagon train of the 1840s, as other reporters claimed.

The proper way to judge this convoy is to compare its achievements with the four objectives given it in the original War Department orders: (1) to contribute to the Good Roads movement for the purpose of encouraging the construction of transcontinental highways as "a military and economic asset;" (2) to recruit young men for the Motor Transport Corps; (3) to acquaint the public with the development of the motor vehicle for military purposes; and (4) to study the terrain and test equipment for various branches of the army. With the possible exception of the second purpose, the convoy far exceeded expectations. (No quota or numerical goals were set for recruits so we cannot measure that program; a few hundred men enlisted during the sixty-two days. No officer complained of the paucity of recruits, for publication at least.) In the eleven states that embraced the Lincoln Highway, the Good Roads messages got out clearly. West of the Mississippi, especially, the movement received a tremendous boost. H.C. Ostermann and the Lincoln Highway planners always considered the quality of existing roads as they laid out the route. The expedition passed through 350 towns and cities. Residents of dozens of others were chagrined to be bypassed because they had not done enough for their own roads and streets. Most vowed to remedy that condition promptly. Several states voted favorably on bond issues that same year, according to Lt. Jackson, and the vast, pioneering Bankhead and Townsend Highway bills were being considered — and passed — by the U.S. Congress in these same months.

The third objective, publicizing the utility of the equipment, was achieved almost literally beyond calculation. While Lt. Col. McClure preferred camping just outside a town, it mattered little where he put his campsite. On nearly sixty occasions the public came out en masse to see his outfit. Men and women of all ages examined the vehicles, marveled at the searchlight, sat behind the wheel of a four-wheel-drive, or yearned for a seven-passenger Cadillac. They could peer into a small Renault tank that had fought in Europe; they could see perhaps the first pneumatic tires ever to reach that county. It was a publicist's dream. The army claimed that 33 million people heard of the convoy, and 3.25 million actually witnessed it.

We can be more specific about the last of the four goals of the expedition. A number of individuals commented about the equipment, giving a good estimate of what worked and what did not. A few conclusions: the three Cadillacs (two passenger cars and the searchlight truck) got high marks, especially considering that the one driven by McClure covered about twice the mileage of the other cars. Dodges, some 20,000 of which were reported to have been used by the army during the war, did reasonably well, but their Stewart carburetors could not cope with the dust, often requiring several cleanings a day. The steering column on all the White trucks worked loose by mid-trip. "Class B" trucks — makers unknown, but built especially for the army — were the "most towed trucks in the Convoy." The Garfords "proved to be the most unsatisfactory," timing gears and connecting rod bearings giving constant trouble. All commentators rated the three four-wheel-drive trucks — also built for the army — the most satisfactory. They had few mechanical problems and could pull through sand and gumbo unaided. They were, however, difficult to steer. The GMC trucks posed little trouble except for their complex carburetors, which the mechanics never seemed to understand. Every big Mack truck had its clutch replaced at least once; otherwise, east of the Mississippi they performed ably, but in the dry country they consumed enormous amounts of water and frequently overheated. They also were harder on tires than any other truck. The Packards gave little trouble of any kind. Rikers were rated the best rear-drive trucks on the convoy. All the drivers without them insisted upon glass windshields for future convoys. Better electric starting systems were also in demand.

The motorcycles got much attention, probably because of the romance attached to their use in the late war. While the British had relied exclusively on the Indian, Americans tried many varieties. By 1919 only Indian, Harley-Davidson, and Cleveland were still in major production, and only the first two were used by the convoy. The riders concluded that the tires were too narrow; all the bikes had carburetor trouble on the desert; all the saddles were — perhaps not surprisingly — very unsatisfactory, as were both the Bosch and Berling magnetos. Perhaps more to the point was Ike's conclusion: in bad terrain the motorcycle was useless. Wheels spun and wallowed in dust and mud. Chains filled with sand and burned out bearings or simply quit. With unusual foresight he recommended replacing them all with a sort of runabout car, preferably four-wheel-drive, holding three or four passengers, capable of going anywhere. (Ike clearly was thinking of something like the World War II Jeep, but there is no evidence he played any role in the vehicle's design.)

As we have seen, everyone had praise for the Caterpillar and the Militor, and no suggestions about their improvement have been recorded, except a recommendation to devise a stronger and larger sprag for the Militor.

Truck and auto makers and their suppliers had scores of lessons to learn, and more importantly, customers, who soon would be in the millions, had objective resources for making their decisions about automotive purchases. For example, Cadillac and Packard, just two among many luxury cars before 1920, emerged in the twenties as the epitome of fine driving. (During the slump of 1920, General Motors suspended manufacture of all but the Cadillac and Buick.) Packard's slogan, "Ask the man who drove one in France," became the more famous, "Ask the man who owns one," a few years later. Military men gave Harley-Davidson much better marks than the Indian motorcycle. The name Caterpillar was almost synonymous with tractor. The brands and types of tires received detailed and serious consideration from the various observers on the convoy. The expedition fairly well brought an end to the controversy over the preferred type of tire; the military drivers strongly favored the pneumatic tire over the solid rubber, and the leaders in the industry battled with one another for years in their claims to have first marketed the pneumatic.

The army did more than meet its four immediate goals, however. The expedition brought a major change in how America thought about its roads. Some of this was totally unexpected. The War Department concluded that the radius of action and the utility of vehicles were limited only by the road. Defense and commerce both required a national, comprehensive system of roads. In particular, west of the Mississippi, federal help was needed because of the great distances and the light population: those roads were national problems. The "Ship by Truck" movement, largely spurred by Harvey Firestone, received a big boost, changing forever the manner in which Americans distributed goods. Americans' love for the open road had wide, new horizons, and tourism replaced the farm as the chief rationale for road building. Advertising exploded if a product were in any way related to cars. *The New York Times* crowed that the Lincoln Highway would be paved from the Hudson to the Missouri in three years. And finally, in 1921 Congress asked the War Department for advice on a federally aided highway program. Much concerned with defense, especially of the Pacific coast against Japan, the measured reply, replete with maps, came from General John J. Pershing, now chief of staff of the army. Pershing wanted a vast network of 55,000 miles, with one or two roads that we later would call superhighways, linked with thousands of miles of feeder roads. Concerned with the rise of Japan, Pershing was thinking primarily of defense. He did not favor building a large number of major cross-country routes, so popular with the public in these years. Twenty-seven years later President Harry Truman sent the same maps to Congress in his proposal for a national highway system.

The winding up of the convoy's business — reassigning the men and officers, shipping most of the trucks by train back to Maryland, dismantling the unit's structure — took place quickly. (After a leave, Ike returned to Ft. Meade to coach football.) "Tech reps," the factory representatives accompanying the expedition, headed for their home offices to make their private reports. One piece of business remained unsettled. Lt. Jackson had insisted upon an investigation of the removal of the Militor from the convoy in Utah, when it was needed the most. The inquiry never took place. What was the mystery of this powerful, ugly duckling?

Every report, every comment from anyone connected with the convoy, stressed its magnificent performance. Most felt that the truck was indispensable. Then why ship it home? True, it suffered damage on the salt flats of Utah, but all the repairs were made quickly except one, a simple bearing replacement. Two answers to the mystery impel themselves, and they are not mutually exclusive. One is old-fashioned politics, the other, old-fashioned interservice rivalry.

The army developed the Militor in 1918, categorizing it as a truck-tractor. After a series of tests, the blue ribbon Westervelt Board recommended the Militor for exclusive adoption by the field artillery. Congress, however, refused to accept the recommendation, in spite of its endorsement by the chief of field artillery, chief of ordnance, and the director of the Motor Transport Corps. By the summer of 1919, several branches were considering its adoption for their use. As we have seen it was the only wrecker-truck on the convoy of 1919. By October, five more had been built and seventy-five authorized.

As the post-war public demanded cuts in military spending, Secretary of War Newton D. Baker told the chief of staff to limit production to the authorized eighty-one Militors, particularly because of congressional insistence upon the utilization of the many vehicles still left in France. His advice was to wait for Congress to rebuild the motor fleet. At this point, politics took hold of the Militor.

In 1916, the brilliant, tough-minded president of General Motors, Charles Nash, left his position to create Nash Motors, one of whose products was a four-wheel-drive truck called the Nash Quad. Military men considered it inferior to the Militor but they reckoned without Charley Nash. Although his major Rambler plant was in Kenosha, Wisconsin, many of his vehicles were manufactured in Indianapolis. His Indiana congressional representative, James Bland, who had considerable clout in military budgets, prevailed upon his colleagues to kill the authorization for the seventy-five Militors. Other manufacturers, thinking of building such a truck, joined Bland, and only six Militors were ever built. (Congress did not start rebuilding the motor fleet until 1933.)

The remaining question, of why the Militor was removed from the convoy and shipped home, has less to do with politics than inter-service rivalry. The commander of the convoy, Lt. Col. McClure, was commissioned in the Infantry. Lt. Jackson was in Ordnance, and all the other officers (except for observers like Eisenhower) were from the Motor Transport Corps. Jackson frequently complained that his opinions were ignored by the MTC officers, although he praised most of them highly in his reports. All of the vehicles on the expedition were also assigned to the MTC, except the Caterpillar tractor and the Militor, both of which belonged to Ordnance. All of the corps in the post-war years were vying for more turf, and nothing looked greener than the future of the motorized army vehicle. No smoking gun has been found, but it appears that the MTC, nearing the climax of a very successful expedition, did not want to share its glory with the two ungainly representatives of Ordnance. For practical reasons, one of the two had to stay in the convoy until San Francisco. The Caterpillar — less threatening to the MTC — was chosen to remain because it had received much less publicity than the Militor and because it would always require another truck to carry it in convoy. Ordnance prevailed upon the War Department to recall the Militor from western Utah with vague, unkept promises about its return. Only E.R. Jackson was left to wonder what had happened, fruitlessly demanding an investigation. (An historical postscript nullified the whole tempest. The National Defense Act of 1920 made sweeping changes in the army, one of which eliminated the Motor Transport Corps entirely and transferred all army vehicles to the new Transport Service of the Quartermaster Corps. And the large cuts in budgets of the next few years meant little testing and no new trucks.)[3]

The army motor convoy of 1919 received splendid support from the federal government, as we have seen. Nevertheless, it totally ignored one region of the nation, in spite of Woodrow Wilson's mild demurrer. In December of 1919, Senator John H. Bankhead, Sr. of Alabama, dean of the Good Roads movement, asked the chief of the MTC to authorize a second coast-to-coast highway convoy, this time to utilize a southern route. The army could not say no to Congress, and so the plan was quickly approved for 1920.

The second transcontinental convoy differed significantly from the first, in part because it was the second (it was also to be the last) and in part because the southern states had no agency so powerful as the Lincoln Highway Association to promote the expedition. Essentially the 1920 campaign was sponsored by the frequently inoperative Bankhead Highway Association, which appears to have been organized in Birmingham in 1917. (Much of its leadership was also participating in the Good Roads movement, and it is difficult sometimes to separate the two.) Southerners active in these groups sought to honor Bankhead, who had served Alabama as representative and senator since 1887. Correspondence among members of the Bankhead Highway Association indicates that they discussed some sort of Bankhead road during World War I, but had not agreed upon any specific route. But after the army utilized the Lincoln Highway in 1919, the southern leaders knew that they, too, must have a transcontinental road, hence Bankhead's request to the army that December.[4]

On March 1, 1920, Senator Bankhead died. His immense popularity in Alabama and Washington guaranteed speedy action on a southern road, specifically a Bankhead Highway from Washington to California. The tribute was not empty; no one south of the Mason-Dixon line had done more to promote the nation's roads, and he was most instrumental in introducing national legislation as well.

The Second Transcontinental Military Convoy was organized by the MTC and ordered to proceed from Washington to Los Angeles eleven months after the first. Its published purposes were the same as those of the Lincoln Highway convoy with one addition, reflecting technological gains of the past few months; the army wanted to test telegraph and wireless communications. Lt. Col. John F. Franklin, Jr. was given command. His organization had about 150 enlisted men, 15 officers, and about 20 officer observers, a somewhat smaller detachment than in 1919. The number of vehicles was reduced also; paying attention to some of the lessons learned in 1919, this convoy had few heavy trucks and fewer service vehicles. Neither Militor nor Caterpillar was represented; towing was to be handled by a Cleveland tractor. There was no band, less representation of manufacturers, and less pretense of being self-sufficient.

The departure date was June 14, 1920. Again the convoy mobilized at the zero milestone in the Ellipse. Again speeches were made. Again one by Secretary of War Newton D. Baker, but this time augmented by words from secretaries Josephus Daniels, Navy; David F. Houston, Treasury; and Joshua Alexander, Commerce. J.A. Rountree, secretary of the board of the National Highway Association and a very active official in the Good Roads movement, spoke in tribute to Senator Bankhead. The army appointed

Rountree field director of the convoy, the counterpart to Henry Ostermann of the 1919 trip. (Rountree was accompanied on the expedition by his eight-year-old son, "Mac.") Drivers were better trained and disciplined than in 1919; there were no "giddaps" and "whoas," no burned out clutches and brakes.[5]

The Bankhead Road proved to be largely myth, lines drawn on scores of Good Roads Association maps. The drafters hoped to have the convoy pass through the major southern cities of Richmond, Raleigh, Atlanta, Memphis, Little Rock, Dallas, El Paso, Phoenix, and San Diego, halting at Los Angeles. Many deviations were to occur because of poor or non-existent roads. One was encountered almost immediately. The convoy intended to spend its second night in Richmond, Virginia, but rains created so much mud that it could reach only Ashland, a drive of about thirty miles for the day. In two days' time the convoy was almost one day behind schedule.

The trucks moved slowly through North Carolina, taking nine hours to drive from Oxford to Raleigh, obviously a political stop since it was out of the way. Several trucks had to be pulled out of the mud before the convoy swung west toward Greensboro and Charlotte. Receptions, large and enthusiastic from the public, included mayors and governors. Communities put on swims, picnics, dinner dances, and speeches, in the manner of the northern towns. The expedition entered South Carolina at Blacksburg, passed Revolutionary War battlegrounds, camped the night of June 28 at Athens, Georgia, and enjoyed a two-day celebration in Atlanta. They were greeted as the "Bankhead Tourists" by the *Constitution*. Heavy rains and collapsing bridges held them up for three days. Recruiters worked the young men of Atlanta with fair success, feeding them barbecued pork and "Chero Cola."

Bad roads brought more detours. Politics and mud decreed that the convoy would visit Birmingham, rather than cross northwestern Georgia into the corner of Alabama. More mud meant more deviations in northern Mississippi and a detour through Oxford. Rountree wrote to another Good Roads official that the "Mississippi route got an awful black eye." Broken bridges also slowed them down.

The administration of the convoy was having serious problems other than the condition of southern roads. Enough complaints about health conditions were made that the Medical Corps was called in to investigate. The findings were bad. The mess officer had to buy foods on the open market, in competition with the public; sources were always insufficient, frequently stale, and sometimes spoiled. Many of the troops suffered from diarrhea. They had no fresh milk for days, and the cooking was poor. The final indignity — 600 pounds of bread from the quartermaster at Camp Lee, Virginia, had been packed in clothing boxes, lined with a tar paper smelling heavily of naphthalene. Five endorsements later the quartermaster general found the right sergeant to blame and declared it did not happen and would not happen again.[6]

Two weeks of rain, broken bridges, and the usual mud put the convoy seven days behind at Memphis. Less than halfway across the country the troops had already rebuilt 269 bridges according to a Texarkana paper. Plans were to cross the Mississippi at Memphis but for unstated reasons Col. Franklin rented barges and ferried the troops across the river near Helena. This meant that the people of Brinkley, Arkansas, were "disappointed" and the folks of Tunica happy enough to load up their buggies and cars and bring supper that night to the boys, who could not leave camp because of the mud. They spent the entire day, July 27, ferrying the White River; one truck broke its ropes entering the ferry, but the driver steered it on board safely. Rountree pronounced Arkansas's roads almost as disagreeable as those of Mississippi. Mud forced another detour, this one around Arkadelphia, whose citizens worried that they were permanently off the Bankhead road. By now Rountree figured he had made his speech about good roads in seventy-five towns. Another day was spent crossing one river — the Red. The delays were so substantial that Franklin now frequently forced night-long drives to try to get within distance of their schedule. He changed another major policy; he told the Texarkana papers that the unit would rebuild no more bridges. He thought it was not the army's job, but rather that of local authorities. Furthermore, some of his men had been injured testing and repairing unsafe structures. Instead, he would simply order more changes in the itinerary. It also meant that some towns that had been told to expect company would be bypassed.

A delighted Texarkana populace welcomed the exhausted men for the weekend of August 7. Some soldiers pitched their tents on hotel grounds, others in the main park. They had so far traveled 1,910 miles, 174 more than planned because of road conditions. They were two weeks behind schedule. Huge crowds visited the tents and inspected the vehicles. Sunday night the officers and enlisted men enjoyed separate, but probably equal, banquets, the enlisted men being promised exemption from speeches. "Best reception yet," and "the farther west we go the better the food," were the usual quotes to be found in the press. Franklin likened the expedition to that of Lewis and Clark.

The vast Texas distances now loomed ahead, but the roads were sufficiently better than those of Arkansas that the drivers looked forward to the open spaces. Leaving Texarkana, the trucks paralleled the Red River across north Texas to Paris and Bonham, then struck southwest for Dallas and Ft. Worth, where the governor addressed the troops, and a loose association of Dodge owners gave them a grand reception. Col. Franklin told the hosts that the Ft. Worth roads were "the best yet." They left Ft. Worth on Tuesday, the August 16 and spent that night in Mineral Wells. They reached Abilene on Friday afternoon. Heavy rains held them up at Trent so that they did not arrive at Sweetwater until August 24. They drove the 83 miles from Sweetwater to San Angelo in 16-plus hours, the fastest average since leaving Washington.

This jog caused the unit to miss Midland-Odessa, on the original Bankhead map, moving the organization through Ft. Stockton to get back to Pecos, a considerable detour. On September 8 the unit entered El Paso and spent a few days at Ft. Bliss repairing equipment, resting and being entertained by the fort's cadre. The convoy left September 11, traveling comfortably on the high New Mexico plateau a distance of 106 miles that day, another record. The night of August 13 was passed in Lordsburg.

Avoiding much of the rugged Chiricahua mountains, Franklin led his men to extreme southern Arizona next, stopping at Silver Creek near Rodeo, and Douglas, where they inspected a vast bowl of a copper mine and enjoyed a dance at the Gadsden Hotel. Before noon of the next day the convoy was in Bisbee and the colonel, suddenly less concerned about his schedule, permitted another day of rest. They camped at a Bisbee park, the officers lunched at the Copper Queen, and everyone picnicked that night while the American Legion band played. Franklin and Rountree gave their usual talks. They had covered 2,834 miles, Rountree boasting that the Bankhead Road was now a reality; each of twelve states had adopted it and connected it to the neighboring states. Within four years, he predicted incorrectly, the Bankhead Road would be paved from coast to coast.

That road next called for stops at Tucson and Phoenix. The trucks reached the former on the afternoon of September 18; the host this time was the University of Arizona, and the men spent most of that leisurely weekend on the desert campus.

Phoenix proved a different story. Governor T.E. Campbell asked Rountree to have the unit pass through Florence and Chandler before

Phoenix. The advanced scouts returned to tell Franklin that the route was impossible because of loose sand in the Gila River bottom. The situation was no better near Buckeye, the only other crossing. In short, there was no open road between Arizona's two largest cities. Phoenix would have to be skipped, to the embarrassment of the governor and the Phoenix residents. Crowed the *Yuma Sun*, "carelessness and stupidity" cost Phoenix the convoy, and the *Arizona Republican* assured its readers that the city would still be on the Bankhead highway — some day. But first, they wanted a state highway commission. The convoy now swung nearly straight west for Ajo, Sentinel, and the vast Arizona desert. Seventeen miles west of Sentinel, the desert began to work on the equipment in unprecedented fashion; trucks stuck in the loose sand were jacked up so often that all the jacks lost their teeth. Corduroy-type roads were fashioned out of cactus. The convoy strung out ten miles, fifteen times its usual length. Col. Franklin began a special report on all the roads of southern Arizona. On September 26 the convoy finally reached Yuma, and the incomparably better roads of California. They entered San Diego on October 2. Most of the men saw the Pacific for the first time. They had picnics in Balboa Park, a banquet at the U.S. Grant Hotel; for two hours, accompanied by "50 pretty San Diego girls," they cruised the harbor on naval ships.

They camped the night of October 5 in Whittier and with men and vehicles scrubbed clean, paraded into Los Angeles. They were met at the city limits by the mayor, representatives of the chamber of commerce, the American Legion, the auto club, and car dealers. A battalion of troops from Ft. MacArthur escorted them through the city while planes from March Field flew over them. They set up camp at Exposition Park, where a "bevy" of girls served them fruit and punch. More smokers, more banquets followed. Technically this was the end of the trip, and the people of Los Angeles made the men most welcome. All that remained was to drive in comfort to San Francisco to disband the unit, send the men on furlough, and turn the vehicles over to the Ordnance Department at the Presidio of San Francisco.

The convoy had covered nearly 3,700 miles through twelve states. The men had driven more than 100 days, and had advertised the army and the highway. They had tested trucks and recruited young men. Rountree and Franklin estimated they had delivered their message of good roads to 300,000 interested listeners.

The army probably learned little about cars and trucks that had not been demonstrated in 1919 on the Lincoln Highway. North and south, the convoys seem to have received the same warm welcome from the thousands of citizens along the way. Newspaper coverage was about the same. But one major difference in the two expeditions can be seen today; the Bankhead group got none of the publicity from the War Department that its predecessor had. As far as official records are concerned, the Bankhead convoy hardly made a mark. No logs, no daily telegrams, no published observations by the attendant officers have surfaced, compared with thousands of documents and photos from the 1919 trip. Nor does there seem to be any reason for the disparity in the military's behavior. But one major difference obtained. The Lincoln Highway Association, which never missed a trick of public relations, had put all its energies and resources into the 1919 convoy. A year later it did not lift a proverbial finger to help the army on its southern route. The LHA wanted the Lincoln road built, not some southern rival. While manufacturers recognized that cars, trucks and parts were going to be sold all over America, no southern agency, public or private, stepped forward to do for the southern route what the LHA did for the northern route. The untimely death of John Bankhead created a leadership void in the southern roads movement, and perhaps that is the best answer that can be found. In 1938, Congressman William Bankhead, the senator's son and father of actress Tallulah Bankhead, wrote to all the governors of the states through which the 1920 convoy had passed, asking whether the road had ever been "legalized." The disappointing replies showed that only Alabama and Georgia had acted. Texas had not, but reported that the people "used the term." There never has been a true Bankhead Highway across the land, but the writer has seen brief strips of road with that name near Ft. Worth and Phoenix, one of the many cities the convoy could not reach. In the 1920s the women's "section" of the Bankhead Highway Commission in Fulton County, Georgia, planted 100 trees along the road in honor of local soldiers killed in the late war.

Never again did the military attempt to duplicate the two convoys of 1919 and 1920. They were entertaining tours; they enlightened the public and educated the army and its men. They collected vast quantities of information on trucks and especially their parts. They clearly demonstrated the insufficiency of American roads, and in particular the total uselessness of trucks for the defense of the West Coast given the current road conditions. But another convoy would merely reiterate the obvious. The days of good roads movements and convoys, even Lincoln Highway Associations, were ended. From now on the issue rested solely with the Congress.

CHAPTER SIX

The Congress

The public, the military, and the lobbies all were ready to attack the problem of highways in America, but no action would result until Congress could agree on something. Legislation did not want for discussion or committee meetings. Professor and Senator Paul H. Douglas of Illinois believed that the first comprehensive federal aid bill for roads had been introduced in 1907 (promptly defeated,) but others followed quickly. He calculated that in the year 1912 alone, 62 highway bills were introduced into Congress. A reading of the popular magazines of 1916 through 1921 indicates that no domestic issue got more publicity than the "good roads" movement. Why did the government do so little?[1]

The reasons were peculiar to the United States, for other major countries had no similar delays. In Italy, Prime Minister Benito Mussolini ordered the construction of the first modern superhighways in 1924; in six years, 320 miles were finished—financed and managed by private interests. Germany seems to have copied the Italians, starting the first autobahn in 1934. Although the roads' chief purpose was military, the Germans pioneered in landscaping medians and borders. By 1942, more than 1,300 miles had been built. The French built good roads as early as the Bourbon and Napoleonic eras, although the use of the corvee often created great bitterness among poorer peasants.[2]

Two matters played significant roles in delaying any comprehensive road building program in the United States, however. Both had their roots in the size and nature of the United States. The lesser of these two was social and might be described as purely anti-auto. Thousands of Americans, mostly farmers, initially believed with Woodrow Wilson that the automobile would destroy the uniqueness of their rural society, that it would inevitably bring the evils of the city to the farm. In 1906, while president of Princeton, Wilson addressed the North Carolina Society of New York. He expressed concern about the growing number of automobile accidents, protesting that he personally would shoot a hit-and-run driver who killed his child. He thought that the car would bring about "immoral businesses." In his own words, "nothing would foster the spread of Socialism faster." The city was evil, and the automobile would bring that evil to the farmer. Wilson said that the city driver on country roads became the picture of the arrogance of wealth with all its "independence and carelessness." Compare this with Senator William Bankhead's 1908 address in which he affirmed that good roads would keep "the misled boys of our American farms" from somehow combining with the "scum of Europe" in our cities and prevent the spread of urbanization. In 1920, Lt. Col. John F. Franklin, Jr., commanding the 1920 military convoy across the southern U.S., declared that "good roads prevented Bolshevism."

An official of the American Automobile Association countered that Wilson was just plain wrong. Cars could be purchased for a few hundred dollars, at least the cost equivalent of a team of horses. Furthermore many farmers now owned cars, rapidly breaking class distinctions. Strange as Wilson's argument reads today, it nevertheless briefly reflected the view of enough Americans before 1920 to bear heavily against the many groups seeking federal funds for highways.[3]

The other issue, far more difficult of solution, stemmed from the nature of the federal form of government, in particular, the question of states' rights. Presidents from Thomas Jefferson to Wilson had tangled with the language of the Constitution which seemed to prohibit road building by the national government except for the delivery of mail. As we have seen in chapter one, the federal government had made sporadic attempts at a national road, but nothing approaching a national system had ever been suggested. By the twentieth century, the United States was the only major nation lacking such a network.

No one questioned federal responsibility toward postal road construction. The U.S. Post Office established the first rural free delivery service in West Virginia in 1896, and within a year there were 44 such routes. By 1903, RFD mileage approached 200,000. In 1906, Congress first loosened the definition of a postal road by enacting the General Bridge Act, permitting the federal government to set standards for certain highway bridges. The Post Office Act of 1912 greatly expanded congressional oversight of postal roads with a $500 million appropriation for what was called experimental construction of highways. The legal justification continued to be the constitutional authority over the delivery of mail, and Congress still played games with the central issue of authority over national highways.

Each subsequent piece of legislation rationalized some expansion of congressional authority. The war-induced paralysis of the railroads helped pass the next measure, the Bankhead Bill of 1916, a blending of many bills. (Huge discoveries of petroleum in Mexico during the first two decades of the twentieth century caused the public to anticipate very inexpensive driving.) Under the name Federal Aid Road Act, the measures went far beyond the 1912 law by laying the foundation for today's policies. The states retained the initiative in selecting roads to be improved, their type, and their specifications — all subject to federal approval. Amounts available were based on a formula of several variables, including the area, population, and rural mail mileage of each state. The measures created immense federal power, still giving lip service to the constitutional requirement to support the mail, classically reflecting in Senator Douglas's words, an "unobserved tendency in American legislation to try to reconcile centralizers and states' righters."

Additionally, the formula, hammered out in months of congressional debate, provided that each state must match the amount of funds distributed to it by the federal government. Each state was required to create a highway department capable of administering these funds, and the state was obligated to assume the task of maintaining the road after construction had been finished. Wartime conditions restricted highway aid to only $5 million in fiscal 1917 and $10 million in 1918.

But as World War I drew to a close, Senator Bankhead and his colleagues renewed their legislative clamor. They demonstrated that good roads would reduce the cost of living — a sop for the city folk who would get little help for their roads in most of the proposals. The distance factor in the new formula would assure the large western states some share, and the southern farmer would be protected by the postal mileage factor. The piecemeal bills were beginning to shoulder aside the notion that the federal government could finance only roads that had something to do with the postal system.

Increasingly, the War Department played a role in road building. During World War I, the nation shivered at the prospect of a "yellow peril," the fear of a Japanese attack on the West Coast. Interception and publication of the so-called Zimmerman note, in which Germany tried to persuade both Japan and Mexico to invade the U.S., helped inflame such emotion. Secretary of War Newton D. Baker advised the secretary of agriculture that federal funds for postal roads should not be used for tourist-related roads to historic or scenic spots; state road commissions should be told that they would not receive federal funds unless their routes linked up with areas likely to be part of a theater of military operations. General John J. Pershing, now chief of staff of the army, appeared before Congress in 1921, testifying for the road legislation of that year. He opposed constructing a few, wide, transcontinental highways, but since federal funds were involved, he favored a network of good roads "all over the country" for national security. Pershing even presented Congress with maps showing more specifically what he meant and where the roads should be built.[4]

In sum, it is clear that money was available and Congress was willing to spend it during that time if the needs of the military, the rights of the states and the role of the national government could all be untangled. Bankhead and other congressmen had their proposals, Pershing had his, and now the national government began to put muscle behind its ideas. Since 1893 there had been a Federal Highway Administration with an administrator, but until 1919 none had exhibited much power and initiative. But in that year a tough new leader was appointed, and he remained until 1953, serving six presidents and almost seven. Thomas H. MacDonald did not devise a magic formula to pay for highways; they existed. MacDonald found unspent funds from the war years and spent them. Supported by the always-powerful American Association of State Highway Officials, MacDonald pushed the Congress for programs he called a federal-state partnership. He traced this to the 1916 Act which recognized the sovereignty of the states. His job, he said, was to harmonize the needs of the factions. He strongly favored a user's fee to establish construction funds and minimize tolls. Most authorities credit MacDonald with much of the success of highway building in the pre–Eisenhower years.[5]

The act of 1921 required the states, in cooperation with the Bureau of Public Roads (then under Agriculture), to designate a system of interstate and intercounty roads which would be eligible for federal funds. Seven percent of these rural roads would receive aid annually. State and federal matching on a fifty-fifty basis was still required. In the 1920s the total amount of federal aid averaged about $75 million annually, and about $200 million in the late 1930s.

President Franklin D. Roosevelt seems to have thought of road building as essentially a means of relieving unemployment. During the Depression an additional sum of more than $1.2 billion for highways was distributed — with little overall plan — along with substantial Works Progress Administration money, which led to a large amount of shoddy and inconsistent construction. What was probably America's first "super-highway," the Pennsylvania Turnpike, built between 1938 and 1940, received some Reconstruction Finance Corporation and Works Progress Administration funds as a result of FDR's policy. (Perhaps not entirely by coincidence, Bankhead's son, William B., another fervent "Good Roads" man, was speaker of the House in the key years 1937–41).

In 1939 the Bureau of Public Roads, then in the Department of Commerce, recommended to Congress a "coordinated national highway system." Virtually all federal road aid was suspended in 1941; the only exceptions were roads with high military priority. President Harry S. Truman lifted the suspension September 6, 1945.[6]

During World War II, as the U.S. gained increasing success in Europe, demand again arose for federal action on the highways. The Federal Aid Act of 1944 was the most ambitious yet and the first to propose special funds for urban roads — a result of increasing freight traffic. This act also was the first to give serious attention to farm-to-market roads. But most innovative was the measure's authorization of the National System of Interstate Highways, a 40,000 mile network to connect as directly as possible all metropolitan areas of 300,000 population or more. The system was also designed to serve the nation's defense needs and to link certain border points with Canadian and Mexican roads. The army's experience with the convoys of 1919 and 1920 is evident here. General Pershing was just one of many military men to make suggestions about national highways. Pershing's latest request sought a network of four transcontinental highways that did not pass through any large city.

President Franklin Roosevelt suggested paying for the network by taxing the unearned increment resulting from the building of these roads; nothing came of that financing scheme. The Act of 1944 went into effect in 1946. The federal government paid out about $500 million a year, until the sum was increased to $875 million by the Act of 1954.[7]

But the nation and its representatives had yet to face up to the vastness of the highway problem. Not until the administration of Dwight D. Eisenhower were Americans ready to bite the proverbial bullet. Why then? A few writers have suggested that Ike's experience with the army convoy of 1919 had burned itself into his memory until as president, he could do something about those bad roads, the same way Lincoln took on the slave trade. This has an element of truth. He had been greatly impressed by the insufficiency of American roads, and he had admired the great German autobahn in 1945. But Ike did not even mention roads in his presidential campaign of 1952, and his inaugural speech of 1953 discussed foreign affairs solely. No highway plan was even rumored until July 12, 1954, when Vice President Richard Nixon addressed a governors' conference on the nation's "obsolete system" and the need for a "grand plan" of road building. Ike's biographers offer no explanation for this sudden pronouncement.

President Dwight D. Eisenhower (Library of Congress).

In any event, the startled governors lauded Nixon and immediately set up a study committee. Ike responded with his own committee, led by General Lucius Clay, then chair of the board of Continental Can. The president asked the committee to draw up a plan that would meet the nation's highway needs, yet do nothing to upset the post–Korean War economy. Clay's group made its study, held public hearings, and reported to Eisenhower by November of the same year. Ike now began giving the road program his greatest personal attention.

Probably most motorists in the nation considered the president's concern long overdue. Ike finally explained his goals in his state of the union speech of January 6, 1955.[8] The need for a road program was obvious. Only the federal government could build a unified system. A carefully conceived plan would level out the economy. And for national security, an evacuation network was needed. He slyly suggested that much of the fault lay with Republican prosperity — too many cars were on the road, approximately 58 million in 1954, with an increase of nearly 50 percent expected within the decade. (After attending a reception for car dealers' wives, Mamie told Ike she had never seen so many furs and jewels.)[9]

Congestion was a nuisance, expensive, and dangerous to human life. It was also a threat to national security. What would happen in case of an air attack by Soviet Union forces? (I recall with little nostalgia driving bumper-to-bumper daily during these years on a New Orleans "evacuation route" whose two lanes twisted alongside the Mississippi levee until the road just disappeared in the morass of Jefferson Parish's equally snarled traffic.)

Before World War II the nation had spent an average of about 1.4 percent of its gross national product on roads. In the post-war years the average was but .2 percent. The nation's transportation system was moving backward, rapidly. Ike's solution was a massive, multi-billion-dollar, ten-year program.

Using the Clay Commission's report as the basis for his requests, Eisenhower asked for: (1) $2.5 billion to modernize the existing interstate roads by 1964; (2) $315 million to continue aid to primary roads "as before;" (3) $210 million to continue aid to secondary roads "as before;" (4) $75 million to improve roads not in the interstate system; (5) $22.5 million for roads on public lands "as before." The annual total federal expenditure would be $3.12 billion. States and local governments might spend twice as much more. All except the first item would be financed "as before," meaning fifty-fifty sharing between the states and the federal government. But the first item would be financed with the federal government assuming $25/27$ths of the cost. How much money each state would get would be determined largely by the formula worked out in the 1916 law, a ratio of its ranking in area, population, and rural mail mileage to the national totals. No state would get less than .5 percent of the total each year. (Primary roads were defined as roads that linked principal cities, county seats, ports, and manufacturing centers. The secondary federal system was essentially farm to market roads.)

Ike's innovation, and the most essential part of the plan, was the expenditure over a ten-year period of approximately $27 billion, completing and modernizing the National System of Interstate Highways. At that moment they totaled 37,600 miles. Few congressmen of either party opposed the construction, but almost every congressman had something to say about the method of financing. For the next year, the problem never got beyond committee rooms.[10]

Eisenhower wanted to pretend that the new system could be completed without new taxes, in today's congressionalese, "off-budget." He asked Congress to create a Federal Highway Corporation which could issue 30-year, taxable bonds, the sums raised to be given to the states for costs of construction of the new interstate system and connecting arterials in urban areas. The corporation would gradually be reimbursed by the receipts from federal gas and oil taxes. The bonds would not be considered part of the federal debt, nor would they be guaranteed by the government. If necessary, the Highway Corporation could borrow from the Social Security fund. The debt could not exceed $21 billion. The corporation would be managed by a board of five, including the secretaries of treasury and commerce without compensation, and three persons named by the president with the advice and consent of the Senate. This group would be concerned with finances only; actual construction would fall to the commissioner of public roads, now in the Commerce Department. The Department of Defense would be the chief technical consultant.

An excited Congress snapped at Ike's large bone. But before any legislative action took place, three major philosophical questions emerged. First, about the bonds themselves — was default a possibility? Without guarantees, would lenders buy the bonds? Were they part of the national debt, no matter how Congress labeled them? Could the federal government sell bonds that are not part of the legal debt?

Second, did Congress have the power to bind future Congresses? Was it legal to create a permanent appropriation from the treasury? (There were minor precedents.)

Third, would the federal government be pre-empting traditional state authority by earmarking the gasoline tax and taking such a high level of responsibility away from the states?

The great debate began. Scores of bills and amendments were proposed, but only three got thorough discussion in committee. In addition to the administration, Senator Albert Gore, Sr., a Democrat from Tennessee, and Senator Francis Case, a Republican from South Dakota, had bills seriously considered. That Republican Speaker of the House Joe Martin and Senator Case had both introduced the administration's bill and then refused to support it helped add to the ironic complexity of the issue. To the extent that party lines mattered, the differences lay essentially in the method of financing the huge project.

Philosophy of government separated many groups. Eisenhower contended that roads were a capital asset, to be treated like the assets of a corporation — meaning that vast funds would not be required at the outset of the program, but would be distributed as needed to help level the economy. Senator Gore affirmed his belief that the roads belonged to "the people;" all would use them and all should pay into the general fund through the usual taxation method. Senator Case, seeking compromise, would use a corporation of some sort but only to buy land; he wanted the taxes based on use in accordance with the benefits received from the new roads. Big truck companies and utilities would be hit the hardest. The three factions also disagreed upon the amount of money needed, Eisenhower aiming high, and Gore aiming low. They all had varying plans for reimbursing owners of toll roads that might be incorporated into the network. Finally, for the new interstate system, Eisenhower wanted 100 percent federal financing, Gore wanted 66.66 percent, and Case wanted 90 percent.[11]

Most Republicans, however, supported the concept of the Highway Corporation and the bonded indebtedness. Most Democrats, led by Senator Harry Byrd, feared the federal government would usurp the states' taxing power and greatly weaken their rights. Senator Richard Neuberger of Oregon presented a less hoary, but equally emotional case. The corpo-

ration, he said, was designed to be a bonanza for the banks, insurance companies, and other financial agencies. He calculated that in the thirty-year period, the $20 billion raised for the highways would accrue more than $11.5 billion in interest. For every dollar appropriated for the road, fifty-five cents would go for interest, not construction. The president's "predilection for financing the responsibilities of government outside the normal government budget" would saddle the nation's children with an unconscionable burden. Neuberger favored straightforward pay-as-you-go taxes on fuel and tires. Gore

Senator Albert Gore, Sr. (Library of Congress).

agreed with Neuberger.[12] Fearing that the "finance men" would dictate engineering standards, the army jumped on the band wagon opposing the administration. When a Senate committee rejected the Clay bill, Representative George Fallon, Democrat of Maryland, brought forth his own bill, the chief feature being an attempt to keep the budget in balance by a series of graduated taxes. Large truck tires, for example, might be taxed at ten times the rate of a standard passenger car tire. Gore, speaking for labor, wanted enforcement of the Davis–Bacon Act, which would assure the payment of prevailing wages on every aspect of the project. Little was acceptable to everyone, and Congress adjourned August 2, 1955, without passing any road law.[13]

Suggestions for a special session collapsed when Ike reported that he could not stand one — it would cause him to lose his sanity.[14] That fall and winter it became increasingly apparent that factionalism might destroy the entire project. According to a major biographer, the president would spend money on roads but nothing else, the interstate system being by far his favorite domestic program, and he frequently asked Congress to give priority to his wishes. Finally, he simply told the leaders of his party that he wanted some law, even if they had to yield a great deal to the Democrats. When the president and the truckers agreed to modify some of their requests, Fallon and Hale Boggs, Democrat of Louisiana, went to work crafting a compromise that would not hurt anyone very much. In April the measure swept through a relieved House 388–19 and through the Senate 89–1. The president signed the bill into law

Congressman Hale Boggs of Louisiana, a leader in winning financing for the interstate highway system (Library of Congress).

June 29, 1956, under the name The National System of Interstate and
Defense Highways. Boggs and Fallon had found a key — plenty of roads
for everyone without pain.

Title I of the National System, labeled the Federal-Aid Highway Act,
committed the federal government to an expenditure of $25 billion for
roads between 1957 and 1969. Title II, the Highway Revenue Act, created
the Highway Trust Fund, and assigned certain user taxes to it. Together
they created "the greatest non-military construction program ever under-
taken anywhere in the world." The president promised that the task would
be completed in 1969 at a cost of $30 billion.

The Highway Trust Fund and the pay-as-you-go principle were not
part of Eisenhower's original plan, but he had promised the nation a network, and this seemed the only way to get one. The acts of 1956 brought
an end to equal federal/state sharing of costs; in some instances the federal government paid as much as 95 percent of construction costs.

The taxes themselves were not onerous. Initially the tax on fuel oils
rose only from to two to three cents a gallon; taxes on rubber increased
from five to eight cents a pound. New cars faced an excise tax of 2 percent; farm vehicles were exempted. All truck tire taxes were graduated but
not enough to create much complaint from truckers. Very difficult decisions, such as how much to pay for old toll roads, were simply postponed.
Some interstate roads, mostly toll, already existed. Generally these were
to be retained, the owners bought out.

About 80 percent of the network was new, however. Precisely where
the new roads would go was not addressed by the new law, and much bitterness would be generated as time went by.

A major issue of great permanent significance to the nation was settled at this time. Eisenhower had intended that the interstate highways
would bypass major cities to provide a smooth flow of traffic from coast
to coast, and according to Stephen Ambrose, the president vigorously
opposed the roads entering cities in any fashion. The system was, after all,
partly a defense measure. But his staff forced him to yield in order to get
the city votes; without interstate roads passing through cities, there would
be no interstate roads. It was that simple. A clear-cut decision made on
purely political grounds was to affect the nation for decades, perhaps much
more. We do not know yet. Perhaps it was inevitable, irrespective of politics. But the impact of this decision — the sociology of the highways —
had not been studied, not even mentioned in congressional debates. That
one decision alone significantly reduced the military value of the roads

that both Pershing and Eisenhower had assumed. It was also to change America's traffic patterns, commuting habits, and style of living for millions of people. (Reflecting the urbanization of the highway story are the bureaucratic changes through the years. From 1893 until 1939 all federal roads were under the supervision of the Department of Agriculture; in 1949 the Bureau of Public Roads was included in the Department of Commerce. And in 1967 the new Federal Highway Administration was incorporated into the new Department of Transportation.) Almost from the start, cost estimates fell short woefully, because city roads meant vast, unexpected purchases of expensive urban lands. The matter is still with us.[15]

Land costs, inflation, and upgrading of standards forced Congress to amend the laws regularly after 1956 to raise more revenue. Taxes were increased in 1958, 1959, and 1961, pushing the interstate appropriation up to $41 billion. The Federal Highway Act of 1968 added 1,500 miles to the interstate system. At the end of 1974, 36,500 miles were completed and 2,800 more were under construction. The bicentennial date of 1976 became the new target date. That proved naive. In 1981, approximately 5 percent of the network was still unfinished, and the federal bill now exceeded $130 billion. Maintenance was beginning to prove more costly than the original construction.[16]

By the mid–1980s, some of the roads had reached the end of their design life, and traffic was immeasurably heavier than anticipated thirty years before. About 130 million vehicles were licensed, traveling an estimated 1.5 trillion miles per year. President Ronald Reagan's administration concluded that an updating of the 1956 act was needed, and he pushed through the 1983 Surface Transportation Assistance Act. By increasing federal fuel taxes to nine cents a gallon, an additional $4.4 billion went into the Highway Trust Fund. Construction began on a few hundred more miles. In 1988, mileage driven equaled 2 trillion, up more than 27 percent in a decade, while the interstate system grew less than 1 percent. Perhaps beginning to see the light, Congress appropriated more than $3 billion for mass transport expansion.

As the decade of the 1980s ended, several assessments of progress could be made. Just a bit more than 500 miles remained to reach the goal of 43,000 interstate miles. (Much delay had been caused by local interests in Louisiana over questions of bypass routes, and that state had the longest unfinished portion.) The federal aid program would expire in 1991. Various groups were beginning to puzzle over the fact that thousands of miles of new road had not eliminated congestion.

Highway experts speculated that the massive building era might be drawing to a close, to be supplanted by a period of upgrading and repair. Many motorists were surprised to learn that the great new roads had a life expectancy of only twenty years; thousands of miles would be obsolete — some in Louisiana — before Louisiana had its quota filled. The secretary of transportation estimated an expense of $75 billion just to repair bridges. Total federal spending on original construction alone now exceeded $112 billion. The Reagan administration withheld portions of the Highway Trust Fund in order to make the overall federal budget look better; the powerful American Automobile Association demanded the fund be used before any new taxes were considered. The AAA also opposed the diversion of funds to finance mass transport of any sort. Yet in less than 35 years, national traffic had tripled. Was Ike's program in danger?[17]

President George H.W. Bush had a comprehensive plan, at the heart of which was simplistic change. He would shift the major financial burden to the states and give them more control over routes and design to make them less unhappy about their increased taxes. The federal budget would look better. Few states could adjust to that scheme; the state of New Jersey, in bad financial condition, privatized four miles of I-95, converting it into a toll road for $400 million. "Massive" increases in tolls followed. Other states considered the same solution.[18]

Oregon's Governor Neil Goldschmidt, a Democrat, attacked Bush, writing that Oregon's gas tax had increased nearly 200 percent in less than ten years and had reached its limit. He calculated that the federal government was carrying only about half its share of the burden. In the Reagan years, federal spending on national transit had declined 50 percent while state and local spending had increased from 64 percent to 80 percent of the total. Bush, Goldschmidt added, had no national policy for roads, truck damage, or use of the railroads, yet billions for infrastructure remained bottled up in the Highway Trust Fund. He concluded that the Reagan–Bush administrations had surrendered the federal government's road responsibility in insuring the nation's economy.

The governor's complaints were echoed in many other states, but more important was general public dismay that while the interstate highway system was superb in many ways, it had increased congestion enormously in most cities. Woe betide the tourist who encountered the flow of commuters at the wrong time of day, even in a relatively small town, if it happened to straddle an interstate highway. And even casual observers could see that the system was in serous disrepair.

But in the meantime the Bush administration had come up with its "landmark" bill. In 1991, the U.S. Department of Transportation had submitted to the president its biennial report on the highways. The report substantiated and quantified what most drivers had guessed. DOT found that 642,000 miles, about half of non-local road mileage, were at or near such quality as to damage vehicles using them. (In some stretches of I-20, heavy trucks were required to use the inside lane because of the damage already incurred on the outside lane.) Seventy percent of peak-hour travel on the interstates resulted in daily congestion equaling 8 billion hours of delays, costing $120 billion in lost time each year. One-fourth of highway bridges had significant deficiencies, the agency concluded.

All these factors impressed the legislators, and in December Congress passed, and President Bush signed, the Intermodal Surface Transportation Efficiency Act, soon to be known as ISTEA (pronounced "ice tea"). (The measure had far less media exposure than Ike's 1956 law, but promised more money and wider implications.)

The 1991 act contained innovative provisions. It changed the 35-year-old method of financing construction. The package contemplated spending $151 billion over a six-year period. Of that, $119.5 billion was designated for road construction and repair, and $31.5 billion for mass transit programs. Individual states could transfer as much as half their quota to mass transit if they so chose. This was mandatory if the state failed to meet clean air standards. The federal-state match for the interstate portion of the roads remained at 90–10. Much would still be financed by fuel taxes. New toll roads could be built with federal help, but not as part of the interstate system.

ISTEA provided an innovation in road building. Some of the road money must be used for restoration or improvement of certain sites along the highways. These projects are called "enhancements," and 10 percent of each state's allotment (or $3 billion total) must be used to make the highways more attractive. By late 1994 more than 2,000 such projects had been approved. They include landscaping, bike and hiking paths, purchase of easements and historic sites, and restoration of old buildings and total more than $650 million so far. States put up 20 percent of the cost.[19]

Another $8 billion was set aside for special projects and research, especially in the field of mass transportation. Among these plans was to be a magnetic levitation train. Proponents of mass transits systems were made reasonably happy by the increased expenditures expected. The government was beginning to recognize that congestion could not be relieved by more miles of interstate alone. "Landmark" or not, however, little change occurred. Highway expenditures for fiscal 1993 were far below those promised by the Intermodal Act, and many states and cities seemed determined to opt for using their share of the fund for a traditional increase in paving, not mass transportation.

President Bill Clinton, proposing a vast array of major legislation, did not place a priority on the highway crisis. He did ask for more help for mass transportation; the American Public Transit Association concluded that he had increased public transit budgeting 20 percent, the best record since Jimmy Carter, but Clinton made no significant proposals about the highway problem in his first year in office. But in 1994, Congress began serious debate on a bill introduced by Max Baucus, Democratic senator from Montana. This would be a new "National Highway System," of 150,000 miles, connecting major population centers, national parks, ports, defense installations and tourist attractions. It would be state of the art, with smart signals and landscaping, with details to be worked out as the costs were studied. The system would include the 45,000 existing miles of interstates and would carry more than half the passenger traffic and 70 percent of the freight traffic of the nation. The administration touted the bill as a major boost to the economy.[20]

Had Congress followed through, the National Highway System would have accomplished that precise goal, for coincident with the road measure, a vast new trade program was pushed through by the Clinton administration, which would rely heavily on motor transportation. Supported in various forms by each administration since Gerald Ford's, the North American Free Trade Agreement was completed in 1992 and signed into law late in 1993. NAFTA, a plan to remove trade restrictions among Canada, the United States, and Mexico, stirred up tremendous opposition in all three nations; in the U.S. the greatest objections came from labor and environmental groups who foresaw great harm from Mexico's cheap labor and weak health and safety controls. Nevertheless, the law passed and went into effect January 1, 1994.

The agreement is complex and still young; its ultimate results must wait for another day. For our purposes, its importance lies in its immediate and future impact on the American road system, for 85 percent of U.S.–Mexico trade moves by truck. The first obvious consequence was heavy investment and the movement of U.S. branch stores into Canada and Mexico, with the attendant shipment of vast quantities of goods from U. S. distributors. Wal-Mart purchased 120 stores in Canada. The Rio

Grande was now less of a border as American franchises moved hundreds of miles south into Chihuahua and Monterrey. Texas, especially, gained by the new law. Laredo and El Paso boomed from the trucks and businessmen passing through. About half the commerce from the U.S. to Mexico passed through Texas. But California, Arizona, Michigan, Illinois, and New York all shared in the growth. In 1986 the city of Laredo had forty-nine freight transit companies; in 1994, it had 300. An estimated 2,000 trucks a day passed through the city, carrying goods to and from Mexico. The post–NAFTA truck crossings into Mexico in 1994 were seven or eight times what they were in 1987. Nightmare congestion demanded new bridges crossing the Rio Grande.

What did all this trade mean to the American highway system? Assuming that the bonanza would continue indefinitely, booster groups with strong ties to NAFTA immediately insisted upon the construction of more highways. For the moment ignoring the cost question, local groups touted their favorite routes, insisting upon the usual federal assistance. The greatest rivalry rather logically appeared in Texas. Pre-empting the field, a group of south central Texans created the Greater Austin–San Antonio Corridor Council and named I-35 the NAFTA Highway, urging others to accept the term. I-35, which extends from Duluth through Kansas City, Oklahoma City, Dallas–Ft. Worth, Austin, and San Antonio to Laredo, allegedly moves more trade in the NAFTA market than any other highway. A Dallas congressman sought unsuccessfully to have the road designated as essential to international commerce, meaning it would get priority funding under the ISTEA. But weakening the argument for I-35 was competition from within the state. El Paso and Midland were but two cities seeking the same advantage. Even some central Texans opposed expanding I-35. Already six lanes in most urban stretches, the road cannot easily be expanded.

The weakness of the I-35 dream is that trade is not heavy at its northern reaches; significant amounts of freight do not flow from Duluth — and Canada — to Laredo. The Mid-Continent Coalition, with its greatest strength in Houston, makes a strong case for I-69, which runs from the Canadian border through Flint, Michigan, to southern Indiana, with plans to continue to Memphis. New roads would have to be constructed to Houston with both Brownsville and Laredo terminals. The great advantage of this road is that it would help the industrial heartland of the U.S. send industrial goods to Mexico; but its disadvantage is that much of it has never been built! Both the I-35 and I-69 plans would take advantage of the recent burst of industrial energy in the Midwest, which is growing much more rapidly than the rest of the nation and exporting twice as much as other regions.

No discussion of road-building legislation should end without some reference to the work of Lady Bird Johnson to beautify the road network. Mrs. Johnson grew up in a singularly beautiful section of Texas, and when she married Lyndon, she wrote, she greatly enjoyed their motor trips between Austin and Washington, but abhorred the trash and billboards along many of the roads. In 1964, when Lyndon ran for re-election as president, Lady Bird campaigned for him with Stewart Udall, former secretary of the interior, and in their travels observed much of the damage highway construction was doing to parks and wilderness areas. Sharing an interest with her in saving and improving the appearance of the land, Udall suggested she use her influence with the president to beautify the capital, which Udall called "shabby."

With influential friends and much private money she succeeded in planting vast quantities of flowers and trees throughout Washington, for few people objected. But the highways proved a tougher task. The Bureau of Public Roads estimated there were 16,000 junkyards on the nation's roads, with more than 1,600 in Texas alone. Their owners provided a formidable block of opposition. The billboard story was comparable. President Eisenhower had thought that the federal government had no authority over them; while in Congress, even Lyndon Johnson had opposed anti-billboard legislation. But now, as he said, things were different. "I love that woman and she wants that Highway Beautification Act, and by God, we're going to get it for her."[21]

The efforts of the two Johnsons created intense bitterness among many Democrats as well as most Republicans. So many amendments were proposed that some of Lady Bird's friends suggested she withdraw the bill rather than see it emasculated. The bill was condemned as "a woman's issue"; Congressman Bob Dole (R–Kansas) tried to get the bill amended to substitute the name "Lady Bird" for the secretary of commerce wherever the measure designated authority. (That failed.) LBJ assigned Bill Moyers to work with the Outdoor Advertising Association of America to seek a reasonable compromise, but the OAAA badly fooled Johnson with their determination and their strength, and simply co-opted Moyers. Lewis Gould wrote that it was surprising any bill passed. But in 1965 the badly battered Highway Beautification Act went into effect. Costs, the OAAA, and Vietnam all meant that the law never achieved its goals, but it was a noble try. Without Lady Bird Johnson there probably would have been no measure at all.

A century and a half after Henry Clay, the nation, overcoming obstacles of all forms, finally had an elaborate system of highways. In fifty-plus years, billions of dollars had been spent on thousands of miles of well-engineered, high-speed roads. All were intended to move Americans safely, quickly, and comfortably from one city or state to another. Most did. Some were even beautiful. But while individual stretches of road were vastly improved, automobiles were choking the cities more than ever before. Experts clamored for more effort on mass transit, but all too many defeated bond issues demonstrated little public support. More pavement seemed to be the only answer, yet it was becoming clear that congestion rapidly followed every new road. Where should we go now?

CHAPTER SEVEN

Pie in the Sky

The 1990s brought significant change in the role of the interstate highways, if not clearly delineated at the time. President Eisenhower had thought of the roads as essential to defense needs. Many congressmen saw them as links between congressional districts larded with pork. The public, with mixed purposes, saw safer and quicker interstate travel, and could hope for easier commutes. All of these goals were soon to be augmented by a worldwide fascination with international trade — the promises of economic globalization. Although in some ways a movement to match some of the economic growth of the United States, globalization could go nowhere without U.S. cooperation, even leadership. And globalization required that resurrected shibboleth, free trade.

Since the time of its inventor, Adam Smith, free trade never disappeared from international trade negotiations until the Great Depression. In futile efforts to reduce competition and support business at home, nation after nation raised tariffs to unprecedented heights. In 1930 the U.S. enacted the Hawley-Smoot tariff, the highest in our nation's history. Then, during World War II, attempting to support Latin America against Nazi commerce, the U.S. reversed the trend with a series of reciprocal trade agreements negotiated by Secretary of State Cordell Hull. These prefaced much of the vast multilateral system functioning today. After the war the larger nations sought to restore commerce by various agreements both bilateral and multilateral. European nations took the lead, with its Common Market forcing American leaders to examine means to compete. The obvious market would be regional and encompass as much of the Western Hemisphere as possible. Problems abounded, among them America's aging infrastructure, but the movement fell into willing hands.

Leadership for a North American trade agreement in the late 1980s came from Canadian Prime Minister Bryan Mulroney and U.S. President George H.W. Bush. Mexico's new president, Carlos Salinas de Gortari, promising economic reform, also brought his nation into the pact. All three leaders faced substantial opposition, yet the proposal elicited enough bipartisan support, including that of incoming President Bill Clinton, that it was signed by him and went into effect January 1, 1994. The measure was called the North American Free Trade Agreement (NAFTA) and has had vast consequences for all three nations.[1]

A dozen years later, NAFTA still bitterly polarizes thousands most closely affected by its dramatic changes. This is not the venue to debate its merits, but one obvious conclusion directly affects the highway story. Trade among the three nations has grown enormously. U.S. trade with Canada and Mexico reached an all time high in 2005, some $790 billion. This was 11 percent greater than the 2004 total and double the pre–NAFTA volume. About two-thirds of the trade moves by truck, and border crossings, now about 12 million annually, rose by nearly half in those years.[2]

The nation, meanwhile, slowly grasped that the interstate highway system had a shelf life, perhaps 35 or 40 years, barely a generation. Popular tastes changed as well, and the public seemed to want a more comprehensive highway program that would encompass some money for rapid transit and even beautification. Perhaps smarting from a lack of success in foreign affairs, President George W.H. Bush pushed Congress for an ambitious "intermodal" (meaning linking different types of transportation) highway bill.

Passed in 1991, the Inter-modal Surface Transportation Efficiency Act, a five-year program, did not lack for goals. It would create a national intermodal system, complete the Eisenhower highway targets, improve public urban transportation, reduce pollution, even make roads more attractive. These somewhat traditional aims were accompanied by a new concept called corridors. Frequently amended, ISTEA changed the number of corridors almost monthly—from as few as three to 80 or more. That these were all labeled "high priority" showed the influence of congressmen. The exact definition was not expressed; corridors could extend border to border or remain within one state. They could be statewide or shorter than a county. Some had fancy names like Heartland Express or Canamex. They must have been fun to draw, but they were not cemented in reality.[3]

ISTEA expired in 1997 after a great deal of noise and modest highway construction. (The Cato Institute condemned it for being anti-auto and too much the product of central planning.) It mattered not. President

Bill Clinton had a new program called the National Highway System Designation Act (NHS). One hundred sixty-one thousand miles of road were "designated "as part of the U.S. system. Guaranteed federal funds could go directly to the states. In 1996 that amounted to a mere $5.4 billion. Help was also promised to long-suffering rail systems.

But President Clinton was not done. In June 1998 he signed into law another highway bill, this called Transportation Equity Act for the Twenty-first Century, or TEA-21, the largest public works act in history, also one of the most complex. In its simplest form it allocated far more funds than the other bills of the late twentieth century. It made available $218 billion in federal funding for highway construction, highway safety, and transit programs for six years. The amount actually appropriated hinged upon moneys received by the Highway Trust Fund, a creation of Eisenhower's days, but the new law guaranteed a minimum return to each state. This averaged about 37 percent above ISTEA funding.[4] Perhaps pressured to match his predecessors in high spending, President George W. Bush in 2005 signed the Safe, Accountable, Flexible, Efficient, Transportation Equity Act (Legacy for Users), known as SAFETY (LU). This five-year measure guaranteed to the states $244 billion, another record. It confirmed 80-plus High Priority Corridors, and perhaps most important, made it easier to convert roads into toll roads and for the private sector to take part in setting their rates.[5]

This spate of legislation strongly appealed to the public. But as time passed it became apparent that not a lot had been accomplished. Every study revealed that highway construction and repair were losing ground, and the demand seemed insatiable. Sampling the press of a few states might be instructive.

- Tuscaloosa, Alabama: too much traffic, highway fund will disappear in three years, gas tax losing to inflation.
- Pine Bluff, Arkansas: need $15 billion, no plans or ideas about solutions.
- Sacramento, California: too many bottlenecks, too much growth, bonds suffer from eastern competition.
- Fort Wayne, Indiana: expensive study concludes long beltway around Indianapolis will not relieve congestion.
- Shreveport, Louisiana: truckers say Louisiana roads the nation's worst.
- *Las Vegas Sun*: state faces a shortfall of nearly $5 billion in highway funding.

- *Oklahoman*: state worried about future NAFTA commerce. Worst bridges in the U.S.
- Lambertville, New Jersey: taxes can't go higher. It's time to consider tolls.
- *Pocono Record*, Pennsylvania: new roads badly needed but need repairs first.
- *Sunbury Daily Item*: state cannot build roads fast enough to keep pace with the growth of traffic.
- *Seattle Times*: state needs $5 billion for one bridge alone. Way short of funds.
- *Martinsburg Journal*: West Virginia's interstates need "major" work. Thirty seven percent of bridges obsolete.

And so on.

Not a newspaper bragged about its state's highways; some seemed to want to compete for the title of state with the worst highway problem. Suffice it to say the needs were enormous and the solutions inadequate. The war in Iraq meant that orderly, substantial federal assistance was no longer to be expected. Increasing taxes, especially on gasoline, which was already selling at very high rates, was considered unlikely by either the federal or state governments. Bonds were always possible, but high interest rates, public reluctance, and an uncertain economy precluded many such possibilities. The Federal Highway Trust Fund calculated that in 2009, for the first time in its half-century history, it would run out of money. There remained that old bugaboo, the toll road. Mentioned, or at least whispered about in every legislative corridor, toll roads would require a lot of selling to get public approval, but to many a governor there was no place else to turn.[6]

After all, a toll was a tax, no matter where collected. But a tax could easily be diverted to other needs than roads; legislatures could guarantee that tolls would be used only on roads. New technological devices such as transponders could eliminate some of the wasted time and social annoyances of the traditional toll booth. But there was another, more materialistic concept. The magic word was privatization.

Perhaps it should not have sounded so revolutionary. After all, most colonial America roads (turnpikes), ferries, and even mountain passes were privately owned, built, and operated. But America had outgrown them, and probably most of the public long since had assumed that some level of government built all the roads.

However, the University of Chicago Economics Department, the World Bank, and various third world governments had found new, far broader definitions of privatization.

Highway privatization has many fathers, but Robert W. Poole, engineer, transportation advisor to several presidents, and one of privatization's chief theoreticians, probably deserves the honor as much as anyone. Admitting he did not invent the idea, he nevertheless popularized the scheme of selling or leasing America's highways to private operators. He claimed, in fact, that his paper of 1988 directly resulted in four private express lanes in Orange County, California. His Reason Foundation has been beating that drum ever since.[7]

In 2006, the Congress removed a number of legal barriers prohibiting charging tolls on interstate highways and gave private investors new access to tax-free bonds for highway work. The way was now clear.

Assuming the soundness of the idea, did private agencies have the vast resources required to take on numerous projects costing many billions of dollars? For the moment, at least (the moment being the early twenty-first century), there seemed to be money for any project — if the terms were right. Perhaps more surprising, foreign investors took on more ambitious projects than did Wall Street. Who owned these deep pockets?

Dozens, perhaps hundreds of companies are currently performing highway and toll road construction, and it is not always possible or worth the trouble to sort them out, but a few of the largest should be cited for the scope of their ambitions. Probably the best known in America because of the size of its projects is a Spanish firm called Concesiones de Infraestructura de Transporte, or Cintra. Cintra is a subsidiary of Grupo Ferrovial, which is primarily held by the Spanish Del Pino family. Grupo, capitalized at more than $5 billion, engages in a vast variety of activities, highway construction being primarily the domain of Cintra. Among their achievements are roads in Canada, Spain, Portugal, Chile, and Ireland. In the U.S. the works are already most impressive. Alone or with other firms, Cintra in 2005 took over the seven-mile Chicago Skyway on a 99-year lease, which gave Chicago $1.8 billion; about the same time it leased the 157-mile Indiana Toll Road, a 75-year lease for $3.8 billion.[8]

Macquarie Infrastructure Group, an Australian company owned by Macquarie Bank, probably has an even larger number of American developments. MIG, as it is called, often works with Cintra and others, so precise responsibility is not always clear, but the company claims operations in 24 countries. For example, it controls and/or owns a dozen British airports. In the U.S., it shares with Cintra the Chicago and Indiana roads mentioned above. It manages the Dulles Greenway in Virginia and a planned road near San Diego. Three or four roads are being contracted to MIG in Oregon. The company operates the Detroit-Windsor Tunnel and an expressway bridge in Alabama.[9]

Another Australian firm, Transurban, has taken over the Pocahontas Parkway in Virginia, paying $611 million for a 99-year lease. Transurban has a long record of similar work in Australia.[10]

Perhaps the first American firm to privatize highway asset management (henceforth HAM), was VMS Inc., founded in 1995 in Petersburg, Virginia, subsequently operating from Richmond.

According to its own handouts, VMS executed thirteen contracts with five states in its first four years. The company did not build complete highway systems but seems to concentrate on HAMS.

What's in highway asset management? Almost anything pertaining to a highway, apparently. Under the public/private partnership (PPP) contract, VMS operates and maintains bridges and tunnels as well as the more prosaic welcome centers, rest stops, toll booths, and high occupancy vehicle lanes—in short the highway infrastructure. In the year 2000, VMS contracted a major five-year program to manage the pavement, bridges, tunnels, etc. of the National Highway System in Washington, D.C.[11]

That American contractors (or governments) lag well behind several other nations in the promotion of PPP's is obvious, perhaps a consequence of our long tradition of public ownership of so many activities. And the partnerships are all so new that profitability is uncertain. But we are catching up. Goldman Sachs and Co. already are involved in many financing proposals; Carlyle Group, Washington's biggest financial firm, has established a committee to study such investments. In December 2006, Governor Ed Rendell of Pennsylvania asked for expressions of interest in privatizing the ancient Pennsylvania Turnpike; within a week he received 48 responses, all offers of some form of professional service. American Automobile Association's telephone poll found that 52 percent of respondents favored introducing toll roads to meet the needs; 21 percent would raise gas taxes.[12]

Where does that leave us? Do we know where we are going? Is privatization the magic solution, a *deus ex machina*, pie in the sky? Or, to mix metaphors a bit more, are we entering a vast uncharted minefield?

The answer may be that all of the above are right. The immediate gains are obvious and substantial. Traditional (public) road building agencies, with rare exception, claim they lack resources to maintain existing roads and fall far short of the highway expansion that the twenty-first century demands. Most drivers, commuters or tourists will loudly agree. Outside capital is needed and it has shown up.

Agreements will vary in detail, but the outline is the same from job to job. The public agency, facing a particular and sizable need, asks for bids. Two or three huge, foreign (largely) firms form a consortium, secure financing from a variety of banks and investment houses and offer a contract. The consortium will rebuild the bridge, repair and expand some roads, remodel the rest stops, or create a grand new highway, anything, all at no immediate expense to the public. The agreements are of long duration. Most seem to be at least thirty years, many as much as ninety-nine.

And what does this cost the public? In short, it's the cost of the toll, and therein lies the rub. Who sets the rates? Are they equitable? After five, ten or 99 years, won't we need a new basis for calculation?

Scanning the few contracts available so far produces little information about rates. Perhaps not surprisingly the contracts are complicated, lengthy and not widely publicized. They discuss snow removal and inflation, toilet management and the bankruptcy of either party. They tell Cintra how much time it has to remove a dead possum from the roadway. But they don't set toll rates. These, like college seminars, are to be arranged.

The Reason Foundation asserts that the developer "may or may not" control rates, but that most allow for annual increases in accordance with inflation. In some, rates are to be set by the state utilities regulating body. Some permit increases based on productivity (unspecified and undefined). None will let the governing agency alone control the rates. (Reason says it distrusts politicians).

The Federal Highway Administration studied the Chicago Skyway partnership and concluded that for two-axle vehicles the 2005 rate of $2 would become $3 by 2008; $3.50 in 2011; $4.50 in 2015. These constitute the minimum. They could be greater if justified by inflation. A vague factor of productivity could enter future calculations. Inasmuch as this is a 99-year lease, further listing is probably pointless.[13]

USA Today believes that the Indiana Toll Road fees will rise from $4.65 to $8 the first year for two-axle vehicles, an increase of 72 percent. Truck rates would go from $14.55 to $18. One can assume that other privatization contracts with these foreign developers would be similar, but pertinent data appear to be classified or unsettled.[14]

It would seem that the die is cast. What state governor can refuse a deposit slip of $3 billion to perhaps $30 billion in cash? The road system could be modernized. Public transportation could be implemented. Certainly thousands of jobs would be created. He could get vast new political action contributions. And he could take the credit.

And yet not everyone was happy. Indiana was the worst battleground. The toll road traverses seven counties along the Michigan state border, and it has its enemies in every county. The *Pittsburgh Post-Gazette* reported that the decision to rent the old highway "has blown into one of the biggest brawls here in a generation." Drivers interviewed at rest stops wanted to know if the big corporations would take good care of the roads. Would they be too expensive to drive? What would happen to competing public roads? What about foreigners owning our roads. Long contracts were frightening to many folk; how high might rates go? What could happen to a highway in 99 years? What if Cintra failed to carry out its obligations? Could Hoosiers find recourse? How? And inasmuch as Governor Mitch Daniels is a Republican, much opposition came from prominent Democrats, who thought they saw President George W. Bush's hands trying to balance an unseemly budget.

An Australian experience cast a frightening shadow. In October 2005, Sydney drivers began boycotting the new Cross City Tunnel, whose toll rates zoomed from $3.50 to $6.80 for two-kilometer stretch. At 4 P.M. one day a reporter could find almost no cars in the tunnel. Instead drivers used an old parallel, free road. The city responded by closing some of the lanes to force drivers back to the expensive tunnel. Startlingly, the once-secret contract provided the city not only with that option, but prohibited it from improving competing public transportation. The international consortium that built and operated the tunnel has been accorded bankruptcy. Sydney is looking for a buyer.[15]

After a short engagement it appears that the most expansive marriage in America is between Texas and foreign developers, with occasional aid from some well-heeled Americans.

That the state of Texas should have the grandest, costliest, largest plan in all America for highway building should come as no surprise. But the plan unfolded at the beginning of the twenty-first century stretches the imagination to its limits. Texas faces the same highway problems as any other state — probably every state. The interstate system is old, congested, inadequate, badly in need of major overhauling. State budgets are strained for a variety of reasons, but badly strained and unable to meet the demands of the times. But Texas has a plan as vast as its plains.

The plan, called the Trans Texas Corridor (among many names), has been linked most closely with Governor Rick Perry, who appears to have hitched his legacy to this proposal.

TTC quietly became possible with the passage of Texas Proposition 15 in November 2001. This measure, in the language of the Texas Department of Transportation, would amend the state constitution to "give the state authority to finance and build transportation infrastructure in innovative ways." It allows the department (TxDot) to make "exclusive development agreements with public and private entities for the construction of large-scale transportation projects." It also permits the creation of a fund (Texas Mobility) that could use "toll equity" for construction costs. The public supported it with a small turnout, but with a smashing 67 percent approval.[16]

Did the public know what it was doing? Given the nature of proposition votes, probably not. Certainly the voters could not conceive of the ramifications. Was the state going to convert some old highways into toll roads? What was a private entity? What was toll equity? Almost immediately, Governor Perry tossed out some clues.

In January 2002, Perry sketched his plan in a brief letter to John W. Johnson, state transportation commissioner, asking TxDOT for a bold and comprehensive plan within 90 days. Five months later the "department's top talent" presented the commission and the governor the basic scheme for a 4,000-mile, multi-use transportation system. With startling speed the report became law. In June 2003, Perry signed HB 3588, which he called a mobility package, permitting "new planning" and "innovative financing options" for a Trans Texas Corridor (TTC).[17]

Before any comprehensive plan could be executed, some investors created the Camino Columbia Road, a modest enough private toll road designed to relieve truck congestion through Laredo. The 22-mile road would cost $90 million, with tolls set at $16 for trucks, $3 for cars. It set a bad example; tolls were too high; traffic was a fraction of expectations. Lawsuits ensued; the bondholders foreclosed. In 2004, the entity was auctioned off to TxDOT. Not a great start for private toll roads.[18]

Nevertheless, corridor plans were underway. HB 3588 in its enormity sparked statewide action. This measure gives little information on the corridor's location, except vaguely that it will run from Mexico to Oklahoma or perhaps Arkansas. Everything else related to the corridor is covered in the greatest of detail.

September 23, 2003, was set as the deadline for high-priority segments of the corridor. Everyone must have been waiting in the wings. Fluor Enterprises of Sugarland, Texas, submitted a border-to-border bid before they were requested. Other Texas firms had less ambitious offers.[19] But the big one, the proverbial gorilla, Cintra, was ready with corridor-like proposals. The short list seemed to include Cintra and two Texas firms, but TxDot refused to release their plans, citing trade secret preservation. Cintra got the contract, forming a Spanish-Texas consortium with Zachry of San Antonio.

Within less than a month work began on Texas 130, a 49-mile toll road, breaking off from I-35 near Georgetown, then paralleling it into southeast Travis County. The cost was $1.5 billion. It was the costliest road contract in Texas history and the largest active contract in the U.S. The first public hearings on TTC were held four months later. About one-third of the job was complete and open to traffic by December 2006.[20]

In December 2004, TxDOT confirmed the contract by which Cintra Zachry would take over the entire Trans Texas Corridor program from Oklahoma to Mexico. The first of presumably many roads is TTC 35, designed to relieve the congestion on I-35, more or less in the center of the state.

Again details were not forthcoming from the state but one paper reported that Cintra would pay $1.2 billion for the right to operate the segment paralleling I-35, then over a 50-year period Cintra would invest $6 billion more for the right to build and operate a toll road from San Antonio to Dallas and relocate some Union Pacific Rail tracks in so doing.[21]

The location and direction of TTC 35 was still not revealed, TxDOT stating only that public input and environmental studies had yet to be concluded. As late as 2005 the state's attorney general was declaring that TxDOT must outline the full contract with Cintra. TxDOT declined.

But combining statements by Governor Perry with smaller revelations of various newspapers, Cintra's promises looked something like this: the Trans Texas Corridor would be a 4,000 mile network crossing the state, the equivalent (not necessarily a single swath) of four football fields wide, more or less paralleling I-35 from Oklahoma to Nuevo Laredo, Mexico. Ranchers, farmers, and businesses in the way would be treated fairly, said Perry.[22]

In March 2006 the Trans Texas Corridor Advisory Committee received a briefing from a Cintra representative, helping to clarify the corporation's expectations. He reported that Cintra Zachry would perform direct development of five Texas toll roads. Cintra would make suggestions only; the precise routes would be determined by TxDOT. From experience, Cintra expected to manage ancillary establishments such as McDonald's restaurants but expected no significant profit from that arrangement. The opportunity lay with the operation of the corridor — essentially, with tolls. TxDOT would decide whether billboards would be permitted along the highways. And Cintra had no interest in planning any rail functions.[23]

In sum, at the end of 2006, relief for I-35 was underway — with perhaps one-third open and collecting tolls. Completion, presumably from Dallas-Ft. Worth to Houston or San Antonio, was a few years away. That would be one corridor. But Perry was committed to others, and Cintra Zachry was committed to build them.

What about the people of Texas? Would they support Perry? No plebiscite on corridors has yet been held and probably won't be. But the 2006 gubernatorial election was one clue. Perry, a Republican, was running for re-election against a stable of candidates, splitting the anti–Perry vote. All of the latter asserted some measure of opposition to the corridor plans. Perry essentially ran on his record, but firmly supported the TTC program. Out of more than four million ballots cast, 1.7 million voted for Perry. With only 39 percent support — a plurality — Perry nevertheless won re-election. What did it mean? Apparently most Texas voters opposed the TTC, but Perry was governor for four more years, and TTC was alive.[24]

Highway building can scarcely be a stealthy operation, but it would seem that most Texans had not given much thought to the impact until the election. Now opposition began to flourish, however much of the argument came from outside the state.

U.S. Representative Ron Paul of Texas complained that the Congress had exerted no oversight at all. "Millions" of people and businesses could be displaced as well as many towns. A secret summit meeting in Waco of the leaders of the U.S., Canada and Mexico, he said, had laid out the scheme, whose ultimate goal was a North American union. All this, said Paul, without a treaty or any congressional involvement. A group of Texas Republicans urged the repeal of HB 3588, which legalized the entire plan. Carolyn Strayhorn, one of the defeated gubernatorial candidates, spoke of Perry's "land grabbing highway henchmen." The apparent secrecy bothered many. Most contracts were at least initially restricted. After two years of argument the master plan was revealed — all 1,600 pages, much of it incomprehensible except to the specialist.[25]

A trucker's magazine was annoyed by the coziness. Dan Shelley had been a consultant for Cintra. Next he became Perry's aid to the state legislature and sat in on many TxDOT meetings discussing Cintra. Then he and his daughter obtained contracts as consultants to Cintra. Apparently he had broken no law, but the drivers viewed it as conspiracy. The magazine, *Human Events*, devoted a number of articles to attacking the corridors. The chief objection seemed to be the loss of individual property rights implicit in the vast program. Ranchers worried that their holdings might be split, making moving from one portion to another seriously complicated or even hazardous.[26]

But the recurring complaint was the matter of tolls—who would set them and what would they be. The *Dallas News* estimated that the rates on the new Texas 130 would be 15 cents per mile for passenger cars and 58.5 cents for trucks, some $56 and $216 respectively for the ultimate 370-mile journey.[27]

Some language in available contracts seems contradictory, so TxDOT was questioned directly for guidance. Their reply: neither TxDOT nor any contractor would set rates. Instead they would be determined by individual Regional Mobility Authorities, agencies created by the state in 2001 and 2003 to give considerable power over road regulation. RMAs are political subdivisions of the state, but can be created by counties. They are governed by a board, whose chair is appointed by the governor. Other members, appointed by county commissioners, represent each county where an RMA project will be built. Each of these boards has authority to set toll rates within its district; no tolls will be determined by TxDOT or by contractors.[28]

Perhaps more important than the pricing power, however, is RMA's relationship to eminent domain, a matter of great financial significance to thousands of Texans, whether they would use the new highways or not.

Eminent domain is authorized by the Fifth Amendment to the U.S. Constitution, and in various forms, probably by every state as well. Until the late twentieth century its use had been tested infrequently. Most commonly a government agency expropriated private property for a highway, utilities or other form of infrastructure of value to the community. Compensation, by law prompt and fair, seems to have been proper enough to keep cases out of the courts. Courts and public alike seemed satisfied with the procedure if the land were taken for "public use." But that process began to change. More and more cases were concerned with the taking of private property and conveying it to another private individual—presumably for the good of the community—for the "public good."

A case in Connecticut brought the issue sharply into focus. In 1998

Pfizer Corporation built a pharmaceutical plant in the Ft. Trumbull neighborhood of New London. Parts of Ft. Trumbull were clearly run down, others neglected. Some old homes had been bought by speculators, others were still occupied by owners with considerable pride in their homes. New London's city government, hoping to add to Pfizer's revitalization, sold the Ft. Trumbull area to a private development company, the New London Development Corporation, giving the corporation the power of eminent domain. Hotels, a mall, and new apartments were some of the improvements promised. The corporation soon began clearing the land and buying out some of the 80-plus homeowners. May 31, 2006, was set as the deadline for all the owners to move. A handful held out. Susette Kelo had bought her home in 1997 and had no desire to leave. Her little pink house in the midst of all the turmoil attracted much public attention and sympathy. With financial help from the Libertarian Institute for Justice, AARP, NAACP, and others, Ms. Kelo filed suit to prevent the expropriation of her home.

By a vote of 4–3, the Connecticut Supreme Court denied her request, so Ms. Kelo pursued her case to the U.S. Supreme Court. That body rendered its decision June 23, 2006. A 5–4 vote upheld Connecticut. The case may yet have enormous consequences; the court agreed with New London that the redevelopment would at least partially be for "public use" as required by the Fifth Amendment, that this was a "carefully considered development plan" not intended to help individuals. Local government could give to a private developer the right to seize private property. In a sense the vote was on strict party lines, for traditional liberals provided the majority against traditional conservatives. Justice Sandra Day O'Connor was vehement in her opinion, declaring that every mom and pop store might be vulnerable to a Home Depot. (Ultimately New London moved the "pretty little pink house" to a new location for Kelo.)[29] Outside Connecticut, responses to Kelo v. New London were prompt and strong, if not necessarily clear. Since the decision, thirty or more states have passed legislation restricting the use of eminent domain, sometimes in language that satisfied no one.

The powerful Texas Farm Bureau met in Arlington in December with its usual full agenda, but uppermost was the Kelo case. The 900-plus delegates unanimously supported such constitutional changes as would protect homeowners, detailing some of the methods needed and limiting the agencies that could wield the right of eminent domain.

Actually, Texas already had a new law, interpreted by Governor Perry to "prevent private profit making," but not "choosing between competing private interests." The law has not been tested.[30]

One more scheme must be considered in the Texas context. Interstate 69 has a life throughout much of the middle of America, but its destination is Texas, and most of its commercial significance is expected to lie with Texas.

The road begins at the Canadian border, near Sarnia, Ontario, in the Michigan city of Port Huron. It meanders across southeastern Michigan, then moves diagonally into Indiana via Ft. Wayne. For now, it stops at the outskirts of Indianapolis, and is a modest contribution to the nation's highway system. Within Indiana there has been a running struggle over the road's extension; no interstate runs from the state capital to Evansville at the state's southern limits, and factions have argued for years about the propriety of I-69 filling this vacuum. But this is not I-69's destiny. The federal government as well as some of the states have dropped hints, or guesses, from time to time, about something grand called the NAFTA highway. Federal and state officials have disclaimed the existence of such a road, or even its likelihood, yet small segments are being built. One such is in Mississippi near Tunica, and in January 2007 a $286 billion highway bill included $111 million to help plan I-69 in Tennessee.[31]

So I-69 continues to grow, even though its destination remains unknown to the public. If it is extended to Laredo, it will truly be a trinational highway, and in that sense could well be called the NAFTA highway. Stiff resistance to that expression probably has little to do with the road (everyone likes new roads), but rather the charges that the three nations plan some sort of free trade area growing into a political union modeled after the European Union. That notion has a few very strong proponents, but a highway does not have to mean political union.

So in Texas there are dreams, plans, environmental studies, and actual contracts. At the beginning of 2007, no blueprint of this maze existed or probably could, but the direction is clear. Politics, taxes, and international relations are getting mixed in the asphalt. Governor Perry likes to say that there are toll roads and no roads, and the state is even considering tax exemptions for toll road owners. Roads will be built.

CHAPTER EIGHT

Tales from a Few Cities

In 1999, the Fannie Mae Foundation declared that the 1956 Interstate Highway Act and the dominance of the automobile were the most important influences on the American metropolis in the past 50 years — ahead of malls, desegregation, sun belt sprawl and other blessings.[1] Perhaps it should not rank first, but it belongs in anyone's top ten for its effect upon so much of our lives. Looking at some of these consequences, this chapter will be devoted to the impact on villages that were bypassed and on cities that were not, but instead were penetrated by the asphalt assault. (No distinction is attempted between the effects of interstates and any other type of U.S. highway.)

Bypassed communities abound along our highway system, but most of them are quite small and their abandonment may not even be noticed except by the local folk. At first glance, however, it would seem that these would have been the most seriously discomfited, the bypassing forcing changes in habits at the least or the loss of a home or business at the worst.

The literature for the field seems broad but thin, that is, a number of social scientists have studied one community or more, but are extremely cautious about making any generalizations. Not unreasonably; preliminary studies show little agreement about the results of bypassing. We are not sure how to define a bypass and most of the work is very parochial, and at the same time, very regional.

Parochial is understandable. Academicians in small towns often have first-hand experiences to examine, or handy local data, making for logical and relatively compact studies. The regional aspect is less clear. Most of the studies emanate from and are about America's heartland, as we like to call it. Much more has been studied about Kansas, Nebraska, and Iowa, than Oregon or Vermont, for example. The answer probably lies in the

114

vast distances and small populations of the Great Plains, but it also may have something to do with the writers themselves.

Let us start with Oklahoma, about which some assumptions must first be made. It is largely a rural state, and several writers tell us that the impact of highways on rural roads is less understood than their impact on more urban roads. Additionally the cities have more money for planning and are often in a position to cope with issues that become evils in rural environments. Unhappy with the results from a purely local, rural study, the authors discussed here expanded their work to cover the whole state of Oklahoma.

The emphasis was on finding the socioeconomic differences, if any, between the towns that were bypassed and those that were not. Much of this data-collecting remains to be performed.[2] The authors also agreed to measure only permanent results, finding the temporary of little value.

Along with de-emphasizing the temporary, the writers had to cope with wild fluctuations in oil prices, an overall decline in state population, and a "stagnant" economy, all of which could superimpose significant change on top of the effects of bypassing.[3] Table one categorizes some three dozen Oklahoma towns divided by size and whether they were bypassed by road construction since 1956.[4]

To maintain consistency across the various phases of this project, a classification scheme partitions the study towns into three categories: "Small" towns have fewer than 2,500 people. "Medium" towns have between 2,500 and 7,500 people, and "Large" towns contain over 7,500 people. Distinct natural breaks occur across the 2,500 and 7,500 population boundaries in terms of business characteristics and overall population sizes. The analysis here includes thirty-five Large towns (twenty-one non-bypassed control towns and fourteen bypassed towns), twenty-one Medium towns (thirteen control towns and eight bypassed towns), and five Small towns (four control towns and one bypassed town). Table 1 lists the towns used in this analysis as well as the various classifications into which towns are placed.

Clearly, the reliability of the analysis will decline with town size, particularly as Stonewall is the only Small town in the state to have been bypassed in the study period. Interestingly, it is also the most recent bypass (1994). Combined with ODOT interest in other similar towns in southeastern Oklahoma for bypass consideration a new emphasis on speeding traffic movement around very small towns may have serious local economic impacts, based on recent evidence collected in an earlier phase of this research project (Comer and Finchum, 2001).

Table 1
Bypassed and Control Towns

Large Bypassed?		Medium Bypassed?		Small Bypassed?	
No	*Yes*	*No*	*Yes*	*No*	*Yes*
Altus	Ada	Alva	Checotah	Crescent	Stonewall
Bartlesville	Ardmore	Anadarko	Henryetta	Morris	
Chickasha	Blackwell	Atoka	Holdenville	Talihina	
Claremore	Clinton	Coweta	Hugo	Waukomis	
Duncan	Cushing	Frederick	Idabel		
Enid	Durant	Grove	Pauls Valley		
Glenpool	El Reno	Madill	Perry		
Guymon	Elk City	Muldrow	Tecumseh		
Miami	Guthrie	Noble			
Muskogee	McAlester	Seminole			
Mustang	Okmulgee	Sulphur			
Owasso	Sallisaw	Tonkawa			
Ponca City	Tahlequah	Vinita			
Poteau	Weatherford				
Pryor					
Sapulpa					
Shawnee					
Stillwater					
Wagoner					
Woodward					
Yukon					

What then do Comer and Finchum conclude about bypassed Oklahoma towns? First, they find a fairly predictable decline in the population of small towns, a fairly flat line in medium-sized, and slight increases in larger towns. But in all cases they concluded that the data was insufficient to make significant distinctions between bypassed and non-bypassed towns.

Second, bypassing and not bypassing seem to have little impact upon a town's ethnicity.

Third, again not very surprisingly, they found more vacant homes in bypassed towns than in non-bypassed towns. (This conclusion could almost be conceded.)

Fourth, again a slam dunk, older people in bypassed towns tended to move away less often than younger.

Fifth, incomes of the bypassed residents were significantly lower than those of the non-bypassed.[5]

Another Oklahoma study concentrated on one tiny community, reaching similar conclusions. The authors using the small town of Stonewall concluded that the bypass highway had no "significant effect on the already declining small town business district."[6]

Up in Iowa, folks watched while U.S. 20 was being widened and rerouted. This time the social scientists could study why some towns survived the change while others could not. Their first conclusion was that no town would be badly damaged and second, nothing could be more useful than creating an economic development board. The board would attract new business to keep the town alive. Second (and just as simplistic) the board should work closely with federal and state programs. How a community could *not* make those contacts is puzzling.[7]

The methodology chosen by Ms. Clapp compared three towns that were going to be bypassed with six that had been bypassed in the 1980s, focusing on retail sales.[8]

The article is accompanied by several charts showing the number of businesses and the value of retail sales over a period of several years following the bypass of a handful of small towns. The conclusions are clear. No town was hurt by the rerouting, and some actually made slight gains in the number of businesses or value of retail sales. Since the effects were so slight, and the writers paid almost no attention to outside economic forces that could have been strong, their study showed little effect from bypassing a small Iowa town. They agreed that Iowa is a nice place to live.

Far more sophisticated methodology was employed by the Institute for Public Policy and Business Research for the Kansas Department of Transportation. Using a variety of models and regressive techniques, the IPPBR collected far more data than these predecessors, and were able to wring much more information from that data. Modestly critical of their own work, they felt that some of the samples were still too small. Their conclusions:

• One: long term, Kansas bypasses have done little harm to the economy. In fact, improved transportation seems to have provided some benefits to the bypassed communities.

• Two: in the short term, towns as a whole suffered little, but in the first two or three years, selected firms, especially travel-related such as bars, service stations, motels, and restaurants, were damaged. Nevertheless, even some of these survived.

• Three: again, not surprisingly, some towns suffered more than oth-

ers. Often these "background variations" were more important in deter-
mining the future of some small towns than the bypass.

• Four: the bypassing of 21 small towns was "highly beneficial" to
through traffic. The scholars estimated time savings to be worth $1 mil-
lion a year.[9]

To understand that bypassing has many ramifications, look at I-39
passing north and south through central Illinois. This road was completed
in 1992, initially bringing some slight harm to El Paso, Oglesby, and
Minonk. Then the unanticipated occurred. The road seemed to be attract-
ing people and business, especially around the I-39 exits. These were not
unmeaningful developments. El Paso attracted new motels, restaurants,
shops and homes, accompanied by hundreds of thousands in revenue.
Sales tax pumped up from $250,427 in 1991 to $567,235 in 1995. The
extra income is being used to improve El Paso's infrastructure, thereby
increasing the attractiveness of the town. The property tax rate declined
about 22 percent during the same years.[10] That the schools have meanwhile become overcrowded is another story for another day.

Anecdotal evidence flourishes of vacant storefronts and streets so
empty a discharged shotgun would hit no one in bypassed towns, but the
academic literature finds little to support that. True, large numbers of villages were bypassed and some changed slightly, but the scholars are pretty
well united in their belief that changes were too minor to prove much and
could well have been brought about by factors other than moving the
highway.

That the impact of the interstate system upon the *city* would be more
complex and surprising should require little proof or study. Bypassing a
small village in the hinterland may mean something to a few, but what
effect does that road have upon the metropolis that it sooner or later
pierces? A rather thorough hunt failed to find any study of this sort performed *before* the interstate system was inaugurated (and perhaps we would
have a different system had that happened), but post-mortem evaluations
abound.

No one seems to deny that our highways led to considerable urban
growth, so on that matter we shall pass. But did the opposite occur? Did
the highways and arteries draw people or business off from the cities? At
least one scholar says yes. Nathaniel Baum-Snow of Brown University has
staked out that claim.

Baum-Snow contends that each new highway passing through a city reduces the city's population by some 18 percent, people who presumably moved to the suburbs. While there are many reasons for America's suburbanization, a major factor in our sprawl and spread is our highways.

Baum-Snow appears to be the first to hold this view, and based on his career and publications, his argument cannot be ignored. He adds that in the cases he has documented, the city's population would have *grown* by about 8 percent had the highway not been built.[11]

Baum-Snow's methodology included data on 139 large metropolitan areas. He used this material to compare cities with new highways built between 1950 and 1990 with cities that had fewer roads built during the same years by measuring "rays."(He defined rays as a portion or segment of a road from a central city connecting to regions outside.) He found that during those years while the national population grew 64 percent, the aggregate population of central cities fell 17 percent.[12] Before examining Baum-Snow's evidence, a trio of scholars questioned his conclusions because of the size of his unquestionably large numbers. Would two new rays help remove one-third of a city? Cox, Gordon, and Redfearn are right in one argument; those are large numbers. Are they right?

Unfortunately for our purposes, the critics repeatedly accept Baum-Snow's research as proper and solid, so we do not get expert opinion on that phase of the work, but let us look at some of his replies to this extended critique. First, they claim his numbers could not possibly be right because not enough housing could be built rapidly enough for a population increase of 8 percent in a given geographic area. Baum-Snow's reply — not so. San Diego grew 70 percent between 1950 and 1990, and 11 other cities grew more than 8 percent in that period.

Second, not the highway, but rising incomes and many more cars account for suburbanization. He says, yes, they are factors, but the changes were far greater in cities that built more highways.

Third, the trio compared Baum-Snow's research to similar conditions in a number of European cities. He found some validity in their conclusions, but insisted his were more reliable.[13] There is more to be said for each point of view, but this is not the place. Suffice it to say that highways, automobiles, rays, and suburbanization all increased enormously in the last half of the twentieth century. Which is the chicken and which the egg will be hard to determine.

More easily studied is how all of these elements have led to another highway problem tied closely to suburbanization. Commuting.

That suburbanization inexorably leads to commuting few will doubt.

(It seems safe to assume that no one moved to the suburbs just for the fun of commuting.) The Census Bureau can help us see just how serious the matter has become. In 2004 the bureau released a study comparing commute time in America's largest cities. Not surprisingly, New York City residents have the worst commute in the nation — an average of 38.4 minutes each day each way. Chicagoans ranked second with a commute of 32.7 minutes. The Dakotas, Nebraska, and Montana just as unsurprisingly had the shortest commute time, around 15 minutes in each state. The national average is 24.4 minutes.[14]

The following year, the bureau changed its release format a bit, but New York and Chicago retained the top spots. The bureau came up with a new expression, "extreme commutes," defined as a journey of 90 minutes or more each way. Some 5.6 percent of the commuters in New York and Baltimore fall in the "extreme" category.[15] In 2007, the bureau dug a little deeper into our driving habits. Its survey revealed that in spite of rising fuel costs, most commuters (90 percent) drove to work, and 77 percent drove alone. (Boston held the distinction of leading the nation in people walking to work, at 13 percent.)[16]

"Extremes" are easy to report — 75-mile bus rides necessitating arising at 4 or even 3 A.M.; a daily 105-mile drive from Chicago to Benton Harbor, Michigan, and so on. Housing costs play such a role that Silicon Valleyites speak "of driving till you qualify." As commuting gets worse, and more workers enter the extreme category, the impact is felt in every direction. One survey found that 45 minutes each way is about the maximum tolerated by most drivers. Communities are likely to spend billions for mass transit, but have encountered the driver, who sharply opposes such expenditures and instead demands more highway.[17] For now, at least, that is the balance we have achieved.

CHAPTER NINE

The Brass

At the end of the nineteenth century, the nation lacked a highway system. The thousands of miles of roads, usually maintained by poorly or unpaid farmers, could scarcely be given the name. For one hundred years an argument had raged over the question of responsibility. An abundance of rivers in much of the nation, providing natural transportation, fortified the stance that the national government lacked constitutional authority to fund interstate roads, and so it built none. Even the arrival of the auto made little immediate difference, for the farmer could see small good in something he could not afford. For some, the Tin Lizzie was the work of the devil, as city slickers raced their new cars through the countryside, scaring horses, drying up cows and spreading dust and mud over the landscape.

Time weakened such attitudes, though, and the states' rights people began to lose to progressivism and modernism led by officers of the federal government and a variety of bureaucrats. Representative of these was General Roy Stone, Civil War veteran and engineer. Stone had supervised clearing channels in New York harbor, had written an army manual on road building, and while in Washington fought for federal aid to highways. His National League (not to be confused with baseball's National League) essentially was a lobby for the same cause. In 1893, President Grover Cleveland appointed him special agent in charge of the Office of Road Inquiry. The ORI had little budget and few duties, in part because it was placed within the Department of Agriculture under J. Sterling Morton, a strong states' righter. But Stone did the groundwork for a change in attitude in Washington. His work was largely one of public relations as he sought to help state engineers improve their roads. In 1898, when America entered the war in Cuba, he took leave to return to the army. He saw little combat but led attempts to give Puerto Rico something of an infrastructure. He retired from ORI in 1899 and died in 1905. Using a small stretch of the imagination, General Stone could be labeled the first federal highway administrator.[1]

Stone achieved little in miles of road built, but he was an accomplished forerunner to other administrators. In 1905, the new special agent was Logan Page, a graduate of Virginia Polytechnic Institute. While still very young he served as geologist and test engineer for the Massachusetts Highway Commission. Then he moved on to a job with the Office of Public Roads Inquiry. In 1895, OPRI became the Office of Public Roads (OPR), with new responsibilities and a budget, and President Theodore Roosevelt appointed Page director.[2] Page served thirteen years as director, dying in office. He was a firm believer in the ability of the technician to solve even the social problems of the nation. His qualifications as well as his strong belief in progressivism turned OPR into a strong agency for technical progress. He worked with the states to hire better highway officials and was one of the founders of the American Association of State Highway Officials (AASHO), still functioning today as AASHTO. In 1914, he used the press to affirm that $50 million, a huge sum for 1914, was being wasted *annually* in the U.S. by inefficient supervision of highway funds. What he was proposing was a merit system for artery directors, superintendents, and engineers. He contended that most states had no requirements at all for the jobs. Often the tasks were performed by local farmers seeking a few dollars but with no idea of how to build or maintain a road. His solution was to ask the National Civil Service Reform Association to help the states get trained manpower. When a county pleaded a lack of funds, Page worked to help two or more counties combine operations.[3] Page used gimmicks, too. Somehow he got command of a railroad car, which he called "government special." He dispatched it around the country carrying speakers and models extolling the virtues of roadways. Said *The New York Times*, "Government's Good Roads Special is said to have stirred up more enthusiasm for the good roads cause than all other plans put together." Page added that freight hauled by truck remained very expensive compared with that hauled by rail and ship, because the roads were so bad. Good roads, he asserted, made for less expensive living. Logan Page made some progress, the federal government even hard surfacing 88 miles of road in his first year.[4] But he needed congressional help. Beginning about 1905, bills he supported were regularly introduced in Congress, only to die in committees with economic and constitutional objections.

But during Page's tenure change was taking place. Ford's cars were beginning to create a new influence for good roads, and lest there still be constitutional problems, the U.S. Supreme Court handed down *Wilson v. Shaw* in 1907. The case essentially dealt with the complexities of U.S. relations with Panama, but clearly stated that Congress had the authority to "construct interstate highways."[5]

Even now, with a majority of Congress supporting federal aid, consensus was hard to reach, for each state touted its own peculiarity — great distances, much freight, low mileage but many people. Could all those needs be met in one bill? The credit for finding an answer belongs to many — Page, AASHO, Rep. Dorsey Shackleford of Missouri, and Senator John Bankhead of Alabama, the "father of good roads," who for so long wanted to "get the farmers out of the mud."

Someday there would have been a law, but Logan Page was the catalyst making it possible in 1916.[6] Even President Woodrow Wilson may deserve a little credit. We have little evidence of his participation in the legislative process, but he often spoke of his love for motoring, which he apparently engaged in for two hours daily. Surely that impressed some folks in the District of Columbia.[7]

Logan Page directed the federal highway program for 13 years, a long tenure in a government office held at the whim of the president. But even more startling is the 48 years encompassing his term and that of his successor, Thomas H. MacDonald. The two men had worked closely during Page's administration, and MacDonald was highly qualified to succeed Page.

Only superlatives seem adequate for MacDonald's var-

Thomas MacDonald, federal highway administrator, 1919–1953, a towering figure in highway construction (Federal Highway Administration).

ious biographers. "Man of the Century." "Creator of Interstate routes." "Towering figure of road transportation." "He has no equal." Thomas H. MacDonald was born in Leadville, Colorado, on July 23, 1881, was raised in Iowa and graduated from Iowa State in civil engineering. He worked for the college for a spell and in 1913 was appointed chief engineer of the new state highway commission. His labors somehow (we do not have details) impressed AASHO and Logan Page enough so that on Page's death, President Wilson replaced him with MacDonald. Incredibly, MacDonald served seven presidents until he was fired by Eisenhower in 1953.

When he took office he declared that the nation had 3 million miles of road but only 350,000 miles of that were hard surfaced. In 1917 the demands of the war for trucks, tires, and fuel were so great that the rail system broke down and had to be supported by trucks in an unprecedented fashion. MacDonald played a major role in this, moving some 30,000 trucks from Toledo to the Baltimore port in three weeks (incidentally destroying many of the roads). Like Page before him, MacDonald helped fund the AASHO, which in turn was extremely valuable to him, serving as the lobbyist that he technically could not be.

In office, the chief claimed to be appalled to find that Page had spent only a fraction of his budget. How he could have been deputy for many years and remain ignorant of the budget is a bit bewildering, but that is what he said. Now MacDonald played the good roads hand constantly. He spoke to state and county officials of the economics of good roads; he opened test farms in Virginia; and he worked with General John J. Pershing on U.S. maps that might meet military needs. By MacDonald's time, AASHO was tightening its membership and its goals, and for the rest of his tenure the chief regularly relied upon the state officials. He served until 1953, when President Eisenhower removed him from office. Never out of work, the chief moved to College Station and at age 71 established the prestigious Texas Transportation Institute, directing it until his death in 1957.[9]

Under MacDonald's leadership the old states' rights question got short shrift. His word for the issue was "partnership." In its simplest terms, the federal government and the states would share in the costs for a national highway; the technical standards would be set by the federal government. How would he pay for roads? It would not be by tolls. We have his answer in a long, detailed letter written in 1947 to a New Hampshire news editor.

The editor was concerned about a state bill pending for a major road and the likelihood that it would be financed by tolls. The chief was adamant. Tolls were a mistake. With small exceptions, no toll road ever "earned enough to cover all costs of the undertaking."

Even the young and famous Pennsylvania Turnpike had needed a $29 million subsidy, he alleged. The competition between toll and "untolled" roads would be bad for society. Proponents of the toll failed to see the true costs. Without revealing his math, the chief continued his attack. He calculated that a cent a mile toll was the equivalent of a twelve- to sixteen-cent per gallon gas tax. Furthermore, he had concluded that the noisy opposition to gas taxes did not come from the public but from the petroleum industry.

MacDonald wrote for several pages. His argument was clear. Tolls were bad.[10]

Most of the men directing the public roads program served for brief periods only, and need not be mentioned here. Holding the job and working closely with AASHO, they became a new, strong force for federal aid. Arguments in Congress continued, generally over the locations of proposed routes.

And putting car costs, farmers' roles, and AASHO aside, state officials were not accustomed to someone in Washington telling them what the road standards should be or setting requirements about working conditions and wages.[11] Resistance was to be expected.

As we have seen, large numbers of highway bills got nowhere in the early twentieth century, usually being assigned to committee for a quiet death. The climate changed slowly, however, perhaps because Ford's reduced costs were beginning to appeal to the farmer. So-called post roads amounted to a mere 600 miles in 17 states as a result of some 1913 legislation. Federal aid had to go only to the states; the Office of Public Roads was simply too small to work with 3,000 counties.

The Shackleford-Bankhead measures were the most prominent and promising as war broke out in Europe. Now they had the support of AASHO, a new weapon with growing nationwide influence. When it was founded in 1914, its very first discussions concerned the drafting of a federal highway aid bill. Regionalism and demographics plagued AASHO just as they did every other roadway proponent, but in 1915 a small number of states led by Thomas MacDonald found a compromise, and AASHO had a purpose in life. The big issues were how to keep cities from getting all the benefits and what formula could be achieved to apportion fairly the funds among the states. A variety of compromises now called the Bankhead Bill was known to many legislators as the AASHO Bill. That was good enough, and on June 27, 1916, both houses approved the bill. President Wilson quickly added his signature. Besides providing funds for building roads, the Federal Aid Road Act of 1916 added some stern measures. It required each state to have a professional engineering agency to supervise all construction. While the state would build the road, it must first get federal approval of the design and quality of construction. In practice, the program favored "enhancing the life of rural America" over the long-distance roads that Pershing thought were needed for defense.[12]

The start of the MacDonald era roughly coincides with the end of the First World War, providing a convenient study aid for the accomplishments of the chief's long tenure. MacDonald's toughest task was to resolve the major issue of long versus short roads.

In essence, one group, let's call them nationalists, thought of a federal highway program in Pershing terms. One lesson of the war had been the vulnerability of California, should the Japanese attack. When doling out millions for roads, they thought priority should be given to the movement of troops and military equipment from the industrial East to the West Coast.

Opposed to these nationalists were "localists," who thought of highways in terms of getting the mail to farmers and getting the farmers' goods to market.

MacDonald's compromise in 1921 denied any chance at a national highway system; but he did not want to lose control of some future system. So the nationalists received a sop; federal aid toward a system of federal-aid highways could be used but would be limited to 7 percent of all roads in the state. The amount of money that could be spent on such roads was also limited.

MacDonald presumably concluded that in most states farm and postal advocates were numerous enough to protect their interests. The legislation worked. In 1922, more than 10,250 miles were finished, triple the average of the three previous years.[13]

The decade of the 1930s did not bring about any revolution in highway building nor any vast expansion in miles finished, but interest was never greater. Some of this interest was grassroot and probably could have been expected. An entirely different factor, however, drawing people to the lure of long highways, was arising in Germany. The attraction was the autobahn.

To be accurate, the first superhighways probably were Italian, work starting in 1913 and culminating with a "Milan to lakes country" superhighway in 1923. A second of about 100 miles was started the following year.[14]

These precursors never received the publicity of Hitler's autobahn, however. The first road, from Cologne to Bonn, began operation in 1932. In the 1930s, engineers and builders came from all the industrial nations to see what Hitler had wrought. American officials argued over Hitler's objective. Many feared some secret military purpose. Others bought Hitler's own contention that he was trying to reduce unemployment. Chief MacDonald and his deputy, Herbert Fairbank, made the requisite visit. The roads were "wonderful" but not something the U.S. might copy. Germany's roads carried small amounts of traffic and stayed out of the cities, he concluded, while the U.S. was straining to deal with roads in the cities.[15]

In 1937, the chief told a group of engineers, "From the development abroad and in the United States the situation is just the reverse and the building of superhighways must be limited to areas where the present and prospective traffic will justify it ... one can conclude that superhighways will be created but only in the vicinity of metropolitan areas, for relieving traffic congestion within those areas and connecting those that are separated by relatively short distances."[16]

This quotation requires some thought. This is Chief Thomas MacDonald speaking, and he is telling the most concerned men in the country that the purpose of superhighways was to relieve municipal traffic — and without tolls, we must reiterate. What shall we make of this? Assuming MacDonald was expressing his personal views, and all who knew him would say that was his habit, how can we call him the father of the interstate system that we have built?

In MacDonald's defense it should be noted that a number of traffic surveys were taken in the 1930s and none found any significant coast-to-coast travel. Consequently the BPR put its attention on metropolitan and regional traffic. On occasion, Congress had expressed interest in a limited number of toll superhighways, but the bureau's report of 1939 declared that especially with the burden of tolls, such a network would not pay. The report went on to emphasize the belief that in the immediate future a toll-free system of regional superhighways should get priority. Rural sections would be improved but remain undivided two-lane roads.

By regional traffic, MacDonald and Fairbank seemed to mean city to suburb, and they spent considerable time lamenting the suburban movement, which was destroying the inner city by "stages" as the homes were "transferred to lower and lower income groups housing the humblest." In the end homes would be taken for unpaid taxes and become parking lots.[17] Into this mix we must add President Franklin Roosevelt's concern for veterans. In 1945 and 1946, troops were being discharged at the rate of thousands per month. Many had an old job to return to, and the GI Bill was proving extremely popular, but that still could not guarantee work for every soldier returning home. The prospect of vast unemployment frightened FDR. He also was keenly aware of the nation's vulnerability on the West Coast at the time of Pearl Harbor.

Perhaps a sweeping highway program might impact all of these issues. In 1941 he created the National Interregional Highway Committee to study these issues and see how much linkage existed. The committee reported that year, but FDR sat on the report until 1944. On finally releasing it to Congress, the president mentioned some of the connections between highways and slums but obviously was not so enamored as MacDonald of the belief that highways were the key to urban revitalization.[18]

Only a few days later MacDonald again spoke to the American Society of Civil Engineers. He reminded them that cities had tried zoning and city planning to cope with a vast number of major problems and failed; they must try something else. The BPR could hope that the something else would be embodied in the Federal-Aid Highway Act of 1944. But the act fell far short of a MacDonald plan. It ignored the matter of coordination with other facilities and provided no special funding for the system.

After the war, the government faced demands for jobs and housing, and until the demand for autos caught up, highway construction lost some of its priority. By 1949, President Harry Truman had killed the BPR suggestions; he thought urban renewal and housing programs were needed, but expressways would not be the centerpiece of such developments.[19]

Through the administrations of five presidents, MacDonald remained the chief, and by the 1950s was giving thought to retirement. He reached the federal mandatory retirement age but because of the Korean War remained on the job as interim head at President Truman's request.

We have no evidence that incoming President Eisenhower had policy differences with MacDonald, but some state highway officials in Massachusetts felt he had not treated them fairly in recent fund allocations. As head of BPR, MacDonald served under the Department of Commerce. The new secretary of commerce, Sinclair Weeks, was from Massachusetts and found a measure of revenge by firing MacDonald the day he took office.

This was a great irony. The man most praised for the American roadways was forced out of office just as the nation was to embark on its greatest construction venture ever. Certainly MacDonald deserves huge credit for foreshadowing the Interstate Highway System. What would have been his role had he remained as chief another five years? The system allowed for no tolls; MacDonald would certainly have concurred in that prohibition. But otherwise it is difficult to see agreement between him and Eisenhower on the very nature and purpose of the roads. Ike wanted to bypass cities. MacDonald saw the roads as tightly integrated into the revitalization of the cities. Compromise would have been unlikely.

A few other men deserve mention, not all in the BPR, who played major parts in the initiation of the interstate roads. Francis DuPont, head of the BPR, resigned in 1955 to help Ike get the bill through Congress. Also instrumental were Charles D. Curtiss, assistant to MacDonald, then chief; and three congressmen, Senator Albert Gore, Sr., who helped draft the interstate highway act; Congressman George Fallon, who was almost indispensible in getting legislation approved; and Representative Hale Boggs, who developed the idea of a "highway trust fund" to finance the new system.[20]

As we have seen, Eisenhower did not assume the presidency planning to start a new highway system on March 5, 1953. But sometime during his first two years in office, he was converted. Certainly he had been impressed by the autobahn during the war. "After seeing the aurobahns [sic] I made a personal and absolute decision that the U.S. would benefit by it."[21]

In Congress, enthusiasm for the highways was great, but Ike could get little consensus on a method of payment. Most sources at this point credit Representative Thomas Hale Boggs of Louisiana with the solution. Boggs was born in Mississippi but grew up near New Orleans. He received degrees in journalism and law from Tulane University and at age 26 captured a seat in the U.S. House of Representatives. He served in the Navy in World War II, then returned to Congress where he became an influential member of the House Ways and Means Committee. With George Fallon he proposed a variety of measures to finance Ike's bill, but most

Democrats seemed frightened by the size of the bill — around $50 billion — and would not support it. Eisenhower and his followers continued to favor an enormous bonding program. But bonds would go nowhere, for the chair of the Senate Finance Committee was Harry Byrd, in those days known for his tight control of the federal budget and for being opposed to any new bond program. Would there be any bill at all if trucking and other associations stoutly opposed new taxes, while so many in Congress opposed bond issues? What was left?

At this point Fallon and Boggs took over and split the bill, authorizing the highways from the taxing bill. Then the BPR entered the fray; it distributed a 100-page book of maps called the Yellow Book, which clearly showed the new roads falling into each congressman's district. Powerful. They could now offer a new approach to constituents and sell it as "pay as you go."[22]

Boggs' bill created the Highway Trust Fund, still functioning today. It is a highway user tax on motor fuel, diesel fuel, special gasolines, truck sales, truck tires and truck use. The taxes were numerous but not heavy. They are not collected by the federal government but paid to the Internal Revenue Service by the producer, retailer, or importer. Prior to the fund, such tax receipts went directly to the General Fund, and there was no relation between these taxes and the funding for highways. But with creation of the fund the money collected had to be expended on transportation.

The original HTF was to expire in 1972, but since then it has regularly been extended. Then in 1983, a Mass Transit Fund was carved out of the HTF.[23]

One final member of the highway brass remains to be mentioned, Edward M. Bassett, sometimes called "the father of American zoning." Probably less well known than most of his predecessors in this chapter, his achievements in his field are unique. Bassett (1863–1948) was born in Brooklyn to a merchant family. He attended Hamilton College and Amherst College and was a member of Phi Beta Kappa. In 1886, he graduated from Columbia Law School and practiced law in Buffalo and New York City from 1892. He married Annie Preston, with whom he had five children. He served one term as a Democrat representing New York in the U.S. House of Representatives. Beginning about 1907 he increasingly took part in New York city affairs, especially as they concerned planning and zoning. Secretary of Commerce Herbert Hoover appointed him president of the National Conference on City Planning. In that capacity he wrote a 1932 article for *The American City* in which he outlined terminology to describe highways:

• A "highway" is a strip of public land devoted to movement over which the abutting property owners have the right of light, air, and access.

• A "parkway" is a strip of public land devoted to recreation over which the abutting property owners have no right of light, air, or access.

• A "freeway" is a strip of land devoted to movement over which the abutting property owners have no right of light, air, or access.

Bassett went on to explain the great advantages of freeways, a term apparently not in general use in the 1930s, and according to one biographer, a term Bassett invented. Bassett saw the freeway as full of virtues. They would have three or four lanes in each direction with "business centers" down the middle. Motorists could purchase "supplies" without leaving the roadway, helping end congestion. Local traffic is *totally* eliminated, so the freeway becomes the safest of roads. Living on a freeway is advantageous, for property values will rise as a consequence of the trees and shrubs hiding the cars from homes and diffusing the noise.[24]

A modern commuter can wonder just how Bassett thought such roads would come about, but he was highly respected in his day even though the terms never fell into general use.

Our highway system has many authors, and perhaps no one of them deserves to be called the "father." The ideas came from everyone — politicians, engineers, social planners, the public. But it was the coincidence of time and the times that brought forth a finished product. It probably was as fine a product as we could get. What would it look like if we did it over?

CHAPTER TEN

Dollars

The highway system is now more than fifty years old and it seems appropriate to consider whether we have gotten our money's worth. Most drivers would agree that much of it is in disrepair. What do we do now? Continue efforts toward a reasonable upkeep or budget some enormous fund to meet all the needs? Start over?

The approach taken by both the Federal Highway Administration (FHA) and the American Association of State Highway and Transportation Officials (AASHTO) was to examine the economic impact of the Interstate Highway System, the link between public capital and private sector economic performance, a daunting task at best. But that link demonstrates more than exercises in econometrics. It is a major element in public policy, for street and highway capital make up nearly one-third of all the public capital in the United States today.[1]

The planners of the interstate system assumed and understood that the system would save lives, speed deliveries, and perhaps lower costs. Beyond that they made few calculations. In the decades following construction, many private individuals prepared their own research, usually confining it to the effects of the highways on a single industry or activity. Dissatisfied with these studies, the FHA looked in new directions. First, the FHA used the research of Barbara Fraumeni, a Ph.D. in economics. Ms. Fraumeni, chair of the public policy program at the University of Southern Maine, served several years as chief economist of the Bureau of Economic Analysis in Washington.[2] Her work pioneered studies to measure the amount of highway capital stock, the basis of most subsequent analyses.

Secondly, the FHA supported the work of Ishaq Nadiri and Theofanis Mamuneas, who sought to learn about the broader effects of spending public infrastructure capital on economic development.

They studied twelve American manufacturing industries to examine the degree to which they were affected by public infrastructure investment. First, they concluded that the benefits varied from industry to industry, making calculations much more complex.

Perhaps more significantly, they found that public investment proved less costly than private.

But the FHA wanted the focus on highway expenditures only. Nadiri and Mamuneas were again sponsored to examine a number of aspects of highway expenditures. This and related research has gone on for decades now, moving toward more and more sophisticated studies of rates of return for highway capital. In the period 1949 to 2000, they estimated an average rate of 34 percent, with a much higher rate in 1949 than in later years. One conclusion was that the country has an ample supply of capital available for highways.[3]

AASHTO also sought some answers about highway investment, using much of the Nadiri and Mamuneas research, but sponsoring other teams as well. Some of their conclusions follow.

They found that interstate highway investments have lowered production and distribution costs in almost every industry. On average these reductions (savings) amounted to 24 percent. Productivity growth during the 1950s averaged some 31 percent, but with time the rate fell to about 7 percent in the 1980s. The net social rate of return, meaning the benefits to private industries that share the use of the public highways, also has declined — from about 35 percent to about 10 percent or less today.

The research does not always bear out every optimistic prediction. Many studies have been made to determine the extent of economic development resulting from highway construction in less developed and rural areas. Most of the work zeroed in on Appalachia because of the great amount of government investment designed to reduce the poverty of the region. The conclusion seems to be that areas with development programs get some small gains from new highways, but merely building roads for the sake of roads does not lead to growth. Interstate highways seem to have the greatest impact on counties with cities of 25,000 population or more, and a greater impact where counties have large cities. Counties lacking a city gained little from new highways.[4] In short, build a road, and they won't necessarily come.

Congestion also affects the economy. Obviously this was of little consequence in the early years of the interstates, but as the years have passed, numbers of cars have increased by the millions, and congestion has become an expensive, aggravating, national scandal. In recent years most agencies responsible for highways have diverted more and more funds away from new construction to expansion and maintenance. Much of this is a consequence of congestion.

Congestion has lent itself to a wide variety of research. The first studies concerned themselves with topics such as the direct costs to users of vehicles — time wasted, extra gasoline, vehicle depreciation, even the costs of pollution of water and air. Most of the studies examine the time element. More sophisticated are the efforts to calculate the costs of uncertainty in travel.

Owners of commercial vehicles find it valuable to know just how much delays cost in wages as well as extra fuel. What does it cost to reduce congestion? What level of expenditure is needed to make a difference? One case study concluded that highway investments designed to relieve congestion can save about $2 for every single dollar spent.[5]

The FHA Office of Freight Management and Operations sought information about congestion-related freight delay and economic performance. In a series of studies the office concluded that truck freight gained the most from highway investment. The effect of highway investment on industrial productivity also was examined. Prior to 1973, the consequences were substantial but after that date increases in rates were similar to normal rates of return. The studies found that the greatest gains were made by the industries that were most transportation intensive, and that it was important to find where most of these savings lay. Less travel time, less warehousing and smaller inventories are in order.[6]

While most statistical studies seem to discern a variety of economic benefits from highways, critics abound. Outstanding among these is Randal O'Toole. An adjunct at Cato Institute, he is a strong advocate of the free market.

O'Toole made manifest his attitude toward the system. It worked, he thought, because of decentralization, engineers, and incentives. The federal government, he claimed, did little but enforce standards and serve as a funnel for the funding. More dubious is his assertion that state highway departments are free of politics. The engineers concentrate on what they do best, improving safety and efficiency. Incentives support the engineers; much of the financing comes from gasoline taxes, thus encouraging the construction of roads only where needed, eliminating the pork barrel kind. This method disappeared, according to O'Toole, when Congress started doling out vast sums.[7]

O'Toole also complained that in 1964, when Congress first started financing mass transit, it abandoned the state/federal formula based on population and road miles. As the system grew and the money poured in, Congress was overcome by catering to special interests. Policy making was taken from the engineers and turned over to urban planners, O'Toole's favorite culprits. Inflation slowed road growth. Neither federal nor state gas tax increases (cents per gallon) could keep up with inflation, which O'Toole claims slowed construction. O'Toole even targets improved fuel efficiency. Between 1973 and 1983, total driving increased 25 percent, while fuel consumption increased only 5 percent, a phenomenon warranting a deeper study than this. Writes O'Toole, "When you fill your gas tank today, you only pay half as much tax for every mile you drive as your parents did in 1960. To make matters worse, inflation in construction costs was greater than the general rate of inflation."[8]

As might be expected, a vastly different view has been presented by Mary Peters, appointed in 2006 by President George W. Bush to be the fifteenth secretary of transportation. Peters had a strong background in transportation, serving some sixteen years in the Arizona Department of Transportation, culminating in her appointment in 1998 as director. From 2001 until her cabinet appointment she was head of the Federal Highway Administration. In 2006 she helped commemorate the 50th anniversary of the Interstate Highway system with an article in *Better Roads*.

After describing the system as a "wonder to behold," she, like O'Toole, examined the complex and varying financing methods utilized during the half century just concluded.

President Eisenhower had created the Clay Commission and somewhat surprisingly suggested to the members that one suitable method of financing might be tolls. The commission vetoed the idea, just as Congress vetoed utilizing bonds. In 1956, agreement was reached on the creation of a highway trust fund supported by an increase of 1 cent in the existing fuel tax. The estimated cost was $25 billion. The federal government would finance 90 percent of the costs, the states 10 percent. At the same time, Congress created the Department of Transportation and moved the Bureau of Public Roads from the Department of Commerce to Transportation and changed its name to the Federal Highway Administration.

Within a dozen years the appropriation reached $56 billion, yet completion remained years away. The 1991 Intermodal Surface Transportation Act (ISTEA) did not change methods of financing much but focused more on the contribution of states and counties to design and location.

By 1998, several states complained that they were paying more to the highway program than they were getting back and insisted upon changes in the formula. The result was the Transportation Efficiency Act for the Twenty-first Century or TEA-21. In the end, all states began receiving more, and the dubious practice of earmarks began to reach substantial amounts.

TEA-21 was extended a dozen times before Congress passed a bill with the ridiculous title of Safe, Accountable, Flexible, Efficient, Transportation Equity Act: A Legacy for Users. By now it appeared that each presidential administration sought to exceed the previous in money spent, ways to spend it, and elaborate titles.

SAFETEA-LU promised all states a minimum rate of return on their contributions to the Highway Trust Fund that would increase from 90.5 percent to 92 percent by 2008. It also promised a 19 percent average increase in highway funding over a six-year period. Congressmen inserted more than 6,000 earmarks, costing $24 billion. (There were 10 in 1982.)[9]

Peters seemed a bit shocked by her own revelations, including the policies she took part in. She said all the country was doing was increasing the amount of spending on highways without facing up to the real question of the proper role of the federal government in the future.

No one had his eye on a vast, wonderful highway system; all everyone wanted was a greater and greater piece of the action.

Peters closed by admitting that a huge gap existed between funds and perceived needs, and that few agreements have been reached about a way forward. Consumers, she feels, see little real benefit from more investment. The only result is more congestion. Her estimate is that 30 percent of the highways are congested today and the figure will reach nearly 50 percent within a dozen years.

She offered little by way of specifics, but talked in terms of the grand, the national, including facing the challenges of congestion, high-priced foreign oil, earmarks, and an aging population.[10]

Secretary Peters had implied that using tolls to finance the interstate system would be impossible as well as illegal. But is it? She was not entirely accurate; the Federal Highway Act of 1956 permitted some 2,100 miles of interstate to be supported by tolls, and the next year the Bureau of Public Roads announced the addition of 2,100 more miles to the exempt list. (Federal funds could not be used for their maintenance.)[11]

Tolls can be collected on both public and private highways. President Ronald Reagan had strongly urged privatization of many government activities, including road construction, but at that time Congress had little interest in such action. By the twenty-first century, many attitudes had changed. The most vocal proponent of private roads was the Reason Foundation (see chapter seven). Privatization implies the use of tolls, whether the builder be foreign or domestic, and it was becoming a popular answer to the road problems of the day. What about tolls on existing roads as a means of rebuilding the state's highway funds?

In late 2007, the state legislature of Maine discussed a plan to place tolls on sections of I-95 and I-295; the governor opposed the scheme—at least for his term of office, he said. The federal DOT seemed ready to approve.

South Carolina had a different approach, receiving federal approval first. In this case an interstate would be built for the first time as a toll road. I-73 would be an 80-mile stretch connecting Myrtle Beach with existing roads near the North Carolina border. Similar proposals in Texas seem to be failing for lack of public support.

In Pennsylvania, Governor Ed Rendell strongly fought for tolls on the turnpike and the state Turnpike Commission has granted contracts to begin installation of booths. Federal approval has not yet been received, however.[12] Rendell also sought the right to grant lease concessions while the legislature moved in other directions or not all. The toll story in Pennsylvania is at best obscure.[13]

Probably most state governors and other leaders look favorably on the use of tolls (as an alternative to raising taxes), but some blocs strongly opposed their use. Among these, not surprisingly, is the American Trucking Association. "Imposing tolls on existing lanes of the interstate system would have a devastating effect on the trucking industry," writes the ATA. Specifically it claims that "the trucking industry's historical average profit margin is between two and four cents per mile." (Depending on the method of bookkeeping, that's $20 for an all-day trip!) The state of Virginia is planning a truck-only toll on I-81 of 37 cents per mile. If all the math is true, the variation is unmanageable.

The association went on to say that tolls amount to double taxation, listing other taxes such as the 12 percent tax on new tractors and trailers, 24 cents a gallon on diesel fuel, and an annual vehicle use tax of up to $550 a year, plus taxes on tires.

Finally, the tolls create two classes of drivers, say the truckers, those who can afford to pay the toll (and after this math one wonders who that is), and those who cannot. The latter group simply find a parallel route, the association asserts.[14]

While tolls offer a simple, unpopular solution to highway funding, more sophisticated mechanisms have been introduced. In essence most of these are a form of toll, but that name is anathema to many so it is concealed. The FHA uses the generic term "congestion pricing" to cover most of these gimmicks, and put out a manual to explain.

It delineates four categories:

1. Variably priced lanes with High Occupancy Toll lanes (HOT) and Express Toll Lanes. HOT lanes require a toll from low-occupancy vehicles, while vehicles with two or more persons travel at lower cost or free. Express toll lanes are similar but there are no high occupancy vehicle lanes. Instead all vehicles are required to pay a toll.

2. Variable tolls on roadways. Existing tolls are changed to a variable toll schedule, higher during peak travel hours and lower during quieter times. Test cases in Florida showed that a 50 percent discount in fees resulted in a 20 percent drop in rush hour traffic with a concomitant increase before the morning rush period.

3. Cordon pricing. This variation charges a fee on all vehicles that enter a specific, heavily trafficked area, usually in a large city.

4. Area wide pricing. The state of Oregon is one of the very few places considering this method of taxing. Fuel taxes would be dropped and replaced by pricing based on miles driven. This would include some form of congestion pricing as well. Stay tuned.

It would appear that every agency is in pursuit of some taxing method that would raise money and reduce congestion. So far there is little agreement on the best way to solve this puzzle, but drivers can be assured that they will have to pay to reduce congestion.[15]

The FHA seemed at one time, at least, to be urging agencies to consider HOT lanes and went to the trouble to explain them to the public and show the advantages of this concept. The agency defined HOT as "limited access, normally barrier-separated highway lanes that provide free or reduced cost access to qualifying HOVs, and also provide access to other paying vehicles not meeting passenger occupancy requirements."[16]

HOT lanes can be created through new construction or by converting existing lanes. They are a combination of value pricing and lane management, two of the most effective tools for controlling heavy traffic, according to the FWHA. HOT lane management usually requires the number of passengers to be two or more per car. Increasingly these lanes are equipped with some form of electronic payment system or monthly pass. Lane markings or physical barriers are normally used to separate the HOT lane from others. The brochure lists a great number of gains provided by HOT lanes, but in essence they boil down to hope for more revenue and less congestion.[17]

When the federal government draws up a plan for helping state or local governments there surely will be disagreements over details and over the philosophy of the project. This has led to any number of unintended consequences in American history and is a major reason for matching requirements. Matching does not mean or imply *equality*. It means each side puts up something. When states deal with the U.S. government, matching can mean very little. Generally, states must put up some share of a project's cost, and that share may be 20 percent or even 10 percent or less.

Why is matching required in highway programs? States must have a share in the funding as an incentive for economy and design. Comparing costs and benefits, for example, states may oppose a project, giving no thought to the other states involved. Hence the federal government may want to spend money collected at the national level rather than from the one state that is benefiting. What share is proper? In theory the state share should reflect the benefits the state receives. Forcing a state to share in the burden with its own money may force more careful consideration of each new project.[18]

What can be expected from matching grants? Does a federal grant tend to make a state spend more or does it substitute for expenditures the state would have made? Does it help states reduce taxes or shift money to other programs? Economists have tried to determine answers to these questions, and have many answers but remain unsure. To estimate states' reaction to federal aid, one could try to calculate what the state would spend on some activity lacking aid compared with its spending in the presence of federal aid. This is complicated enough, but some economists have found that local and state governments do not treat federal aid the same way they treat money from other sources. Casual, unscientific observation would lead one to think that government aid tends to stick where it lands, giving us the term "flypaper effect."

What has been concluded by the specialists? Harry Meyers concluded that federal aid largely replaces state highway expenditures. He believes that the state will spend 63 cents of the federal dollar on something of its own choice, leaving 37 cents for its original purpose.

Edward Miller found that only eight states stayed within the limits of their grants. They assumed that the marginal dollar spent on highways was "theirs to spend as they saw fit."[19]

In the 1930s, several bills had been enacted for some kind of a national highway system supported by tolls. The Federal Aid Act of 1944 called for a national system of up to 40,000 miles. In 1947, the states proposed 37,700 miles, which were reviewed by the Department of Defense. But in neither year were funds authorized. It was not until the administration of President Eisenhower that a systematic program was inaugurated. Money from states as well as the federal government was dedicated to the new Highway Trust Fund, and road construction was then on a pay as you go basis, one of Eisenhower's aims.

Beginning in 1958, Congress appropriated billions for the states to build their roads. The share received by each state was in proportion to the work done. To make sure all the states' work moved forward at approximately the same speed, the Bureau of Public Works regularly checked the progress of construction in every state. The act also required certain standards to be uniform; many of these were designed by states or the American Association of State Highway and Transportation Officials. These included such items as speed limits and the width of shoulders. Lanes could be added but could not be paid for with Interstate Construction Funds.[20]

At this point a brief summation of the toll story might not be amiss. The first federal aid highway program back in 1916 prohibited the use of federal funds for any form of toll road. In 1927, Congress permitted the use of federal aid funds for tolls on bridges. As years passed, legislation made for more flexibility. The Interstate System, under different rules, was mostly free of tolls, but in time approximately 2,900 of the 46,730 miles had toll facilities. Federal aid funds can now be used to improve a toll facility. Half a dozen exceptions have been built into the system annually that makes the expenditure of federal aid funds on toll roads fairly simple.[21]

In the twenty-first century the story changed but little. In February of 2008, eight governors went to Washington to ask the federal government for highway funds. "We are going to ask the federal government; we are going to inspire them; we are going to force them to rebuild our infrastructure." So was quoted California's governor Arnold Schwarzenegger, who apparently led the group. The group was to meet with President Bush. They were armed with a study by the American Society of Civil Engineers declaring that the nation needed to spend $1.6 trillion in the next five years to bring its roads above mediocre condition.

The governors got little support for their movement. The money could probably not be raised without an increase in taxes, which President Bush would oppose.[22]

Evidence of the states' problems lay in the sudden rise in the use of Grant Anticipation Revenue Vehicle bonds. Since 1998 when they were first permitted, $5.7 billion in Garvee bonds have been issued with an increase every year.[23]

CHAPTER ELEVEN

Innovative Highway Financing

In 1998 the states received about $20 billion a year from the federal government for highway construction grants. This amounted to about one-fourth of the total highway expenditures of all levels. Most of this money was raised by taxes on fuel, lesser amounts from user fees. Rarely have these sources been adequate, however, for most agencies have been reluctant to raise user tax rates because of strong public objection to price increases at the pump. As we have discussed elsewhere several states have turned to the private sector, often foreign, for help. Results so far have been mixed, but it is one solution to be considered.

No longer is it the only life vest, however. Politicians are imaginative souls, and in recent years have sought, and apparently found, some new ways of raising highway money.

For decades most roads were financed by states with federal assistance. States would employ user fees, often earmarked for transportation, matching federal funds, and pay-as-you-go financing. Any variation from this is considered innovative, even though many of these plans involve fairly traditional bond issues of some kind.

Every few years since 1916, the federal government has granted federal money to the states for new road construction. Along with these funds came a large and often confusing set of requirements that the states must obey. During the 1990s, many of these were relaxed by the Federal Highway Administration or acts of Congress to give the states more freedom and options.

The Federal Aid Highway Act of 1956 created a system of 41,000 miles to "promote commerce, provide for more expeditious movement of military supplies and personnel, and expand and improve travel opportunities for citizens."[1] The same act created the Highway Trust Fund. The

1956 act required enormous infusions of cash to pay for the thousands of new miles to be built, so the federal fuels taxes were raised one cent a gallon (50 percent).They have been adjusted upward frequently in the years since. In 1983 a new act set aside one cent per gallon in fuel taxes for transit purposes. From time to time fuel tax receipts have been diverted from the trust fund and placed in the general fund, putting the money at the mercy of the Congress, unprotected by the fund and not necessarily to be used for highways.[2]

The amount of money granted by the federal government to the states varies from state to state. This has always been a source of much debate as each state makes its case for a greater share. So far, no easy formula has been devised to meet these needs. Beginning in 1997 the allocations have been based on the amount of money in fuel taxes paid by a state, need, and the effort made by a state to do its own financing. These elements obviously can be most subjective and probably provoking.[3]

After allocations have been sorted, the state has the option of accepting the money and the numerous restrictions accompanying it or refusing the money. No one would expect the latter to occur often. The states were given a large variety of options on projects and the requirements for each. Few could miss out on such opportunities.

The eight categories or programs authorized under ISTEA included interstate construction, interstate maintenance, the National Highway System, mass transit, congestion and air quality control, bridge construction and repair, and federal lands highways and interstate substitutes.[4] All of this is a far cry from the authority originally assumed by the federal government. It is made even more complicated by provisions to stimulate construction of mass transportation works.

Most federal aid programs require matching. A better word might be sharing or helping out, for the state share is often only 10 or 20 percent. In certain instances even smaller shares have been acceptable.

States may also be required to support certain national objectives if they want to receive their allotment. For example, during short periods national policy has required helmets for motorcyclists, or set speed limits determined by oil shortages. Even small business gets a break through some provisions.[5]

For years, many acts of Congress meant serious slowing of delivery time for a number of projects. Not the least of these was a stipulation that a state must have in hand the full amount of both state and federal money needed for the project before work could begin.

Bypassing Interstate 40 at Clayton, North Carolina (North Carolina Department of Transportation).

In the 1990s, the FHA created four methods of speeding things up. Their brief titles are: advance construction, partial conversion of advance construction, phased funding, and tapered match.

Advance construction permits states to use their own funds at once based upon the promise of federal money at some time in the future. The utility of this option is obvious; months, even years, might be saved on some projects.

Partial conversion lets a state receive advance federal funds in stages as the work progresses without having to wait for the completion to get full federal funding.

Phased funding is so similar to partial conversion that the practice seems to have been halted.

With tapered match, the amount of federal funding will vary with the stage of development of the project. That is, the state can draw varying amounts or percentages, depending upon the immediate needs.[6]

All of the above options granted the states far more flexibility in road financing than ever before. As might be expected, however, the national government did not release all of its strings. Under ISTEA, interest rates were to be set by federal legislation, one powerful string.

Since the 1990s, most of these innovations have been confirmed by congressional action or executive decree, and most of the states have given them consideration. One state official told the author that his state was studying every method of financing that it could find.[7]

Evaluation

These forms of innovative financing, often modified, have proven quite successful. They not only make funds available sooner, often much sooner, but with greater flexibility frequently open up funds not otherwise available. States are more free to act when the time is right, often meaning a bargain. By its own calculations, the FHA states that these initiatives accounted for a net increase of more than $1.1 billion in construction funds in the first two years.

This is not the proverbial free lunch, though. Most of these innovations mean a more rapid distribution of funds, meaning a quicker draw upon the federal treasury, meaning heavier burdens upon the taxpayer.

Net costs are going to rise, also. It is costly for the federal government to set standards and check to see that they are maintained. It can also be extremely costly for the programs to pursue social goals. For example, the wages under the Davis-Bacon Act required by the federal government may well exceed local rates and prove to be a burden in some communities.

Another source of serious contention is the federal requirement that 10 percent of the allocation must be used for beautification, bicycle routes, and historic preservation, loosely called enhancements. These are bitterly opposed by some states and towns.

Predictions are risky and we will make none here. Let us say instead that the trend is for the states to ask for, perhaps demand, more authority and flexibility in their dealings with the federal government. The resolution is likely to be based on who has the dollar. Does the state need the dollar so badly that it will yield or can it find solace in some of these other sources?[8]

State Infrastructure Banks

Seeking yet more means of funding highway needs, President Bill Clinton and the Congress in 1998 authorized the secretary of transportation to make agreements with ten states to set up state and multistate infrastructure banks. The ten banks were chosen. The following year more banks were approved and $150 million (taken from the HTF) was allotted to capitalize these banks (generally referred to as SIBs.) Then the DOT invited the states to submit proposals for more banks. At the same time the agency began spelling out more specific requirements for the states to meet, most concerning funding by the state, and too complex to justify their examination here.

The institution proved popular and by 1999 thirty-eight states had asked permission to run an SIB. DOT accepted them all. The author's calculations indicate that each bank was to receive very small sums, however.[9]

What have these banks done? Even the DOT has trouble answering this question, for some of the banks simply did not use the money the way they had put in their proposal. A few used funds for mass transportation or what some called multimodal, meaning *some* funds went to highways. Two built parking facilities.

But most of the money did go to road construction — interchanges, bypasses, connectors, nothing of a major nature. Most will be repaid by borrowing from tax revenues. A few planned tolls or special assessments. Various schemes leveraging bond issues were launched and considered permissible.[10]

Since the purpose of the SIB program was simply to increase available construction money, one would have to declare it a success. Are there better ways? Can more money be raised through SIBs differently managed? Probably, but we keep trying the old ways. At the heart of an SIB is new, private money. Are SIB offerings enough better to draw such money away from other investments? The mere creation and operation of an SIB can alter local plans and the existence of enough of them can have implications for the federal budget, as well.

Why would a state use its SIB for bonds rather than directly floating a bond issue as some had done before SIBs were permitted? The answer is that by using an SIB the state may avoid its own debt limitations.[11] Also, the money distributed by an SIB is a loan, not a gift, and must be repaid, a virtual guarantee that the state will choose the project carefully. The state retains control of the funds and can keep them recirculating on projects the state prefers.

State officials can also hope that each project will be sufficiently successful to generate other economic activity, perhaps lure a large industry or employer to the state.

Since 1998 the FHA has published its *Innovative Finance Quarterly*, occasionally including updates on the condition of SIBs. As of 2006, the program was clearly flourishing. During the last half of 2005, thirty-four new loan agreements were concluded. In total, this brought to 33 the number of states with agreements, their sum exceeding $5 billion. The most active states in order of dollars involved are South Carolina, Florida, and Arizona. FHA classifies the Arizona program as one of the most active in terms of numbers and value of its loans. Arizona's SIB is called the Highway Expansion and Extension Loan Program or HELP. A seven-member committee (FHA does not say how they are appointed) accepts and judges the applications and makes its recommendation to the state transportation board. As of 2005, the board had approved more than a half-billion dollars in projects. Fourteen of the fifteen counties have had aid from HELP. The board makes sure that each region of the state has its fair share of the funds. Perhaps the most significant of the projects is the addition of high occupancy lanes on I-10 near the city limits. Many works begun by HELP have used other funds to finish the job; HELP's great contribution appears to be expediting works that otherwise might never have left the drawing board.

Arizona and other states have in one fashion or another found ways to continue building roads without resorting to the usual bugaboo, tax increases. All of this has been done with the sanction of the U.S. government.[12]

Garvees

Among these innovations is the Garvee, still relatively quiet but figuratively explosive in its potential. Brookings Institution calls it "today's roads with tomorrow's dollars." How did this blockbuster come about? It began with Section 311 of the National Highway System Designation of 1995, then became permanent highway law in 2000. A large number of bond-related costs now became eligible for repayment. These items included such things as principle and interest payments, insurance, administrative costs, and a number of other minor items.

The chief intention of these changes was to expedite construction. Among the many new approaches is the Grant Anticipation Revenue Vehicle, immediately branded Garvees. The government defines a Garvee as a "bond, note, or other financial instrument issued, based upon future projections of federal-aid transportation funding." States can begin work for which they have no funding, but anticipate some future funding.[13]

How Garvees work can be best understood by examining the traditional methods of financing. In 2002 the federal government assessed gasoline taxes at 18.4 cents per gallon and the states averaged about 20 cents per gallon. In the year 2000 they together amounted to more than half the non-local money spent on highways. (The federal portion of gas taxes is collected by the IRS and retained by the Highway Trust Fund under the direction of the FWHA.)

For many years the gas tax receipts increased annually, providing the states with an ever-increasing fund for the state DOTs. In the 1960s the average increase in miles driven was 4.4 percent, but in 2000 it dropped to an increase of 2 percent, meaning the states began to fall behind in their road maintenance needs.[14]

In addition to user taxes, states rely heavily on bonds for revenue. Since they have a fixed date for repayment of the bond (loan), purchasers can count on private sources to provide ratings about a state's ability to repay by the promised date. In 1990 the return on highway bonds amounted to $3.2 billion; in 2002 the figure had reached $13.2 billion.

Some kind of bond has been used for highways since 1893 in Mass-achusetts. Today every state uses them with the exception of Nebraska and Wyoming. Bonds have the advantage over taxes of giving an agency the opportunity to move ahead on its road plans far more rapidly.

For many years the states could borrow against their own state funds, but they could not borrow against federal highway funds not yet appro-priated until 1991. Into this paper opportunity stepped Garvees. They dif-fer from typical municipal bonds or bonds backed by the state's authority in that the principal and interest are repaid with future federal highway funds.[15] Garvees can be used for virtually any highway project, making them popular and highly useful. But there is no guarantee of repayment. Uncle Sam's strong arm can not be used to enforce repayment. The fed-eral government does nothing more than advise buyers to consult experts before purchasing bonds of this type. Any default becomes the problem of the state.

After a proposal has been selected for Garvee treatment, it is presented to the FHA for approval. Once granted Garvee status, the project is given the advance construction label. At this time the state must prepare a debt service schedule, prorating and prioritizing the schedule if more than one project is included.[16]

No government program can exist long without classification or amendments so there are different types of Garvees: (1) short term. Bonds that have been backed by obligations of federal funds that already have been authorized. (2) long term. More risky than short term, they go beyond authorization periods. Historically Congressional failure to reauthorize has been rare. Nevertheless payment is not guaranteed. (3) backstopped. Whereas in the above cases the backing has been federal funding, in these instances a state can pledge other sources, such as tolls or vehicle registra-tion receipts. (4) naked. The bonds are entirely dependent on future fed-eral funds. Their acceptance is often substantially enhanced by the purchase of bond insurance.

Garvees have been permitted since 1991 but until 1998 no state had taken advantage of the law. By 2005, 16 different states and territories had done so. The legislatures of New Hampshire and Vermont tabled any authorization of Garvees, and in 2002, Wyoming for the moment at least, banned Garvees. The greatest number of these bonds, five, has been issued by Colorado. As of 2004, the value of all Garvees was $7.5 billion, and they are growing. One job under consideration in Maryland is valued at $1 billion. Most projects seem to be designed for the suburbs and the edges of large cities. They also tend toward new and very large projects and not maintenance and repair.

Is there any question of the legality of a Garvee? It is a radical departure for many. Even though it has not always been a matter of law, in practice, state legislatures have not permitted one legislature to bind a subsequent legislature. Georgia and Oklahoma were sued on the grounds that Garvees created a state debt which had to be approved by the public. The Supreme Courts in both states ruled that Garvees were legal because the debt was to be paid with federal money, not state. The Colorado court however, concluded that voter approval was required because they amounted to multi-year obligations. At this writing the largest Garvee debt so far ($1 billion) is held up in Maryland apparently on the issue of legality and size.[17]

The popularity of Garvees shows that the nationwide scarcity of highway funds accompanied by massive new needs for roads have greatly increased the need for highway funds. The gap between needs and resources has grown beyond traditional methods of support. Officials responsible for these finances have needed to seek other sources, even some that in years past would have been considered too risky, perhaps illegal. So many states have turned to "innovative financing," just one form of which is the Garvee.

Let's make a final judgment on them. In their favor is speed, or what Brookings calls "accelerated project delivery." Brookings quotes the Federal Highway Administration as reporting that an Arkansas reconstruction job was accelerated nine years and an Ohio interchange will be accelerated by a scarcely believable 25 years because of the support received from Garvees. Speeding up a project can have important, even unexpected side effects. Brookings cites an instance in Alabama where a Garvee bridge program that eliminated weight-restricted bridges made possible far shorter driving distances for school buses with concomitant savings.[18] Additionally, significant savings can be realized by earlier hiring of services, or purchases of real estate, materials, and rights of way. Further savings can accrue by acceleration on rehabilitation projects. According to the FHA, the sooner repair work can begin, the lower the job costs will be, and the longer a job is delayed, the more likely it is that roads and bridges will have to close during the rehabilitation. Garvees also enable bigger projects. Massive projects are apparently becoming more popular with the states, Boston's Big Dig being the best example. Garvees make possible the financing of such projects because of their access to so many more additional sources of funds. They also allow states to avoid state debt limits. Garvee funds are federal so do not count against state limitations on what it can borrow. This is not guaranteed, however, since rating agencies might well take *all* debt into consideration, irrespective of the source, making it difficult to sell the bonds. And they allow states to avoid bond referenda. Most traditional municipal bonds are subject to the approval of the public. This is a decision of the state, and most have exempted Garvees from such a requirement with obvious savings in time and money.

What are the drawbacks to Garvee financing? Costs, for one thing. Garvee bonds borrow from the future and do not add any new money. These long-term commitments mean that future federal funds must be used by the state for repayment and could adversely affect the ability of the state to make or remake plans. They also must have federal reauthorization, which carries risks for the bondholder. What he lends to the government will be returned to him from some future federal aid legislation. Garvees are distinguished from other bonds in that the holders are gambling that such legislation will be forthcoming and the Congress will continue to vote enough aid to cover all obligations. This has been labeled "a key credit weakness" by Standard and Poors.

Modern heavy highway equipment (North Carolina Department of Transportation).

A prime example concerned the funding of Boson's Big Dig. The project was to receive $200 million a year from the federal government each year from 2003 through 2005. However, Congress appropriated far less than promised, leaving a shortfall of about $100 million, roughly one-half. In addition to its impact on the Big Dig, the reduction delayed or eliminated about 20 percent of other state highway programs. Congress generally has appropriated fully, but it makes no promises.

The pertinent legislation is obscure, but in practice Congress has supported the obligations of states and the DOTS, but not counties and cities. (I have found no legislation that prohibits aid to the lesser political subdivisions, but the practice is quite clear.)

Simply stated, Garvee money is easier to obtain than returns from a new tax. Garvees play no part in planning. As a result, critics say that this has led to less careful planning, and considerable trouble down the line. This accusation has not been supported by much documentation, but it obviously could become a very serious matter.[19]

If Garvees are to continue to flourish, a few changes should be made. First, Congress should make clearer the requirements for a loan. The agency should demonstrate savings or benefits or both and should know more specifically what is needed for such loans. Second, there seems no reason why Garvees should be available to states only. Metropolitan planning organizations are increasingly important today and should be able to work without waiting for gifts from the state. Specific legislation is needed to clarify this proposition. Third, specific guidelines should be drawn to make clear just how many Garvees are permissible for one agency, and any limits to the amount of money it might borrow.

The dictionary tells us that innovation means something new, a change. It can be incremental or radical. In any case it should be something better, or, in the business world, more profitable. All of the methods of financing highways covered in this chapter are new. Whether they are going to be profitable or better, we lack the gift to know.

CHAPTER TWELVE

Congestion Pricing

"Midnight Madness!!!! Come early. Bargains galore." Between midnight and 8 A.M. some merchandise would sell for "up to" 65 percent off. Prime Outlets was announcing its post–Thanksgiving sale, sending notices throughout a radius of 100 miles in western Pennsylvania. The 145-store mall is strategically located near the junction of I-79 and I-80, and they both reported heavy traffic Thanksgiving afternoon for sales still several hours away. By 10 P.M. both roads overflowed. Interstate 80 eastbound was backed up four miles; I-79 was choked for ten miles in its northbound lanes. The parking lot soon filled, and drivers resorted to parking on the interstate shoulders. The mall's manager concluded that this was the perfect gridlock; cars simply could not move in any direction.[1]

Even the Census Bureau can not tell us how many such congestions we will enjoy in a lifetime; probably most of us have encountered at least one. That is only one type of congestion, and presumably avoidable. But there is another kind, likely happening every workday to many drivers, in most cases unavoidable.

We call it "driving to work." It occurs all over America, in varying degrees, and appears to be getting worse.

The solution since the 1950s had been to build more roads. But even vast construction has not kept pace with increases in travel. The Texas Transportation Institute (TTI) estimated that between 1980 and 1999 the number of miles of highways increased a mere 1.5 percent, while miles of travel jumped a whopping 76 percent. The agency also calculated that in 2003, the 85 largest metropolitan areas experienced 3.7 trillion vehicle hours of delay plus billions of gallons of wasted fuel. Further, the problem was spreading from the biggest cities to small towns and rural areas.[2] Much of the enormous increase in truck freight has been the result of

NAFTA opening free trade among Canada, Mexico, and the U.S. Between 1993 and 2005, Mexican exports to the U.S. grew 400 percent and U.S. exports to Mexico grew 245 percent. NAFTA has many problems, but growth in total trade is not one of them. The three governments and NAFTA have concluded that this trade would grow even faster were it not for delays in traffic along the borders. As an example, many auto parts are manufactured in Mexico, assembled in Canada, and distributed from the U.S. Congestion at any spot along the way can run up costs and perhaps lose someone a competitive edge.[3] In the summer of 2007, *Public Roads* devoted an entire issue to the matter of congestion, its causes, and its solutions. In the category "dimensions of congestion," the journal declared that congestion was increasing in duration, extent, and intensity. The duration has expanded from 4.5 hours per day in 1982 to 7 hours in 2003. Duration is defined as the percentage of the day with speeds below 45 miles per hour on a freeway and below 30 on an artery.

The extent of congestion grew from 33 percent to 67 percent of highway travel between 1982 and 2003. The very largest cities have sections of road where stop-and-go traffic can occur at any hour of the day.

The intensity of congestion is measured by the average extra travel time due to congestion. This has moved from 13 percent to 37 percent between 1987 and 2007. In short, by every gauge the congestion problem is growing worse.[4]

Citing TTI, the journal claims that the expense of these delays in the 85 largest urban areas was $65 billion. The figure was determined from the costs of 3.7 billion hours of delay plus 2.3 billion wasted gallons of fuel. But TTI believes that these amounts are too small because they do not include (a) the costs of congestion in rural areas as well as in smaller cities beyond the 85 (b) loss of productivity (c) vehicle damage and (d) costs from delays in freight shipments.[5]

The U.S. Department of Transportation through the Federal Highway Administration presents us with some ideas about how to reduce the level of congestion.

The first is as old as the system, and probably favored by most motorists at one time or another — increase capacity. In the early days of interstates, vast amounts of federal and state money seemed always available to build new highways. No longer is that so. Costs have gone out of sight. Noise, pollution, and environmental concerns have pretty well wiped out that method without the infusion of great amounts of new money. (Where this might come from will be discussed later.)

Second, increase productivity. In highway terminology that means getting peak performance from the roads by coordination of traffic signals, removing bottlenecks, keeping travelers informed of road conditions, and managing temporary disruptions, the bane of all drivers.

The highway administration believes that much improvement can be made in this area once agencies recognize that the era of endless building is over. This is especially pertinent when decisions must be made about distributing state funds.

The third idea is to reduce demand or alternatively speaking, provide better transportation choices. These tactics include parking pricing, benefits to car poolers, changes in work scheduling and better transit options. And probably many others.

A fourth consideration is road pricing. The magazine contends that travelers do not pay the full cost of travel or even consider their lack of payment to it. A driver will calculate his own time and fuel but does not consider their effects on other users. In this instance market demand exceeds supply, and the travel "is distributed according to the time users are willing to wait."[6] The purpose of congestion pricing is to charge a price that will bring demand and supply into balance. Would congestion pricing (or parking) have prevented the stalemate at Prime Outlets? Perhaps. It would probably depend on the level of the pricing. The Department of Transportation says that in the U.S. priced facilities are so far too rare to form a judgment but in two cases — I-394 in Minneapolis and I-15 in San Diego — have proven "highly popular."[7] In other areas the public is skeptical. Such programs obviously require a high level of acceptance or they will not work.

Mary Peters, secretary of transportation, told the U.S. Chamber of Commerce that we are being increasingly strangled by gridlock. While some believe there is no solution to our highway problem, Peters' department has come up with a drove of programs and slogans that sound like solutions. One can too easily become cynical here, but a few of these suggestions are probably worthy of mention.

Probably no plan is bolder and bigger than "Corridors of the Future." (The reader should be warned that "corridors" with their grand vagueness, are now very popular with politicians.) What are these corridors? More than just a highway, a corridor is "a broad geographical band with no predefined size or scale that follows a directional flow connecting major sources of trips. It involves a normally linear transportation service area that may contain a number of streets, highways, and transit route alignments."[8]

Whether they understood that language or not, the states were quick to respond when the USDOT asked them for corridor suggestions. In particular the USDOT sought routes that were badly congested and critically in need of funding. Interestingly, USDOT wanted information about the possibility of private financing for each project. The department received 38 responses, usually from a coalition of states, varying from three to eight in number of states. After a series of screenings the applications were narrowed to eight corridors containing 14 projects.

While little may come from all this, it is worthwhile to sum up what has been done. First, USDOT has made clear its priorities. In no meaningful order they are: I-95, Florida to Virginia; I-70, dedicated truck lanes, Missouri to Ohio; I-5, Washington to California; I-10, California to Florida; I-69, Texas to Michigan; I-80, California to Nevada; and two others apparently in California, but not specified.[9] What does this all mean? One is tempted to say very little, for most of the projects have yet to be allocated any funds, and the precise routes are unknown. USDOT says it will help raise money, and its imprimatur will certainly help the Congress determine priorities, if and when it gets involved, for a reasonably impartial bureau has with great effort decided where the highway need is the greatest.

But the USDOT is not through. Its huge umbrella called Congestion Initiative also includes something called Urban Partners. USDOT likes to organize its agencies by numbers. In this case "up to five" metropolitan areas, called Urban Partners, will join with USDOT to demonstrate successful means of coping with congestion. The partner can be a government agency of any nature or even a private transportation provider. They must agree to four steps that have worked in the past. The first is a promise to apply principles of congestion pricing including new tolls, tolls on existing lanes and bridges, and even cordon areas. Second, the partner must modernize or create a transit system that will be coordinated with its street congestion program. Third, the partner must secure promises from major employers to install or expand flextime and telecommunications programs for their employees. And fourth, the partner will support regional programs to improve traveler information such as signals and accident reports.[10]

In June 2007, Mary Peters announced that she had invited nine Urban Partners to make their case for participation. Then in August she reduced the number to five finalists who would share some $850 million in federal grants. The five are New York, Miami, Minneapolis, Seattle and San

Francisco.[11] At the time of this writing that is as far as the program has gone.

The next effort of federal transportation authorities is probably the most innovative, radical, and potentially vast of all their proposals so far. It has also been subject to more debate, for it is sweeping in conception and costs. It is called Public-Private Partnerships or PPP, and has been referred to in other parts of this book. The origins seem to be British. About 1992, Prime Minister John Major, trying to bolster the economy by increasing private investment, introduced a Private Finance Initiative. It did not shake Britain greatly, but it was, in modified form, retained by Tony Blair's Labour government. It spread, however, to Australia, and was especially popular within Partnerships Victoria.[12]

In America, most of the states had depleted their highway budgets in the 1980s and 1990s, spending heavily on expansion of the system or maintenance of the old. They sought some new sources of revenue, and urged on by investment firms as well as the federal government, some government agencies took the step.

In 2005, the U.S. Congress passed the six-year bill known as SAFETEA–LU, providing minor assistance to the road program. In addition, however, the measure made possible, set guidelines for, and actually promoted PPPs. This was followed by a series of acts encouraging the states to participate in the partners programs. Among these the federal government made possible relatively inexpensive loans with delayed repayment. The Congress meanwhile authorized refinancing some debts.

Then new legislation attacked the toll question. States may now toll new, non-interstate highways, reconstructed toll roads, and many other roads. This legislation and much more was designed in part to "open doors for states and private sector entities to begin exploring PPPs."[13]

The federal government having taken many steps to facilitate partnerships, the task now fell to individual states to determine their degree of risk.

A dozen or so states seem to have taken no action at all; a large number have passed enabling legislation, and a few have started digging. Sources rather strangely vary in describing these last, but using USDOT as the most authoritative it would appear that the Chicago overpass, the Indiana toll road, and the Pocahontas highway in Virginia are the major completed works. Texas has contracted for several different projects, Trans-Texas Corridor 35 being the farthest along. Georgia, Florida, and Oregon seem to be making the next most progress.[14]

***Above and opposite*—** Two views of Interstate 26 (North Carolina Department of Transportation).

The precise contractual arrangements will vary from state to state, but three broad types of PPPs are developing. The first in frequency of use are long-term leases of existing tolled assets. They must be well maintained, enjoy low economic risk, and in general be a going concern. The Chicago Skyway and the Indiana Toll Road both readily met those requirements.

The second is the planning, constructing and operation of a new long-term facility. Pocahontas road in Virginia and most of the many Texas plans fall into this category.

The third is a somewhat vague combination of the above two. FHA believes that the partners programs in all their variance will grow and expand, and officials will learn with each new project. Specifically, the department expects that PPPs will not meet all needs but should be able to manage some 10 to 20 percent of need.[15] (Ignored in this study is the use of PPPs for other than transportation needs. For example, hospitals and defense facilities in Australia; hospitals in Canada; schools in Great Britain, and so on. Almost all the PPPs in the U.S. are road related.) Goldman Sachs, the American leader in PPP participation, has put out a number of fliers extolling the benefits of these agreements.

Up to this point, little effort has been made to distinguish among vehicles. No discussion of congestion could be complete without reference to freight and its role in the problem. Many drivers, in fact, would maintain that freight is the congestion problem. Many a trucker would just as quickly blame the drivers of the "four wheelers." This narrative takes the point of view that congestion is congestion, and what may help four wheels may also be good for 18.

Not surprisingly, USDOT has a good deal to say about freight hauling and traffic and has suggestions about road relief. A few facts first. Says USDOT, almost everything made, bought, or consumed in the U.S. is at some point moved by truck. Anything stopping a truck slows some element of the economy. Can we measure its size? FHA says that in 2002, freight carriers hauled 17.5 billion metric tons of freight worth $13 trillion. Miles traveled by truck are expected to increase 3 percent per year, some 20 percent faster than passenger traffic. About two-thirds of all freight is carried in trucks; the rest by rail, air, and water. It would seem that any measure expediting freight movement would also help other highway traffic.

Congestion has two main types, recurring and nonrecurring. The former is provoked by a simple lack of capacity, the second by unexpected or unanticipated disruption of the infrastructure. Other delays can result from administrative decisions, security matters, or just poor work. USDOT estimates that delays can double and triple the costs of transport of goods.

Delays can greatly affect inventories and therefore create additional costs. Suppliers regularly hampered by delay learn to keep more goods on hand than immediately needed to cope with emergencies. Insurance and storage fees will increase proportionately, sharply reducing capital otherwise destined for production. This has become especially significant in recent years as "just in time" practices have become more prevalent in the U.S. One estimate has inventory carrying costs increasing by 17 percent in 2005 alone. Three of the worst districts — Detroit/Windsor, New York/New Jersey, and Los Angeles/Long Beach — have become special USDOT targets to reduce recurring freight congestion.

The latest strategy attempted by FHA to reduce this chaos is Truck Only Toll Lanes (TOT). The amount of the toll would have to be negotiated according to distance and demand. Ideally, this information would be provided to the driver en route, so he could decide which choice to make at the moment. Using stretches of I-10, tests were begun to study the effect of the TOT; the concerned states' preliminary conclusion indicated the savings would be about $6 million a year.[16]

Implicit throughout this chapter is the acceptance of pricing of some type for revenue as well as for congestion control. Most authorities seem to believe that the good old days of large bond sales are gone. Pay as you go is the fashion. Drivers do not like tolls, but neither do they care for increased taxes on fuel. Perhaps pricing, which can come in a large variety forms, will be more acceptable.

This form of pricing is usually denominated congestion pricing, although some agencies have pushed other names — value pricing, peak period pricing, time of day pricing, and variable pricing, all probably designed to conceal the word toll. Whatever its name, the method or program is clearly market-based, fitting so much of the political attitude of the 1990s and since. Congestion pricing charges the driver a fee (toll) for using a bridge, a piece or all of a highway, a tunnel, or even a selected section of a city. Its purpose is to encourage and make possible shifting routes, time of travel, perhaps even destinations away from heavily traveled roads to less busy roads. (This should not be confused with road pricing, which is designed to fund roadways.) Its methodology is to monetarize costs associated with congestion.[17]

Irrespective of benefits and costs, congestion pricing falls into three categories. (1) Variable tolls placed on existing and new toll roads, bridges, and tunnels. The level of traffic determines precise rates. (2) Lane changing tolls, controlled electronically by transmitters from drivers in HOT or added lanes. (3) Cordon tolls, with a fee for entering and driving in certain heavily traveled, urban areas.

Electronic toll collection technology is used for most of these systems.

The vehicles contain identification tags and transmitters. Without stopping or slowing, the car reports to the "reader," which bills a credit card or account. Other methods use cameras photographing license plates.[18] Anthony Downs's *Still Stuck in Traffic* is probably the most thorough as well as objective study to be found on the matter of congestion. After carefully explaining the variety of tolls, Downs concerns himself with the matter of equity. Too easily a route can "price off" a substantial number of drivers, or create "Lexus lanes." Downs suggests that some of the funding raised by congestion pricing be set aside to help low-income drivers. He also points out that HOT lanes are less hard on the low income driver, because they can use them with added passengers.[19]

Congestion remains the motorists' curse. It can be created by nature or by man. It can occur anywhere, any time. Governments at every level have sought some clever new means to wipe it out. It stays. Various financial tricks can reduce it, but not greatly. After decades of study, research, and expenditures we have little to show. Congestion appears to be on the increase. Is there some powerful measure we have yet to try? Or are we just going to try our best to cope?

CHAPTER THIRTEEN

The Private Sector

At various points in this book reference has been made to the subject, merits and demerits of private money invested in public highways. Today, highways can scarcely be mentioned without the topic of privatization arising. In this chapter the use of the private sector will be more thoroughly studied, particularly in the light of recent congressional investigations and surveys made by the General Accountability Office.

At the outset we will examine the work done by the GAO at the request of the Congress and follow that with some specific studies of privatization in an attempt to find a balance of opinion of its utility. There was no constitutional prohibition of highway privatizing, but until the 1980s interstate highways have been more or less prohibited by law and practice from privatization schemes. This is changing, and a very few exceptions have already been permitted. This chapter will discuss privatization of interstate and well as national and local highways.[1]

We can start with one fairly safe assumption, that most public and private stakeholders agree that more money must be found to keep up with badly needed new construction, not to mention maintenance of fifty-year-old roads. The FHA estimated in 2004 that the nation as a whole must spend about $76 billion per year, or an average of some 18 percent more than was spent in 2000. This rate of expenditure must continue to 2020 just to keep up with past conditions. This is made worse by the demographics, which forecast vastly increased mandatory spending on health care and Social Security programs. And people are living and — presumably driving — longer. How can this much money be found?

Privatization is not new, as its proponents like to say. Nearly all the earliest toll roads and bridges in America were privately owned. For many decades state and local governments have built highways with private funds by simple contract arrangement with the builders. Further, billions of dollars in tax free bonds have been sold to private investors in order to finance highway work. The GAO calculated that in 2001 the total bonded debt for state and local roads exceeded $100 billion. Is there more such capital available? The GAO's response was to study the objectives, the obstacles, the advantages, and the sources of financing in general, then to examine minutely some specific cases to highlight real usages. They also included some foreign cases.

The GAO even explained its methodology to the Congress — to leave no doubts, no doubt. Special economists of the GAO studied all the literature that could be found, and interviewed leading economists, bankers, bond market analysts, and a variety of industrialists to get as many views as possible. For case studies they elected to examine only projects they called "major," meaning having a cost of $100 million or more. There proved to be only six such projects in the United States. Social benefits were not of concern nor whether the project should have been undertaken at all. Also excluded were privately owned roads designed to reach privately owned properties.[2]

The six projects had all been planned over 7 to 30 years, indicating a fairly low priority to the agency involved. Each of the states had to make compromises to obtain a privatization contract. Some lost control of the right to set to toll rates, a politically dangerous loss. Others were prohibited from improving competing publicly owned highways. In one California case this handicap proved so unpopular that the state had to buy the road back from the private contractors.[3] In other instances the political subdivision was required to share costs such as purchasing rights of way, environmental studies and housing the consortium. Half of the cases used some federal funding. Some lost federal and local tax revenue. In 2003 the total tax loss was estimated as running between $25 and $35 million. And in case of financial failure of the privatized road, a state can often be required to take back responsibility for the road.

But the privatizers have their problems as well. According to GAO, three of the six cases studied were in financial trouble because the traffic level failed to achieve expectations. The only one to make a profit — SR 91 in California — was built in a heavily congested area. Obviously no profit is likely during construction days, and several years may pass before the traffic is sufficient to make a profit or break even.

Traditionally the federal government had been prohibited by law from assisting private contractors in financing or building, but it could aid state and local governments. Increasingly, federal assistance is becoming more available, however, especially in the wake of the omnibus SAFETEA-LU act of 2005. The GAO study traces its own version of how this came about. Drivers' demands increased with the burgeoning of automobiles in the early twentieth century, the consequence being the Federal Aid Road Act of 1916. This was the first piece of legislation designed to provide states with federal funds to build highways. Then, after years of congressional wrangling over states' rights, an interstate highway system was authorized in 1944 by the Federal-Aid Highway Act.[4]

Then, to quote the GAO, "By expanding applications for tolling, federal programs have gradually become more receptive to private sector participation and investment."[5] By 1956 the Congress and President Eisenhower were ready to change the highway revenue system from a tolls- to a tax-supported system with motor fuel taxes being placed in a Highway Trust Fund. This method prevailed until the administration of Ronald Reagan. He found several objections to the Surface Transportation and Uniform Relocation Act of 1987. It seemed to him that the bill gave too much power to the federal government vis-à-vis the states. He also declared it too expensive by $10 billion. Above all, it contained 121 "demonstration projects," the 1987 version of pork. Said Reagan, "I haven't seen so much lard since I handed out blue ribbons at the Iowa State Fair."[6] He vetoed the bill, But by a very close senate vote, the veto was overridden, the public preferring more roads and a 65 mile-per-hour rural speed limit.

In 1991, ISTEA had permitted a federal subsidy of 50 percent on toll roads, whether public or private. Still there was more. In 1998 the Transportation Infrastructure Finance and Innovation Act introduced another federal financing program. For the period of 1999 through 2003, TIFIA made available some $10 billion in direct loans, limited only to 33 percent of the total bill.

TEA-21 expired in 2003 and after long congressional discussion, was replaced by SAFETEA-LU. This monster provides nearly $300 billion for highway and transit spending, guaranteed for the next five years.[7] It also requires the secretary of transportation to carry out fifteen demonstration cases between 2005 and 2009 to expedite toll collection on interstate highways. The law went on at length to explain how this would be done, including methods of pricing as well as how to collect the toll. HOV pricing would be required. With minimal quibbling, the idea of tolls on the interstates became acceptable.[8]

Three of the privately sponsored highways were for profit, using special purpose corporations to carry out that one job. The other projects created non-profit, private corporations. Who will perform what specific function during private ownership is a matter of contractual detail and varies greatly from case to case. However, all except the

Dulles Greenway contract have one stipulation in common. The state may not build a new road or improve any old road that "competes" for traffic with the new one. In other words, the private is protected from the public. In the case of Dulles, traffic on the private road seemed to be hurt to some degree by improvements in the old.[9]

Usually the agreements provided for the state to permit concessionaires to "design, build, own, and operate." They also would collect tolls for long periods — up to 50 years in these cases. Responsibility for maintenance and concessions is usually worked out in the contract.

State Highway Financing

Project	Mileage	Arrangement	Financing
SR 91 express lanes, California	10	For profit	Equity, commercial debt
Dulles Greenway, Va.	14	For profit	Equity, commercial debt
SR 125, California	10	For profit	Equity, commercial debt. TFIA, federal funds, local government
Southern Connector, South Carolina	10	Non profit	Tax exempt debt
Pocahontas Parkway, Va.	9	Non-profit	In kind contribution, tax exempt debt[10]

(Financing arrangements for privately sponsored projects in millions)

Project	Equity	Commercial Debt	Tax Exempt Debt	Other
Dulles Greenway, Va.	$40	$298		
SR 91 express lanes, California	$20	$100		$5.6 Subordinated
SR 125, California	$160	$321		$140 TFIA. federal, $20 local

Project	Equity	Commercial Debt	Tax Exempt Debt	Other
Southern Connector, South Carolina			$200	$17.5 state
Pocahontas Parkway, Va.	$5		$354	$18 state

As indicated above, each of the six projects had a different method of financing, the non-profits taking advantage of tax-exempt funding, and the "profits" more often having to borrow. The GAO went on to explain the advantages and disadvantages to the states of using private methods. The first of the former was a matter of timing. The GAO found, for example, that the five highway cases studied were considered reasonable and needed, but the funds were simply not there for completion. As the years passed, private sector assistance became imperative. For example, the Southern Connector in South Carolina had been in the planning stage for thirty years before the state contracted with private funders.[11]

Second, while the states could have borrowed and collected tolls for these projects, private funding meant that they could preserve their funding capital and utilize it for other roads. Further, many states have limits on the amount of debt they may incur, and this method gets around that problem. Closely related is that states are protected from highways that create serious debts. Dulles Greenway, for example, could not repay its debt in 1996. Virginia was not held responsible, nor required to help in the repayment.

But not is all rosy for the states. Governments have their share of problems from privatization.[12] In the case of two California roads, SR 91 and SR 125, the consortium has complete control of the toll rates. Dulles Greenway has a ceiling on tolls, but can control the rate under that figure.

Third, states usually lose the right to compete with a new highway. This may mean closing or not improving an existing road or not having the right to build a new one. So much objection has been raised by the California public that amendments had to be made. The state now can make some changes but only after rewarding the consortium for loss of revenue.

Fourth, even though most of the cost of the new road is borne by the developer, some expenses accrue to the governing agency. These might include environment studies or acquiring the right-of-way. These can be very costly and unexpected. For example, new corporations often must be created, and tax problems have proven to be expensive in time and money.

Fifth, even more incalculable is the matter of state liability. Again, each contract will be different, but states may have to step in if the private road proves unprofitable. For example, Virginia was not reimbursed for the several millions paid to Pocahontas Parkway when the road failed to prove profitable and the state was forced to bail the consortium out.

Finally, half the projects were financed with tax exempt loans, the result being a loss of revenue for the federal or state governments or both. The amount is difficult to calculate but certainly represents many millions.[13]

The GAO report ends by explaining why there have not been more privatization attempts, and gives suggestions of what can be done to encourage more such projects.

The first challenge is from the states themselves. At the time of this report only 20 states had granted the legal authority to agencies within the state. Additionally, several of these limited the number of projects. Private developers want design-build projects. They find it simpler and more profitable to combine planning and building. The federal government permits this, but less than half the contracts allow consortiums to combine the two operations. Then, political pressure often prohibits privatization. In particular, the public exhibits great concern about tolls, feeling that fuel taxes should be sufficient to pay for highway construction. The GAO found, for example, that traffic on the Southern Connector in South Carolina was well below expectations because drivers in that area were not accustomed to tolls and resisted using the new road. States and the private sector often cannot agree on priorities. States tend to use their own funds for highly congested districts, the very ones that the privatizer would also prefer to use. Finally there is no guarantee of profit. Environmental requirements can slow developments for years, during which period developers must be paying for their money. Toll roads can experience additional delays in profitability until a sufficient number of drivers decide the cost is worth while. Those projects using bonds may find that their bonds are being downgraded and becoming more difficult to sell. In the case of the Pocahontas Parkway, bond value dropped a damaging 50 percent.[14]

The report concludes with a number of suggestions for the Congress, essentially to make privatizing more palatable to the public.

Let us examine a few of the most important and key players in this game. Who are these privatizers? Are they a cabal of contractors yearning to build highways to nowhere? Are they a group of oily bankers hiding behind barrels of asphalt? Hardly. Their chief spokesman is probably Robert Poole, who is always available for the public. Poole is director of transportation for the Reason Foundation, which he founded in 1978. He holds an engineering degree from MIT and has advised four presidents on transportation issues.

Poole has done a great deal of writing and consulting in matters of air traffic and airport security, but is probably best known for his work on the privatizing of surface transportation. In 1988 he wrote a paper proposing privately financed toll lanes. This paper is generally credited with the passage of California's private tollway law, from which emerged four private tollway projects. Since then more than a score of states and the federal government have passed similar public/private legislation. In 1993, his team introduced the High Occupancy Toll lanes (HOT).

Poole has been a member of many agencies and commissions, especially in California, and has probably influenced more people and governments to consider privatizing than any other individual. Politically, he seems to be a libertarian with some conservative tendencies, but his record would indicate an ability to function readily with any party.[15]

Unofficially, the highway world has several parts; the financiers, the designers, the builders, and the operators. Some of the larger corporations perform more than one of these functions. In each category their numbers are substantial. A handful of examples is all we can give here. Among the investment companies, one of the largest and most active is the Macquarie Infrastructure Group, a wholly owned subsidiary of the Macquarie Bank of Australia. The group is primarily an investment company, with a wide variety of holdings in Australia, Canada, the U.S., and several European countries. But the group does more than lend money. It builds and operates toll roads, tunnels, and bridges. It is the world's largest operator of toll roads, sometimes alone, sometimes in partnership with other giants. Its first American project was opened in 2007 near San Diego. It holds long term joint leases on the Indiana East/West Toll Road and the Chicago Skyway, as well as full leaseship of the Dulles Greenway in Virginia.[16]

Several privatizers have commented on the absence of American capital in major highway construction. The simple answer is probably the right one. Money managers could do better elsewhere. But that seems to be changing, although evidence is still thin. Leadership rests with Goldman Sachs.

But America is not lacking for contractors and builders. One of the largest in this league is Zachry Construction Company of San Antonio. Zachry began as a family company in 1924, building roads and bridges. It has since expanded into power plants, dams, airfields, and much more, starting in Texas and the southeastern U.S. before becoming a major international builder. Zachry is also in the hospitality business and even owns a professional basketball team, the San Antonio Spurs. The company can lay claim to 1,000 heavy construction projects, 800 miles of paved highway, 30 international contracts and 1,500 telecommunications projects.[17]

One of the pioneers in highway asset management is VMS Inc., founded in Petersburg, Virginia, in 1995. It is now headquartered in Richmond. It seems to have been the first to form a public/private partnership, a performance-based contract for transportation infrastructure. Working closely with Virginia DOT, VMS assumed entire responsibility for the comprehensive maintenance of major portions of the interstate highway system. The firm has 600 employees and 10 branches, and operates or maintains highways in Alaska, Florida, Oklahoma, Texas, Virginia and Washington, D.C. The scope of its work is enormous, including, bridges, tunnels, tolls, rest areas, welcome centers, canals, and airports. The company claims to manage 3,000 lane miles in four states. In the District of Columbia alone, VMS contracted to manage and preserve for five years 118 bridges and seven miles of drainage ditches. In Florida, the company maintains 902 lane miles of highway, and 271 bridges.

In 2007, VMS was bought by an Australian firm, Transfield Services, for $29.5 million. VMS's revenue is nearly $100 million a year. Transfield announced the purchase as an opportunity to break into the American market.[18]

Similar functions are in the domain of Transurban, another Australian corporation. It does not build highways, but can perform any other function related to the road. As of 2006, it owned three Australian toll roads valued at $6 billion (American). It has several more in the U.S., including a 99-year, $611 million lease arrangement with Virginia for the Pocahontas Parkway. (It opened an office in Atlanta in 2007.)[19]

Frequently mentioned in this book is the Spanish giant Cintra. It appears to be ready to take on the most massive highway construction jobs that America can dream up. It is the property of Grupo Ferrovial, also Spanish, 60 percent of which is owned by the Del Pino family. Cintra is the acronym for Concesiones de Infraestructura de Transporte and is the building arm of Grupo. Grupo, which has nearly 100,000 employees, invests in construction, airports, toll roads, and car parks. Its specialty is developing, maintaining, and managing transport, urban, and services infrastructure. The company invests in Europe, Chile, the U.S., Canada, and Australia.

It was founded by Rafael del Pino in 1952 as a railroad construction company called Ferrovial. Beginning about 1995 the company began to purchase other contractors, especially in Poland. Major projects include a portion of the Madrid airport and the Bilbao Guggenheim Museum.[20] Our concern with Grupo, however, is Cintra, most active in the U.S.

Headquartered in Madrid, Cintra has subsidiaries on three continents and is one of the world's largest private-sector developers of transport infrastructure. It has some 4,000 employees, and its 2006 revenue was about $1 billion. Cintra has combined with Zachry for some huge highway projects in Texas, many of whose details are still being withheld from the public.

Cintra is capitalized at about $5 billion. It has operating interests with Macquarie in the Chicago Skyway, as well as highways in Canada, Chile, and Europe The company has committed $6 billion toward the Trans Texas Corridor system, and has paid $25 million and a share of tolls for the new T 130, designed to bypass Austin. In March 2006, Cintra negotiated a 75-year lease for the Indiana Toll Road, 156 miles across northern Indiana from the Illinois to the Ohio state lines.[21]

Is all this march toward privatization good for the nation or bad? Is it a bit of both? Every contract is different, of course, so they would have to be examined carefully before a safe answer is possible. Proponents have several arguments.

Chief spokesman Robert Poole says there are three lessons to learn. First, at this moment when state departments of transportation are badly in need of funds, capital at the global level is "awash" with funds for good highway projects. Second, because of the potential for large long-term gains, 50- to 100-year leases are feasible, and can be afforded by the private sector. Third, some of the public may look upon investor-owned highways as odd, even frightening, because the concept is unfamiliar, yet it is little different from privately owned electric utilities or telecommunication firms, whose success record is far greater than that of state owned corporations in so many other nations.[22]

A Progress and Freedom report wants the federal government to phase out all federal funding for highways and fix responsibility with the states. The report alleged that nearly 20 percent of a highway project was lost to "cumbersome collection and divvying up funds." Bureaucracies, unions, and minority companies also came in for opprobrium. State gasoline taxes should be replaced by tolls, and the federal tax eliminated entirely.[23]

Back in 1995, the Cato Institute, always worried about a strong federal government, was one of the first and most vocal supporters of privatization. In a long article by Peter Samuel, Cato presented its case as well as outlining something of a history of privatizing. He began with the apparently required comparison of our highway system with Russian communism, both of which failed badly, according to Samuel. The enormous costs of congestion are cited, and he quotes the Transportation Research Board as saying that congestion ratios are getting worse every year.[24]

Mass transit can be helpful, but fails to meet many needs, especially as family demands become more diverse and far flung. Samuel cites Anthony Downs, who found that from the mid–1970s until 1990, the U.S. population increased 16 percent while the number of vehicles increased 46 percent and travel increased 62 percent.[25]

How would Samuel bring about Nirvana? Free marketeers should begin by seeking wide political support. Progressive privatization of *major* highways would be paid for by "time-flexible toll pricing and concession rights, combined with the phase out of gasoline and diesel taxes and the federal and state highway agencies that live off them."[26] Mr. Samuel is asking for quite a bit, but he adds that the politics, the technology, and the economics are all ready for these changes.

Samuel concludes by backing off a bit: "Entrepreneurs do not want to bite off more than they can chew." They do not want to appear as threats to government agencies. He does not much like public/private partnerships. "The Projects that would not fly without subsidy usually should not fly." But in the short run some such arrangements may be necessary, he thinks. In the long run all highways should be private.[27]

In opposition to privatization, *Mother Jones* magazine echoes the Reason Foundation. One issue is largely composed of excerpts from letters complaining about the "pirates" and "highwaymen" who are going to make so much money off the rest of us.[28] If the letters have anything in common it is that somehow the little guy is going to be taken by the foreign money interests, and since the government is partnering with them, we, the little guy, must defend ourselves. "Sweetheart deals" must be thwarted. The Indiana Toll Road has been leased, says *Mother Jones*, for 75 years, earning the state $3.8 billion, but one economist estimated that in state hands the highway could earn as much as $11.38 billion.[29]

A chronic issue is the privatizing of the Pennsylvania Turnpike, which is nearly 70 years old. According to the governor, many billions of dollars were at stake. But an editorial in the Pittsburgh *Post Gazette* thought too much was at stake for the studies being made and urged delay of the whole process.[30]

In conclusion, a quick evaluation of the results of a few road contracts might help. Very little attention has been paid to Latin America in this book, but some Yale economists have reviewed some of its experiences of note. Studying highway privatization in Argentina, Colombia, and Chile, they found that private financing of new highways freed up less public money than expected because public funds were often diverted to programs other than those planned. The writers found also that contracts were poorly drawn, with expectations too high.[31]

The two famous Cintra contracts were beginning to suffer. The Chicago Skyway toll rose from $2.50 for passenger cars to $3.00 in 2008, and Cintra announced a revenue decline of 13 percent in May 2008 compared with May 2007. By contract, the Indiana Toll Road rate was to rise from $4.65 to $8 (72 percent) in the first year. The decline in revenue was 10 percent on that road. Whether the fall off is due to general business conditions or the rise in tolls is difficult to state so far.[32]

The safest posture at this point is to be cautious. Enormous sums of money are at stake, and in the words of Gertrude Stein, will move from pocket to pocket. Some communities will find relief if not profit. Others will find they have made a bad contract. At the moment, business conditions are not encouraging daring investment, and so we must unhappily conclude, "Wait and see."

CHAPTER FOURTEEN

L'Envoi

Just west of Topeka, the Kansas State Highway Department threw open eight miles of Interstate 70, officially completing the first portion of the interstate system. The date, November 14, 1956. Less officially, two years later, the Century Freeway, technically I-105, opened to great fanfare, linking some seven sun-baked California cities. Seventeen miles long, at a cost of more than $2 billion (approximately the same amount President Eisenhower first sought for the whole nation back in 1956), this was to be the ultimate highway, the costliest ever. Thirty-five years of injunctions, lawsuits, congestion, severe inconvenience or worse for thousands of people, the dislocation of the equivalent of a small town — these were the essential social costs of urban highways.[1]

But the job was done. Now drivers could relax, get to work on time, and enjoy a comfortable ride home from work every day. Everywhere.

Not quite. In state after state it soon became apparent that extension or expansion of a freeway failed to reduce traffic in the long run. The number of cars seemed to expand as rapidly as the available new roadway. The fundamental law of traffic congestion declares that any new, more attractive route will quickly founder on its own success.

A long perspective (and anything about highways is tenuous) seems to show three chronological phases of public attitude toward our highway system. First, great enthusiasm, even awe over the technical achievement; second, very common in the 1970s and 1980s, questioning — a maybe we shouldn't have done it, attitude; and third, predominant in the twenty-first century, resignation; we have to build more — and it will cost money.

Let's take a look at these feelings. First, the system is magnificent; there can be no argument. Probably never in history, anywhere, has there been such construction, so fast, so broad, so influential in a peoples' daily lives. Some of it is just plain beautiful. Sometimes it meets our needs.

Among the flag wavers was John Mitchell, editor of *Audubon*, who drove from upper Michigan to Miami and was struck by the wonder of it all. While he found flaws, and gloried when the public defeated the "highwaymen," he ranked this among the greatest achievements anywhere.[2]

Then in the 1970s, the critics came alive. Literature abounded, although much of it is technical and not often read. The pioneer highway critic was Helen Leavitt, who in 1970 published her scathing *Superhighway—Superhoax*. Leavitt blamed the many lobbies (she appears to have invented the term "highwaymen" for builders, developers, and anyone favoring more roads), MacDonald and the AASHO, contractors, auto manufacturers, and road user groups for building beltways and commuter roads and forcing the public to scuttle all forms of transportation except the auto and the airplane. Communication was not solved. Worse, some of the unintended consequences proved dangerous. Riots in Watts and Detroit she blamed on districts being "sealed off" and neighborhoods being destroyed by interstates. And she reminded the public that President Eisenhower had never expected interstates to pierce the heart of a city.

Leavitt did not specify Austin, Texas, but the city provides a classic example of a highway dividing a city. Interstate 35 passes straight through town and suburbs with scarcely a curve. East Austin, settled a century ago largely by blacks, now finds itself rigidly separated with the completion of the highway in the 1970s. Simply travelling from East Austin to downtown Austin, a short distance, to find malls, major hotels, businesses, and theaters is impossible for the pedestrian and a serious nuisance to the driver. East Austin leaders complain of isolation, lack of services, and high crime.

A different type of division often exists in the suburbs. A suburban city manager compares it to living on a roaring river, as hundreds of eighteen-wheelers pass through each day and night creating new and unanticipated dangers. For example, a popular movie rental store a quarter mile from any overpass daily draws crowds of teenagers, who, living on the wrong side of I-35, risk their lives climbing fences and running across the highway to reach the store and return home again. The manager says he lives in fear of a 70 mph Laredo-bound truck wiping out a group of teenagers.[3]

In *Dead End, the Automobile in Mass Transportation*, Ronald Buell Lewis Mumford quoted to the effect that when the American people through their Congress voted for the 1956 highway program, the most charitable assumption would have to be that they had not the faintest idea of what they were doing. Buell was much concerned with the racial consequences of interstates. He wrote that in Nashville, construction of I-40 disrupted 80 percent of all black businesses in the county, leveled hundreds of homes, and "walled off" 100 square blocks. But the road was carefully "fitted" around Vanderbilt, Peabody, and Scarett colleges. He also reported that in Chicago's black districts, crowded housing badly increased while rents soared.[4]

Bruce Seely in 1987 complained that the system had no rational planning and no input from experts, but merely evolved from compromise after compromise among the special interest groups. Justification for certain roads kept changing; rural influence lost out to urban; states lost to the federal government; and the Bureau of Public Roads grew into an enormous agency that ceased providing expertise and merely bowed to the purse of the national government.[5]

Mark H. Rose probably has the most thorough coverage of the politics of the interstate system. Rose agrees that the roads did not turn out as planned, that poor and black districts lost out to the suburbs and much environmental damage occurred. Until the mid–1960s, he wrote, "experts" determined the flow of traffic. After that, environmentalists and "localists" began to flex their muscles and question the engineers' authority. More importantly, an act in 1973 moved the initiation of urban routes out of the hands of state engineers and into the hands of city officials. He concludes that the situation today is "impossible."[6]

Stuck in Traffic, by economist Anthony Downs, is one of the more sophisticated studies examining the highways. He says studies agree for once with popular conceptions; traffic is getting worse every year. The growth in the number of automobiles has often been about three times faster than population increases. The American demands two incomes and a better way of life. We prefer living in the suburbs; we need two or more cars just to get to work. The result is that most people commute an hour or more each day, each way. We sit in our cars eight weeks a year, not counting recreational driving.[7]

This spate of criticism pretty well stopped in the 1990s to be replaced by a national resignation that we must build more miles. They will cost much more, with new sources of funds required. And the roads of the Eisenhower era have worn out and must be repaired at great inconvenience and expense, much greater than the original.

Is the plan of 1956 yet complete? A fair question, but hard to answer. Congressmen of 1956 generally looked upon the project as a matter of a decade or so. Several communities in the 1980s and '90s claimed title to being the end of the project. But technically speaking it is hard to overlook Boston's Big Dig, a major portion of which was directed to two intersecting interstates. A look at this monster might be instructional, and even portend the future.

Boston is one of the many cities and towns claiming to posses the last mile built as a part of President Eisenhower's original interstate program. The technicalities in this bit of trivia make moot the answer, but no one can dispute Boston's assertion that the Big Dig is the costliest, the most complex, and the most troublesome, if not the last segment of that system. Big Dig is the popular name, now frequently borrowed, for the enormous project officially called the Central Artery/Tunnel Project (CA/T). It falls under the interstate category by virtue of the unfortunate confluence of I-90 and I-93 in the heart of the city.

For years, history and geography critically congested Boston traffic, enough so that in 1948 a master plan was devised to correct all the problems at the same time. Work was begun by tying the downtown with the waterfront. In 1959, an elevated six-lane route through downtown was completed, as were two tunnels connecting it with Logan Airport. But much went wrong. Thousands of homes and businesses had to be destroyed to make possible the construction, greatly disturbing many residents. Highways built for 75,000 cars a day soon groaned with 200,000. The major expressway had too many off/on ramps and tight turns for smooth driving. The accident rate was quadruple the national average. Neighborhoods were separated from one another or destroyed. In the 1950s, some improvement was made by placing a portion of the expressway underground. Meanwhile, I-93, passing north/south through the heart of the city, had become a commuter's nightmare. Their trips to work were badly exacerbated by traffic from the west having to use portions of the Central Artery to reach Logan Airport.

In the 1960s, placing the entire project underground became a popular proposed solution. In 1974, the whole master plan was scuttled, and the state highway department came up with a far bolder scheme, designed, again, to solve all the problems at once.

Official planning for the Big Dig began in 1982. The major change would be to replace the Central Artery with an underground expressway directly under the old road, culminating in a pair of multi-lane bridges across the Charles River. Secondly, I-90, the Massachusetts Turnpike, which ended south of downtown, would be extended to the airport, in part by a new tunnel under Boston Harbor. Mass transit plans were included, but several of them have since been dropped.

Funding for the project required years of lobbying; in 1987, President Ronald Reagan vetoed an entire highway bill that included the Big Dig, but the Congress passed it over his veto, and by 1991 contractors were ready to go.

The Big Dig is not one vast tunnel as the outsider might suspect, but is a combination of several projects; conversion of the Central Artery from an elevated to a tunneled expressway; a new, third harbor tunnel to handle East Boston and airport traffic; improvements to and extending I-90; and work on several other routes in the city. Financial, engineering, and environmental problems delayed work and ran up the costs right from the start. Archeologists wanted to study the homes and even the ships uncovered by the digging. At the same time contractors faced the overwhelming task of keeping traffic moving on the old road directly above. In 1985 the overall estimated cost was $2.5 billion; by 2006 about $18 billion had been spent and costs were still mounting on the most expensive highway project in America's history.[8]

The Ted Williams Tunnel, from South Boston under the harbor to East Boston and Logan Airport, was more or less open in 1995, and became a major element in reducing congestion downtown. In 2002, twin bridges (ten lanes) over the Charles River to Charlestown were completed along with sweeping ramps leading to state route 1. Then the old Central Artery above ground was turned into a tunnel accommodating I-93 through the length of the city. Most of this was available to motorists by 2005. About 95 percent of the Big Dig was now complete.[9]

But its troubles were not. As early as 2001 state officials had become aware of thousands of leaks scattered throughout the main tunnel. Another $10 million was expended (possibly improperly) to repair the leaks. Still they continued. Faked records covering the quality of the concrete were discovered by state police in August 2005. A few months later the state attorney general revealed his intention to sue Bechtel/Parsons Brinckerhoff, the major contactors, over scores of complaints of shoddy material and workmanship. Then, on the evening of July 10, 2006, several sections of the ceiling fell onto I-90. The three-ton tiles landed on a passing car, crushing it and killing the passenger, Milena del Valle. Her husband, the driver, was not badly injured.

Chaos followed. Charges and countercharges filled the press. The immediate cause of the collapse was determined to be the failure of bolts to support the concrete slabs in the ceiling. Twenty of them popped out on the day of the accident. The issue became a test case for safety standards, the contractors alleging that two bolts per slab, rather than the four some inspectors required, met safety requirements. Subsequent inspections found 200 or more questionable fastenings.[10] New accusations arose when the press learned that Bechtel had been paid to perform the remedial work. Repairs, political fallout, and charges continue to burgeon. At the beginning of 2007, most of the Big Dig was operational, but much of it was also in litigation, with the state's attorney general contemplating criminal charges.

Among the many unexpected consequences is the condition of highways elsewhere in Massachusetts. A Springfield paper alleged that the western part of the state normally received $40 to $50 million each year for its highway infrastructure. The Big Dig siphoned off so much funding that the area now has only $2.5 million and a backlog of $300 million in unfunded projects. The same paper declared that the state debt was the worst in the nation and more than three times the national average.[11]

Probably most Bostonians are fond of the Big Dig, especially those who were driving some years ago. Is it worth $18 billion? Calculating the opportunity costs in this instance might be impossible, but the Big Dig has been dug, and once again we can state that the Eisenhower roads have been finished.

One could hope that no other city will be subjected to the turmoil of Boston, but there are no guarantees. A fatal flaw became part of the network back in 1956 when the first interstate laws were drafted. Eisenhower had asked for a system that would not pass through cities, but would necessarily bypass them in the interest of national defense. However urban politicians demanded urban highways for their districts or there would have been no interstate system. Seeking cheaper land, more space, or just an escape from the city, homeowners in every city and state followed the roads away from downtown, even if the job remained behind.

Totally different results are apparent when a new interstate bypasses a small town that had been on an older highway. This can be deadly, depending on the distance involved. If feasible, homes and businesses will move inexorably into the gap over a period of time; but if the distance is great, the town often dries up and is no longer viable.

Cannot public transportation relieve these headaches? Some, of course. Advantages and demurrers are obvious; location, costs, management, and so on. But there are some powerful factors against mass transit that are not so apparent. Two Arizona transportation specialists completed a revealing — and discouraging — study of women commuters in Phoenix and Tucson who regularly drove to work alone.

Their finding: 85 percent of the women could not use mass transportation or even carpool. They had no alternative. Employer-sponsored incentives, free transit passes, fewer parking spaces, higher tolls — none of these made a difference in the drivers' attitudes. With considerable logic they insisted they needed a personal car — to take children to school or day care, transport babysitters, pick up laundry, shop, see doctors and dentists. They were in agreement that these were daily *necessities*.[12] We must also consider that we love our cars too much. They are our prized possessions. In our car we are free, safe, in control. A German social scientist put it succinctly; the car is the womb and we are too frightened to leave it.[13] And we really prefer not to share it.

Millions of Americans now live in the suburbs and work in the city, averaging a commute, as Downs says, of more than one hour a day, each way. Such a driver, and many commute much more than that, spends the equivalent of more than eight weeks each year, sitting in his car, just going to and from work.[14] That's eight weeks lost every year, not counting driving to the store, school, church, and recreation. In addition, people are increasingly working in the suburbs, but not necessarily the one in which they live. It is also apparent that many workers live in the inner city and work in the suburbs. These are often construction workers, day workers, laborers, yard men — helpers with no permanent job, who really cannot afford a car, but for lack of public transportation must carpool, if possible. All of these add to the traffic problem.

So we have reached an impasse; transportation experts, economists and a small portion of the public believe that more paving can bring nothing but diminishing returns. We cannot build our way out of the congestion problem — the costs would be staggering.

But the huge majority of American motorists believe that our congestion can be solved by pouring just one more road, preferably more or less paralleling the one we now use every day.

What about mass transit? The Intermodal Surface Transportation Act of 1991 (ISTEA) was designed to reduce federal controls, letting the states use federal funds to make their own decisions about mass transit. Backers of the law hoped that something like half the money would be set aside for mass transit. Nothing of the sort occurred. Virtually all the money went to the highway portion of the equation.

Traffic experts have other hopes. They'd like to simply reduce traffic, especially at peak hours. Regulatory means — police power limiting the number of hours or days that certain percentages of cars are allowed on the street — probably will not work. (It has been tried in Mexico City and a little earlier in Rome by Julius Caesar, without notable success.)[15] But a market-based approach offers some hope. In essence, a community makes drivers pay a fee to use certain roads at certain peak hours. Hong Kong, Singapore, and Oslo have all tried this with results still uncertain.

Congestion pricing has its merits and can appeal positively to local governments. It is unfair to those less able to pay. It can also be inefficient, especially if the fee is collected at something resembling a toll booth. A big improvement is the transponder placed on windshields or the back of the inside mirror, transmitting an electronic message to receivers at the entrance and exit points of the restricted zone. The commuter is billed and pays by mail.[16]

Unlike the public, most traffic specialists seem to believe the problem is nearly out of hand and the only solution is a combination of heavy taxes and some form of congestion pricing.

Before listening to our experts, real and imagined, let us examine how our road system is structured today. It totals about 160,000 miles and is composed of five subsystems:

1. The Interstate System also known as the Eisenhower Interstate System of Highways.
2. Other principal arteries. "A network of highways rural or urban, which are important to the U.S. strategic defense policy and which provide defense access, continuity and emergency capabilities for defense purposes."
3. Strategic Highway Network (Strahnet). This is a network designed to carry out America's strategic defense policy.
4. Major Strategic Highway Network Connectors. Highways which provide access between major military installations and highways which are part of the Strategic Highway Network.
5. Intermodal Connectors. These highways provide access between major intermodal facilities and the other four systems composing the NHS.[17] That is the system. Now who are the experts who will "suggest" us out of our problem? Gary Toth, director of transportation initiatives of

the Project for Public Spaces, says in the future we must go back to our basics. During his years with the New Jersey DOT he preached that the solution to congestion was to build more and bigger roads. Now PPS is working with a group of regional DOTs to perform functions that individual states can not afford. In the 1940s, '50s, and '60s, presidents and Congress ignored opportunities to subsidize mass transportation as well as regional planning.

According to Toth, by the 1990s the "transportation profession" had hit the wall. That is, its practitioners knew something was wrong but clung to the old formula of maintaining the free flow of traffic at the thirtieth busiest hour of the entire year. Communities began resisting the notion of the national interest predominating. Meanwhile construction costs have gone up at precisely the same time that the aging system is in need of more attention and repair. Little attention was paid to planning for bikes, sidewalks and mass transportation. Revenues are flat because legislators are afraid to use the word tax.

What do we do? We plan. At least that is what Toth stresses. Any major road investment should be "pursued only in communities and regions with effective land use plans in place."[18] And this should be performed at the community level. Create places people will want to visit. We must put schools, grocery stores, and affordable housing in "nice" neighborhoods. He seems to suggest that we should return to the good old days when the streets belonged to the children, not the cars.

While it is always nice to yearn for the good old days, they are not coming back Of course, planning is necessary, but there is nothing in this article to help us cope with congestion. Rodney Slater was appointed federal highway administrator in 1993. A few years later he announced the National Highway System's "Commitment to America's Future." His theme: the NHS is the "centerpiece" of the safe, modern, and efficient transportation system. It is also the backbone of our transportation system. The 256,000 km. of NHS include only 4 percent of the nation's roads, but they carry more than 40 percent of all highway traffic and 75 percent of all heavy truck traffic. The NHS does many important things, he says, so "America can move forward." It is not quibbling to note that he has no solid suggestion about how to manage traffic in the future.[19]

Every related agency and probably most of the concerned public has an opinion or even a map showing the location of dozens of future highways. It is probably fun to perform this ritual and probably a waste of time.

At this moment it makes more sense to ask where will the dollars come from.

For many decades both the states and the federal government have relied on fuel taxes as the main source of funding for the construction and maintenance of highways. These revenues were reasonably popular because they correlated, roughly, with highway usage, and the amounts raised were stable and predictable. In addition, they were generally not entangled with the rest of the agency's budget trading. But that honeymoon has ended. Fuel taxes have been raised too often of late and the increasing crude oil prices have made tax increases far less acceptable. So we must look elsewhere.

To look more closely at some of these matters, former Federal Highway Administrator Mary Peters in 2004 convened a roundtable on future highway financing. The members first traced the familiar stories of fuel taxes and the relationship of state and federal governments in highway financing.

Completion of Interstate 85 near Greensboro, North Carolina (North Carolina Department of Transportation).

Not too surprisingly, the states have been happy to let the federal government play a greater role. One method would have the federal government collect the highway taxes and then dole them to the states. This might save costs but was not very popular with the roundtable.[20]

Considering the matter to be of some significance, the roundtable spent much time on the sources of highway funds. The Federal Highway Trust Fund comes almost entirely from highway use taxes. Ninety percent of those are fuel taxes. State highway taxes also rely heavily on use taxes, but local governments also use sales taxes, property taxes, and the general fund to supplement the fuel tax. Most of the roundtable attendees opposed these sources because they have no relevance to individual driving habits. The roundtable summed up the question like this:

1. Using general funds for highways draws those funds away from other programs that do not have potential direct revenue streams.

2. Because of long term development associated with road building and the shifting priorities associated with general tax dollars, it is difficult to plan and contract for higher cost, long-term transportation projects.

3. Users generally are more receptive to paying charges that are tied to specific improvements.

4. General taxes do not reflect external costs associated with highway use, such as vehicle emissions that affect air quality, other environmental costs, and some safety costs.

5. Using general funds to supplement or replace user charges can lead to inefficient use of the highway system because general funds are not tied at all to highway system use.[21]

The roundtable found an increasing reliance on the sales tax for highway use. It is politically more acceptable than most taxes, but the public wants the money dedicated to a particular project, not just a general fund. Another roundtable suggestion would force developers to pay at least a part of the cost of new roads serving a development. It is assumed that these fees would ultimately be passed on to the new homeowner.[22] But perhaps not too surprisingly, the majority of attendees favored tolls or some other form of direct user charge that permits charges to relate more closely to the costs of operation. Objections were raised to tolls that continue after the bonds have been repaid and the surplus toll is used for some other, possibly new, function.

Tolls and mileage based taxes have their objections, too, such as the following:

- Administrative and collection costs are higher than fuel taxes.
- Variable charges by lane disturb many who refer to tolled lanes as Lexus lanes.
- The public often believes that the lanes have already been paid for through taxes and the agency should not collect a second charge.
- The public will use a good, free alternative if possible.[23]

Technology has made possible some of these recommendations, and doubtless more will occur. But they cannot solve the basic problems, and they pose the danger of exacerbating the "we versus you" syndrome already in place.

What is the real future of the interstates and other highway systems in the U.S.? A.A. Roads, which publishes something called "Future Interstates," has an opinion. In elaborate, official-looking form the company publishes a list of all new roads and extensions, showing the states they pass through as well as the two terminals. They have a couple of dozen new interstates in mind. There is, however, a large, however. In their words, "The following routes are approved or involve corridors where the number has been agreed upon by planners, government, or other organizations." The secret lies in the language. These roads are proposed, according to, slated for, tossed around.[24] One can be skeptical.

More serious is "What Comes After the Interstate?," an article by Robert Dunphy of the Urban Land Institute. Much more realistic than other experts, he agrees with those who say we need a new vision. But one gets the impression that Dunphy is serious. Fifty years ago we had a major highway plan resulting in the Eisenhower roadways. Now we have no serious plan, meaning a major national commitment, something most of the public would want. It would be difficult today to find any major highway program with national support. We just want the problem settled. A common vision, says Dunphy, is not to be seen.

Nor, looking toward the future, does he see any sign of a massive investment program, in spite of an unanticipated increase in America's population.

What is the likelihood, he asks, of a new federal transportation program emerging that will serve the needs of the twenty-first century? His one-word answer—bleak. We have programs, but they are late or thin or poorly planned. The latest one was loaded with pork—6,000 congressional earmarks. Not the way to build a highway. Few will vote to raise gas taxes, and some estimates are that the Highway Trust Fund will be gone by 2010.

Offshore money seems abundant, but where does it want to go? The cheap dollar encouraged foreign investors to shop around for American bargains. Further, there is yet no evidence that the huge sums paid for the Chicago Skyway and the Indiana Toll Road have been dedicated to new highways as promised. In Chicago, for example, the huge fund was used to reduce taxes.

In Congress, current ideas floating with some enthusiasm are greater encouragement of foreign investment (meaning the private sector), spurring foreign trade and reducing urban congestion, all of which have been treated in this book. As examples, Dunphy cites Texas Governor Rick Perry's ambitious highway/trade program, and an even more expensive scheme proposed by Governor Arnold Schwarzenegger.

Dunphy concludes by stressing the need for the federal government to regain its sense of purpose. Otherwise some states and localities will succeed and others will fall into economic backwaters.[25]

Mother Jones is unhappy also, if for different reasons. Not editorializing, the magazine simply lists a state by state accounting of privatization schemes set for the future. Many of these seem not to have been reported in the press nor mentioned previously in this book. Here is a list by state:

• Florida. The first for the state, valued at $150 million, proposed by Australian, Canadian, New Zealand, and Spanish firms. A 3.1-mile toll road in North Tampa Bay connecting two interstates.

• Oregon. A consortium of several builders, foreign and American, will study the needs and the possibilities of three new highways — location vague.

• Colorado. A long suggested 210-mile privately funded toll road from Ft. Collins to Pueblo. Now called the Prairie Falcon Expressway, its major opposition is from farmers fearing the use of eminent domain.

• Illinois. A Swiss group is studying the economic feasibility of a 74-mile tollway on a 75-year lease. Opposed by the governor.

• Indiana. Governor Mitch Daniels announced plans for the Illiana Expressway, a toll road connecting the two states. He also wants to extend the infamous I-69 to Mexico. Indiana has 75 miles that bypass through five counties of southern Indiana.

• Missouri. The largest proposal believed to be under consideration now is an eight-lane, $910 million Mississippi River bridge connecting Missouri and Illinois just north of St. Louis. Illinois has a bridge plan as well, but the two states have no agreement on a single step.

• Nevada. Boulder City is considering a $4.4 million bypass, but privatization deals are not currently permitted under Nevada laws.
• New Jersey. Several major roads are considered targets for privatizing, but no steps have yet been taken.
• New York. Australia's MIG has an offer to build a Tappan Zee bridge, but New York laws do not permit public/private partnerships.
• Texas. A consortium has proposed building a highway from Shreveport through Texarkana and Houston into Mexico. Studies are under way for extensions of I-35 near both Dallas and San Antonio.
• Virginia. An agreement has been made between the state and an American and Australian contractors for high-speed lanes on I-95. The estimate is $913 million.
• Utah. The legislature is considering a privately funded road from Salt Lake City airport into Utah County.
• Georgia. One project would expand the Northwest Corridor to four lanes, at $2.1 billion. Several other projects are being considered.[26]

By way of comparison, we can read some of the local press from several states as the 50th birthday of Eisenhower's dream rolled around. Most of this information appeared in 2006. It is worth study because the comments are more realistic as they talk about needs rather than the privatization dreams recounted by *Mother Jones*.

• Alabama. Between 1990 and 2004 traffic increased 62 percent in Alabama and lane miles grew 3 percent. The state could not expect the federal government to make up that difference.[27]
• Arkansas. Over the next 10 years the state expects $4 billion in highway revenue. The need will exceed $19 billion.[28]
• California. Several highways need expansion because they shrink from 10 to 6 or 5 to 3 lanes. No money is available.[29]
• Indiana. One of the busiest states for highway building, Indiana faces studies and lawsuits concerning "corridors." The major issue is north/south traffic. They talk a lot about Canada to Mexico.[30]
• Louisiana. Truckers "Highway Report Card" evaluates this state's roads as the *worst*. Half are "poor" or "mediocre," and half the bridges are inadequate. The accident rate is 40 percent above the national average.[31]
• Minnesota. One-fourth of the state's bridges need repair, says U.S.DOT.[32]
• New Jersey. State and federal authorities quarrel over the use of

tolls. The feds insist tolls must be used for transportation and cannot be used to reduce New Jersey taxes.[33]

• North Carolina. The state has much "faulty construction," especially on I-40. At least 10 miles must be replaced. Who will pay for repairs?[34]

• Oklahoma. The state alleges its bridges are nation's worst, and even the better ones are too narrow for anticipated NAFTA trade.[35]

• Pennsylvania. The major issue for years has been the use of tolls on the turnpike. The state lacks authority to use them on that road, but whole system is behind in building.[36]

• Texas. A bitter struggle over the governor's corridor proposals is closely tied to international trade and eminent domain.[37]

Likely these samples could be matched by stories from almost every state. The twenty-first century has brought no revolutionary solution to our staggering problem. And is there anything new coming from Washington? Not much has changed there, either, other than some ideas about pricing. In September 2006, USDOT made its awaited announcement about corridors. In a year of jockeying, 38 applicants have been reduced to six. Of course, there is a new bureaucratic name — "Corridors of the Future Program (CFP). The proposals were to be innovative, improve freight delivery and reduce congestion.

The winners were:

• I-95 from Florida to Canada, $21.8 million.
• I-70 in Illinois, Indiana, Missouri and Ohio, $5 million.
• I-15 in Arizona, California, Nevada, and Utah, $15 million.
• I-5 in California, Oregon and Washington, $15 million.
• I-10 from California to Florida, $8.6 million.
• I-69 from Texas to Michigan, $800,000.

Obviously those sums will build few miles of highway. Sometime in 2008 the federal government and the states will "finalize" agreements detailing commitments. They will also formalize the role of the private sector in these vast undertakings.[38] Are we looking forward to a road from Laredo to Winnipeg built by a consortium of the U.S., several states, an Australian bank and a Spanish contractor? What are the terms? And who sets the tolls? This is meaty stuff that should be watched by us all, drivers or not.

There it is. Do we need more asphalt? More mass transportation?

Less travel? Suggestions of every quality abound. In the meantime, if you are a commuter, here is the author's recommendation: get the best hybrid you can afford, an attractive traveling companion, top notch air conditioning, and a radio. Then learn to relax. From now on you will spend your vacation driving to work.

Epilogue

World events occurring while this manuscript was being finished made it seem necessary to include a brief epilogue. Coinciding with the writing of the last few chapters has been the unprecedented rise in the price of crude oil followed by a somewhat rapid decline. What, if any, would be the impact of crude prices on road construction? A rereading of the pertinent chapters of the book convinced me that the development did not nullify any of my study, but neither could I ignore changes of such magnitude. Pump prices rose from around $1.50 per gallon to as much as $5 in some communities. Was there to be no limit? What was the future of travel in an America so accustomed low-cost petroleum? Some folks demanded more drilling, offshore or in Alaska. Others sought alternative sources of fuel or vast conservation programs. There was much furor and not much result. That story is yet unfolding and cannot be considered here, but a few factors before our eyes today seem significant enough to justify inclusion at this point. What will be the price of gasoline five years from today? Of course we do not know, but this year's extravagance brought about unexpectedly rapid and far-reaching results. They could recur.

In September 2008, Mary Peters, secretary of transportation, announced that by the end of that month the federal highway trust fund would be exhausted, with some $200 million in projects yet unfunded. Its balance in 2007 had exceeded $8 billion. The reason for the exhaustion? Simple. Public response to high prices was to drive less — much less. Whether people were walking, carpooling, bussing, biking, or staying home, the net reduction in miles driven was over 50 billion for one six-month period. The probable loss in federal tax would be in the hundreds of millions of dollars. Secretary Peters also blamed congressional earmarking for savaging the highway budget. In this fashion, some $24 additional billion leaked away in 2008. That is, $24 billion approved for highways went instead to some congressmen's pet projects.

In September the Congress passed a measure moving $8 billion from the general fund to the highway trust fund. Contrary to his declaration of a few months before, President George W. Bush signed the bill. The sum, substantial as it might seem, is probably more related to elections and jobs than to construction, but it will keep some projects viable. Which states will enjoy this largesse will probably depend on horse trading.

By coincidence, during that same week, the Associated Press announced the reopening of the famous collapsed bridge on I-35W in Minneapolis. The "state of the art" structure (it has new sensors to report weaknesses) was completed in just over a year after the bridge failure that killed thirteen people. The replacement cost — $200 million, for just one bridge. The nation has 600,000 bridges. One fourth are considered "structurally deficient," bureaucratic jargon for a bridge that needs work but is not necessarily immediately dangerous. The problem varies from state to state. According to the Associated Press, the worst conditions were found in South Dakota, Pennsylvania, and Oklahoma. In each of these, about one-fourth of the bridges needed repair. Now. Louisiana and Nevada did not bother to respond to the study. Arizona and Delaware seemed to have the best record for bridge maintenance.

Whatever the rankings, the problem is national and vast, equaling some $10 billion a year for the next twenty years, just for bridges. The record of the past few years would foretell expenditures far below that, short of another terrible catastrophe. The national roadways have not received the close examination given the bridges, but we must assume their condition is not too different from the bridges. Where will we go? It would appear that the nation is in need of another Manhattan Project or Marshall Plan devoted to transportation.

Glossary

AASHTO	American Association of State Highway and Transportation Officials
ATA	American Trucking Associations
CINTRA	Concesiones de Infrastructura de Transporte
DOT	Department of Transportation
FHA	Federal Highway Administration
GAO	Government Accountability Office
HOT	High Occupancy Toll Lane
HOV	High Occupancy Vehicle
ISTEA	Intermodal Surface Transportation Efficiency Act
NAFTA	North American Free Trade Agreement
NHS	National Highway System Designation Act
OPR	Office of Public Roads
PPP	Public/Private Partnerships
SAFETY-LU	Safe, Accountable, Flexible, Efficient, Transportation, Equity Act
SIB	State Infrastructure Bank
TEA-21	Transportation Equity Act
TIFIA	Transportation Infrastructure Finance Act
TTC	Trans Texas Corridor
TTI	Texas Transportation Institute

Notes

Chapter One

1. William Kaszynski, *The American Highway* (Jefferson, NC: McFarland, 2000), 9–15.
2. Thomas L. Karnes, *William Gilpin, Western Nationalist* (Austin: University of Texas, 1970), 118.
3. For road conditions in early America see Stewart Holbrook, *The Old Post Road* (New York: McGraw-Hill, 1962), 1; Richard B. Morris, ed., *Encyclopedia of American History* (New York: Harper and Row, 1976); Seymour Dunbar, *A History of Travel in America*, (New York: Tudor, 1937); U.S. Department of Transportation, *America's Highways, 1776–1976* (Washington, D.C.: Federal Highway Administration, 1976.)
4. *Encyclopaedia Britannica II* (Chicago: Encyclopaedia Britannica, 1995), 198–200; *The New York Times*, Nov. 16, 1906, 11; Mark H. Rose, *Interstate: Express Highway Politics* (Lawrence: University of Kansas, 1979), 7–8.
5. Morris, *Encyclopedia*, 617–7; Kaszynski, *American Highway*, 22–24. The auto industry is believed to have settled in Detroit because of the long-established carriage industry located there. T. Harry Williams, Richard N. Current, and Frank Freidel, *The Essentials of American History* (New York: Knopf, 1972), 238, 271; U.S. Department of Transportation, *America's Highways*, 42–52.
6. Rose, *Interstate,* 1–9.
7. Williams, *Essentials*, 238, 271.
8. U.S. Department of Transportation, *America's Highways*, 41–52 and U.S. Department of Transportation, *Bulletin*, sum-mer, 1996; *Dixie Manufacturer*, 1903–6; *General Motors, the First 75 Years of Transportation Products* (Princeton: Automobile Quarterly Publications, 1983).
9. John Bankhead, Jr. to his father, Jan 28, 1908, and Feb 15, 1908, Bankhead papers, Alabama Archives.
10. Fourth assistant postmaster general to Bankhead, March 24, 1908; Bankhead to George B. Cortelyou, secretary of the Treasury, March 23, 1908; Bankhead Papers, Alabama Archives.
11. Kaszynski, *American Highway*, 23–35, 52, and 53 discusses early road-building problems as well as the fate of the Shackelford and Bankhead bills.
12. Bankhead's obituary is in the Walker County (Ala.) *Mountain Eagle*, Feb. 12, 1922, and *The New York Times*, March 2, 1920, 11.

Chapter Two

1. Glidden's obituary: *The New York Times,* September 12, 1927, 23; Western Motor Car Club of America, *History of the AAA Glidden Tours*, n.d.
2. Several Glidden tours are described in *The New York Times*, July 30, 1903, 1; Feb 7, 1906, 7; and April 27, 1906, 52; and in *Scientific American*, July 20, 1907, 47 and Aug. 3, 1907, 77–78.
3. David Duncan, "Horatio's Drive," *Texas Journey*, September/October 2003, 36–38.
4. *The New York Times*, Aug. 16, 1903, 1 and Aug. 22, 1903, 1; Carey S. Bliss, *Autos Across America* (Austin: Jenkins, 1922).

5. Alice H. Ramsey, *Veil, Duster and Tire Iron* (Covina, Calif.: Castle, 1961).

6. Bliss, 14–16

7. Effie P. Gladding, *Across the Continent by the Lincoln Highway* (New York: Brentanos, 1915).

8. Emily Post, *By Motor to the Golden Gate* (New York: Appleton, 1915).

9. Maud Younger, "Alone Across the Continent," *Sunset,* May/June, 1924, 25, 43; *The New York Times,* Dec. 20, 1920, 3. Her obituary: *The New York Times,* June 28, 1936, 11 and 9.

10. Sinclair Lewis, *Free Air* (New York: Harcourt, 1919); Harroun's obituary: *The New York Times,* Jan. 20, 1968, 29.

11. *The New York Times,* May 24, 1916, 22, discusses Hammond's driving.

12. Nelson Pringle, "U.S. Army Truck Test, 1912," *Translog,* March 1970, pp. 17–20.

13. Haldeen Braddy, *Pershing's Mission in Mexico* (El Paso: Texas Western Press, 1966); *Motor Trend,* December 1967; *The New York Times,* Feb. 20, 1966, Travel section.

14. Norman Cary, Jr., "The Use of the Motor Vehicle in the U.S. Army, 1899–1939," Ph.D. dissertation, University of Georgia, 1980; *General Motors, the First 75 Years of Transportation Products* (Princeton: Automobile Quarterly Publications, 1983).

Chapter Three

1. Mark Foster, *Castles in the Sand* (Gainesville: University of Florida Press, 2000), is the best study so far of Fisher.

2. Accounts of the Lincoln Highway and the association abound. Among the best is Lincoln Highway Association, *The Lincoln Highway* (New York: Dodd, Mead, 1935). Ford's demurrer is on page 14 of Drake Hokanson, *The Lincoln Highway* (Iowa City: University of Iowa Press, 1988). Unless otherwise indicated, I follow these narratives in discussing the LHA and its work.

3. The appendix of the LHA study contains biographical information about the board and officers.

4. I have found no biography of Ostermann, but obtained much information about him from the LHA studies in note 2, above, and Pete Davies, *American Road*

(New York: Henry Holt, 2002); Michael Scott, *Packard* (Blue Ridge Summit, Pa: Tab Books, 1985); and J.C. Long, *The Man Behind the Hudson Motor Company* (Detroit: Wayne State University Press, 2004). LHA Museum Publications, "Hoosier Tour, 1913," (Galion, Ohio, n.d.).

5. LHA Museum Publications, "Choosing a Route"; LHA, *The Lincoln Highway,* passim.

6. Seedling miles and Idea Sections are discussed in "The Lincoln Highway" by Richard F. Weingroff, Feb 16, 2007, online at http://www.fhwa.dot.gov/infrastructure/lincoln.cfm.; and Alice Howell, "The Lincoln Highway," in *Buffalo Tales* (Kearney, Neb: Buffalo County Historical Society, 1983), 1–5.

7. Hokanson, *Lincoln Highway,* 109–112.

8. For Wilson's and Harding's roles, see, 158–161.

9. The bitter and complicated story of the route laid out through Nevada is in LHA, *The Lincoln Highway,* 164–196; Robert Laxalt, *Nevada: A Bicentennial History* (New York: Norton, 1977); and *Scientific American,* December 1922, 127.

10. Davies, *American Road,* 217.

11. Ibid, 221–231.

12. Hokanson, *Lincoln Highway,* 112–113.

Chapter Four

1. A necessary source for the highway, biographical sketches of the members, the background of the convoy, and even pertinent photos is the association's study. *The Lincoln Highway*; Hokanson's *The Lincoln Highway* offers good personal acquaintanceship with the road accompanied by superb photographs. Pete Davies, *American Road* (New York: Henry Holt, 2002), is a full-length, popular account of the 1919 convoy.

2. Alfred Lief, *The Firestone Story* (New York: McGraw-Hill, 1951) 97–101.

3. Woodrow Wilson to Henry B. Joy, June 19, 1919, Joy papers, Bentley Library, Ann Arbor, Mich.

4. One could scarcely find more complete and detailed records than those that exist for the 1919 military convoy across America. I found an abundance of both of-

ficial and personal accounts which I used for my narrative. The first three are the most complete. "Report on First Transcontinental Motor Convoy, Daily Log" (daily telegrams) by 1st Lt. E.R. Jackson, July–Sept. 1919; 1st Lt. E.R. Jackson, observer, to Col. L.B. Moody, Ordnance Department, Oct. 31, 1919; Major Charles W. McClure, Quartermaster Corps., "Long Distance Motor Convoy Operation," *The Quartermaster Review* 6 No. 1, July/August 1920, 26–31. McClure was the commanding officer of the convoy. Lincoln Highway Association, "First Transcontinental Motor Convoy," an album created in 1960 as a gift to President Eisenhower, which is in the Bentley Library, Ann Arbor, Mich.; Lt. Col. William S. Graf, "The Great Overland March," *Soldiers*, October 1975, 47–50; Alfred Lief, *The Firestone Story*, 108–110, sketches the patent issue; Diary of O.E. Forsling, sheriff, Kimball County, Nebraska, Aug. 5–7, 1919; Warrum Noble, Charles W. Moss and W. Brown Ewing, *Utah since Statehood* (Salt Lake City: S.J. Clark Publishing, 1919); Russell R. Elliott, *History of Nevada* (Lincoln: University of Nebraska, 1973).

5. Jackson, telegrams, letters, "Daily Log," July 18, 1919.

6. In addition to the official reports cited above I have used the following for the almost daily record of the convoy from Washington to San Francisco (in geographical order):

PENNSYLVANIA: *Bedford Gazette*, July 4 and 18, 1919; *Chambersburg Public Opinion*, July 7 and 9, 1919; *Greensburg Daily Tribune*, July 9 and 11, 1919; *Pittsburgh Sun*, July 11, 1919; *Pittsburgh Post*, July 11 and 12, 1919; *Sewickley Herald*, July 19, 1919.

OHIO: *The Daily Leader* (East Palestine), July 9, 10, 12, and 14, 1919; *Alliance Review*, July 12 and 14, 1919; *Delphos Herald*, July 14, 15, and 17, 1919; *The Firestone Non-Skid* (Akron), July 18, 1919; *Wooster Daily Republican*, July 11, 12 and 15, 1919; *Wooster Daily News*, July 14, 15 and 16, 1919.

INDIANA: *Ft. Wayne News and Sentinel*, July 17, 1919; *Ft. Wayne Journal Gazette*, July 18, 1919; *South Bend Tribune*, July 17, 1919; *La Porte Daily Argus*, July 19, 1919; *Valparaiso Daily Messenger*, July 8, 17, 19, 1919.

ILLINOIS: *Aurora Beacon News*, July 20, 1919; *Joliet Evening Herald News*, July 21,

1919; *De Kalb Daily Chronicle*, July 14 and 21, 1919; *Dixon Evening Telegraph*, July 22, 1919.

IOWA: *Clinton Herald*, June 28 and July 8, 12, 18, 21, 22, and 23, 1919; *Denison Review*, July 23 and 39, 1919; *Daily Non-Pareil* (Council Bluffs), July 25, 1919.

NEBRASKA: *Omaha World Herald*, July 25, 28, 29, and 30, 1919; *Fremont Evening Tribune*, July 30, 1919; *Columbus Telegram*, Aug. 1, 1919; *Grand Island Daily Independent*, July 31, 1919; *Lexington Clipper Citizen*, Aug. 7, 1919; *Gothenberg Times*, Aug. 6, 1919; *North Platte Evening Telegram*, Aug. 1, 1919; *Keith County News* (Ogallala), Aug 7, 1919; *Chappell Register*, Aug. 7, 1919; *Sidney Telegraph*, Aug 8, 1919; *Western Nebraska Observer* (Kimball), Aug. 7 and 14, 1919.

WYOMING: *Wyoming State Tribune*, (Cheyenne), Aug. 7, 1919; *Laramie Boomerang*, Aug. 9, 1919; *Rawlins Republican*, Aug. 14, 1919; *Green River Star*, Aug. 15, 1919.

UTAH: *Ogden Standard*, Aug 12, 15, 16, 17, 18, 19 and 20, 1919; *Salt Lake Tribune*, Aug. 15, 17, 20 and 22, 1919; *Desert Evening News*, Aug. 12–16, 19 and 20, 1919.

NEVADA: *Reno Evening Gazette*, Aug. 25, 1919.

CALIFORNIA: *Stockton Daily Evening Record*, Sept. 3–5, 1919; *Oakland Enquirer*, Sept. 5, 1919; *San Francisco Chronicle*, Aug. 25 and Sept. 4, 1919.

7. Lief, *Firestone*, 121–123.

8. Ibid, 108–110.

9. Dorothy Brandon, *Mamie Dowd Eisenhower* (New York: Scribner's, 1954), 105–108.

Chapter Five

1. Major Charles McClure, "Long Distance Motor Convoy Operation," *Quartermaster Motor Transportation*, April 1992, 1–13.

2. A number of officials and newspapers analyzed what they called the significance of the 1919 convoy: McClure, "Long Distance"; U.S. War Department, *Annual Report*, 1920; *Quartermaster Review* 1, July-August, 1926; *The New York Times*, Oct. 26, 1919, x, 3; Graf, "Overland March"; George Lear, *Motorcycle Mechanics* (Englewood Cliffs, N.J.: Prentice Hall, 1977); Nelson Pringle, "U.S. Army Truck Test," *Translog*, March 1970, 17–20; and automobile advertising in the early 1920s.

3. Cary, *Motor Vehicles,* 138–9 and 156–60; and McClure, "Long Distance," passim, have useful information about the fate of the militor.

4. A number of letters from a variety of agencies demonstrate the military's lower regard for the 1920 convoy as compared to that of 1919. For the promoting and planning of the 1920 convoy see Good Roads, *Bulletin,* February 1920; Bankhead Highway Association papers, Alabama Archives. For the trip itself see Scrapbook VC-5, Alabama Archives; Virginia Hart, *The Story of American Roads* (New York: William Sloane, 1950); letters from William B. Bankhead to the secretaries of state of eight southern states (all 1938), cabinet VB 24, Alabama Archives; U.S. War Department, *Annual Report,* 1920 and 1921; J.L. Land, "Alabama Highway Department History," *The Alabama Roadbuilder* 2 (March 1958): 10–29; Marsha Perry Hataway, "The Development of the Mississippi State Highway System, 1916–1932," *Journal of Mississippi History* 28 (November 1966), 286–295.

5. The narrative of the 1920 convoy is largely taken from the following: *The New York Times,* June 15, 1920, 4; Good Roads, *Bulletin,* July, September and October, 1920; E. David Cronon, ed., *The Cabinet Diaries of Josephus Daniels* (Lincoln: University of Nebraska, 1963); *Bankhead Scrapbook,* Alabama Archives; *Greensboro* (N.C.) *Daily News,* June 20, 25, 1920; *Raleigh News and Observer,* June 20, 1920; *Charlotte Observer,* June 25, 1920; *Atlanta Constitution,* June 27, 30, July 12, 1920; *Birmingham Argus,* July 22, 1920; *The South Reporter* (Holly Springs, Miss.), July 16, 23, 1920; *Lonoke Democrat,* July 19, 1920; *Texarkana State Press,* Aug 8, 1920; *Daily Texarkanian,* July 13, 23, 27, and 30, and Aug. 3, 6, 7, and 9, 1920; *El Paso Morning Times,* July 11, 1920; *Bisbee Daily Review,* Sept. 15, 16, and 17, 1920; *Tucson Citizen,* Sept. 18, 1920; *Arizona Republican,* Sept. 11, 20, 26, and 28, 1920; *Yuma Sun,* Sept. 24 and Oct. 1, 1920; *Imperial Valley Press* (El Centro), Sept 20, 22, 23, 27, 29, and 30, 1920; *Los Angeles Daily Times,* Oct. 5, 6, and 7, 1920.

6. The Medical Corps's investigation of the convoy's mess is narrated in a long series of letters and endorsements between the office of the quartermaster and the convoy, almost daily, from June 16 to August 4,

1920; military concerns for the post-war highway conditions are described in Capt. Edward K. Smith, "Road Development for National Defense," *Alabama Highways* 1 (September 1927), 3–8.

Chapter Six

1. Geoffrey Hindley, *A History of Roads* (Seacaucus, N.J.: Citadel, 1972); Paul H. Douglas, "The Development of a System of Federal Grants-in-Aid," *Political Science Quarterly,* March 1920; John B. Rae, *The American Automobile Industry* (Boston: Twayne, 1984); Alfred Lief, *The Firestone Story* (New York: McGraw-Hill, 1951); U.S. Department of Transportation, *America's Highways, 1776–1976* (Washington, D.C.: Federal Highway Administration, 1976.)

2. The beginnings of federal aid are reported in "National Highway Bill," *Outlook* 124 (March 31, 1920); *Literary Digest* 63, Oct. 11 and Nov. 22, 1919; *Literary Digest* 66, Sept 11, 1920, and *Literary Digest* 77, May 26, 1923; *The American City,* February 1920 and August 1921; *The New York Times,* May 28, 1916, V, 10 and April 18, 1920, VII, 10; Cray, *Chrome; Peoria* (Ill) *Star,* Feb. 20, 1916. Roy Chapin's correspondence is in the Chapin papers, Bentley Library, Ann Arbor, Mich. Other reports are in *The Atlanta Constitution,* June 17, 1920, 8; Carl Hayden papers, Arizona State University; *Wooster* (Ohio), *Daily News,* June 14, 1919, 3; *The New York Times,* Feb 2, 1919, IX, 4; Charles Dearing, *American Highway Policy* (New York: Arno Press, 1978); letter, Secretary of War Newton D. Baker to Secretary of Agriculture David F. Houston, April 24, 1917, in the Chapin files, Bentley Library. *Congressional Digest* 34, no. 5, May 1965. Pershing's role is analyzed briefly in "Highways for National Defense," *Translog* 12, April 1981, 2.

3. Some of Woodrow Wilson's unusual fears about highways can be found in *The New York Times,* Feb. 28, 1906, 2 and March 4, 1906, 12.

4. Kaszynski, *American Highway,* 54.

5. Ibid, 59; Rose, *Interstate,* 2–12.

6. U.S. Department of Transportation, *America's Highways,* 152.

7. *Congressional Digest,* May 1955, 131–160.

8. *American Scientist,* September/October 2006.

9. Dwight D. Eisenhower, *Mandate for Change, 1953–1956* (Garden City, N.Y.: Doubleday, 1963), 501–2 and 547–9.

10. *Congressional Digest,* May 1955, 131–160.

11. Ibid.; Rose, *Interstate,* 69–92.

12. *Congressional Digest,* January/February 1956, 66.

13. Eisenhower, *Mandate,* 502.

14. Stephen E. Ambrose, *Eisenhower 2: The President* (New York: Simon & Schuster, 1984), carefully follows the tortured legislation and near-legislation on a highway bill.

15. *The New York Times,* July 19, 1981, Travel section.

16. *Christian Science Monitor,* Dec. 26, 1989, 7; *Americana Annual* (New York: Grolier, 1989), 534.

17. "Weekly Report," *Congressional Quarterly,* Feb. 1, 1992.

18. *Ibid.,* March 9, 1991, p. 597; *Americana Annual* (New York: Grolier, 1992), 392 and 530–1.

19. *Congressional Record,* Nov. 19, 1993; *Congressional Quarterly Researcher,* May 6, 1994, 403.

20. *Business Week,* Nov. 21, 1994, 48–9.

21. Lewis F. Gould, *Lady Bird Johnson and the Environment* (Lawrence, Kan.: University of Kansas, 1988).

Chapter Seven

1. *Business Week,* Nov. 21, 1994, 48–9.

2. U.S. Bureau of Transportation Statistics, June 2006.

3. Kaszynski, *American Highway,* 207–10.

4. Ibid, 201.

5. Federal Highway Administration Office of Safety, Oct. 18, 2005.

6. Jack Basso, "The Future of the Highway Trust Fund," presentation to the Institute of Transportation Engineers, Aug. 8, 2006, online at http://www.transportation.org/sites/aashto/docs/Basso-2006-08-08.pdf.

7. Robert W. Poole, Jr., "Three Lessons in Highway Privatization." *Budget and Tax News,* March, 1, 2005.

8. Cintra Reports; Cintra Fact Sheet; *This Money Magazine,* June 7, 2006. Ferrovial Fact Sheet, 2005; *Hoover's Reports,* 2007.

9. *Wright Reports,* Dec. 27, 2006; *Indianapolis Star,* Nov. 15, 2006; *The Washington Post,* March 20, 2006.

10. Transurban flyer, May 3, 2006; *Roads and Bridges,* Dec. 11, 2006.

11. VMS flyer, Dec. 23, 2006; *Meteorlogix,* 2003; Texas Department of Transportation handout, January 2001.

12. *Forbes,* Oct. 25, 2005 and March 23, 2006; *The New York Times,* Dec. 27, 2006; Daniel Schulman and James Ridgeway, "The Highwaymen," *Mother Jones,* January/February 2007, online at http://www.motherjones.com/politics/2007/01/highwaymen; *Pittsburgh Post Gazette,* Dec. 2 and Dec. 23, 2006.

13. Federal Highway Administration study, Dec. 29, 2006; *Tollroads News,* Nov. 23, 2004.

14. *South Bend Tribune,* March 22, 2006; *USA Today,* Oct. 16, 2006.

15. *Sidney Morning Herald,* Dec. 28, 2006; *Inside Business,* Oct. 16, 2005.

16. Texas Department of Transportation, "History," http://www.txdot.gov/.

17. Ibid.

18. *Corridor Watch,* Jan. 18, 2005.

19. Texas Department of Transportation, "History."

20. *Austin Chronicle,* Oct. 6, 2006.

21. Texas Department of Transportation, "History."

22. *Human Events,* Nov. 6, 2006.

23. Texas Department of Transportation, "History."

24. *Houston Chronicle,* Nov. 8, 2006.

25. *Human Events,* Oct. 31, 2006.

26. *Land Line Magazine,* Aug. 22, 2006.

27. *Dallas News,* Sept. 28, 2006.

28. E-mail, Texas Department of Transportation to author, Jan. 11 and 16, 2007.

29. *Christian Science Monitor,* Feb. 16, 2006; Cornell Law School, Legal Information Institute.

30. *Southwest Farm Express,* Dec. 6, 2006; Gov. Rick Perry, "Gov. Perry Signs New Law Protecting Property Rights," Press release, Texas governor's office, Aug. 31, 2005, online at http://governor.state.tx.us/news/press-release/3239/.

31. *World Net Daily,* Jan. 10, 2007; Texas Department of Transportation, Trans Texas Corridor, Jan 19, 2007.

Chapter Eight

1. Richard F. Weingroff, "The Genie in the Bottle: The Interstate System and Urban Problems, 1939–1957," *Public Roads* 64 (September/October 2000). 2, online at http://www.tfhrc.gov/pubrds/septoct00/urban.htm.

2. Jonathan C. Comer, "Socioeconomic Impacts of Highway Bypasses in Oklahoma, Applied Geography Conference, Colorado Springs, Colo., 2000, 58–59.

3. Ibid, 60.

4. Ibid., 61- 62.

5. Ibid., 62–66.

6. C.I. Rogers and R. Marshment, "Measuring Highway Bypass Impacts on Small Town Business Districts," *Review of Urban and Regional Development* 12(3): 250–265.

7. Tara Clapp, "Sustainability and the Highway 20 Environmental Corridor, unpublished article, 2007, Iowa State University.

8. The writers' objectivity can be questioned as they suggest ways of overcoming the fear of bypasses.

9. David Burress, "The Impacts of Highway Bypasses on Kansas Towns." *Institute for Public Policy and Business Research*, research report prepared for the Kansas Department of Transportation, Ames, Iowa, October 1966.

10. Pat Harrison, "The Road to Riches," Illinois Issues 2 (February 1996): 28–29, 1–3.

11. Nathaniel Baum-Snow, "Did Highways Cause Suburbanization?" *Quarterly Journal of Economics* 122 (May 2007): 775–805.

12. Wendell Cox, Peter Gordon, and Christian Redfearn, "Highway Penetration of Central Cities: Not a Major Cause of Suburbanization," *Econ Journal Watch* 5 (January 2008): 32–45.

13. Nathaniel Baum-Snow, "Reply to Cox, Gordon, and Redfearn's Comment on 'Did Highways Cause Suburbanization?'" *Econ Journal Watch* 5 (January 2008), 46–50.

14. U.S. Census Bureau News, "New York Has Longest Commute to Work in Nation, American Community Survey Finds," Feb. 25, 2004, online at http://www.census.gov/Press-Release/www/releases/archives/american_community_survey_acs/001695.html.

15. U.S. Census Bureau News, "Americans Spend More Than 100 Hours Commuting to Work Each Year, Census Bureau Reports," March 30, 2005, online at http://www.census.gov/Press-Release/www/releases/archives/american_community_survey_acs/004489.html.

16. U.S. Census Bureau News, "Most of Us Still Drive to Work — Alone: Public Transportation Commuters Concentrated in a Handful of Large Cities," June 13, 2007, online at http://www.census.gov/Press-Release/www/releases/archives/american_community_survey_acs/010230.html.

17. *The Nation*, Nov. 19, 2004, 1–5; *Business Week*, Feb .21. 2005; *Investopedia*, n.d., 1–2.

Chapter Nine

1. Federal Highway Administration, "Portrait of a General: General Roy Stone," online at http://www.fhwa.dot.gov/infrastructure/stonetoc.cfm.

2. Richard F. Weingroff, "Federal Aid Road Act of 1916: Building the Foundation, Sidebars," Summer 1996, online at http://www.fhwa.dot.gov/infrastructure/rw96b.cfm.

3. Ibid.; *The New York Times*, Jan. 4, 1914, 1.

4. *The New York Times,* June 1, 1913.

5. Weingroff, "Federal Aid Road Act of 1916," 1–2; Justia.com, U.S. Supreme Court Center, Wilson v. Shaw, 204 U.S. 24 (1907), online at http://supreme.justia.com/us/204/24/case.html.

6. Weingroff, "Federal Aid Road Act of 1916," 1–3.

7. Weingroff, "Sidebars," 2.

8. Tom Lewis, *Divided Highways*, New York: Viking, 1997, 8.

9. Weingroff, "Sidebars," 1; Lewis, passim.

10. Federal Highway Administration, "Thomas H. MacDonald on Toll Roads." Online at http://www.fhwa.dot.gov/infrastructure/mcdonaldtoll.cfm.

11. Weingroff, "Federal Aid Road Act of 1916," 1–5.

12. Ibid., 4.

13. Ibid., 1–4.

14. German Way. "The Autobahn." n.d., 1–3.

15. Richard F. Weingroff, "The Genie in the Bottle: The Interstate System and Urban Problems, 1939–1957," *Public Roads* 64 (September/October 2000), online at http://www.tfhrc.gov/pubrds/septoct00/urban.htm.

16. Weingroff, "Genie," 4.

17. Ibid.

18. Ibid., 5–6.

19. Ibid., 9–10.

20. Richard F. Weingroff, "Federal-Aid Highway Act of 1956: Creating the Interstate System," online at http://www.fhwa.dot.gov/infrastructure/rw96e.cfm.

21. Larry Copeland, "U.S. Interstate System Marks 50 Years Today," *RedOrbit*, June 29, 2006. Online at http://www.redorbit.com/news/business/554109/us_interstate_system_marks_50_years_today/index.html.

22. Lewis, *Divided Highways*, 117–120.

23. Northeast Midwest Institute, "What Is the Highway Trust Fund?" 1–3, online at http://www.nemw.org/HWtrustfund.htm.

24. Richard F. Weingroff, "Edward M. Bassett: The Man Who Gave Us 'Freeway.'" Online at http://www.fhwa.dot.gov/infrastructure/freeway.cfm.

Chapter Ten

1. PB Consult Inc., "The Economic Impact of the Interstate Highway System" (technical memorandum prepared as part of the Transportation Research Board's National Cooperative Highway Research Program Project 20–24(52), Future Options for the National System of Interstate and Defense Highways), June 13, 2006, online at http://74.125.95.132/search?q=cache:B-QN7iVxKC8J:www.interstate50th.org/docs/techmemo2.pdf+P.B.+Consult,+%E2%80%9CEconomic+Impact+of+the+Interstate+Highway+System.&cd=1&hl=en&ct=clnk&gl=us.

2. Information about Ms. Fraumeni is from the Muskie School of Public Service.

3. Federal Highway Administration Office of Transportation Policy Studies. "Highways and the Economy." Online at http://www.fhwa.dot.gov/policy/otps/highways.htm.

4. P.B. Consult Inc., "Economic Impact," 4–52.

5. Ibid., 51–53.

6. Ibid., 53–54.

7. Randal O'Toole, "The Interstate Highway System: What Works, What Doesn't," posted at NewsWithViews.com, July 19, 2006, online at http://www.newswithviews.com/O'Toole/randall.htm.

8. Ibid., 3.

9. Mary Peters, "The Now and Future Interstate System," *Better Roads,* May 2006, online at http://www.betterroads.com/content/Issue-Story.45.0.html?&no_cache=1&tx_magissue_pi1[keyword]=Mary%20Peters&tx_magissue_pi1[pointer]=2&tx_magissue_pi1[mode]=1&tx_magissue_pi1[showUid]=197.

10. Ibid.

11. Federal Highway Administration, March 5, 2007, 2.

12. The Newspaper.com, Oct. 9, 2007.

13. *Toll Roads News*, June 24, 2007.

14. American Trucking Association, "Tolls on the Interstate," n.d., 1–2; Daniel Schulman and James Ridgeway, "The Highwaymen," *Mother Jones,* January/February 2007, online at http://www.motherjones.com/politics/2007/01/highwaymen.

15. Federal Highway Administration, *Congestion Pricing—A Primer: Overview.* October 2008. Online at http://ops.fhwa.dot.gov/publications/fhwahop08039/cp_prim1_00.htm.

16. Federal Highway Administration, "A Guide for Hot Lane Development," March 2003, online at http://www.its.dot.gov/JPODOCS/REPTS_TE/13668.html.

17. Ibid.

18. Harry Meyers, "Displacement Effect of Federal Highway Grants," *National Tax Journal* 40 (June 1987): 221–235.

19. Edward Miller, "The Economics of Matching Grants: The ABC Highway Program," *National Tax Journal* 27 (June 1974): 221–229.

20. Federal Highway Administration, "Design, Dwight David Eisenhower National System of Interstate and Defense Highways," 2002.

21. Ibid.; "Highway Finance Information," *Public Roads*, 1–6; FHA, Federal Highway Administration, "Special Federal-Aid Funding," June 26, 2008, online at http://www.fhwa.dot.gov/specialfunding/.

22. *The San Jose Mercury News*, Feb. 23, 2008.

23. Federal Highway Administration, "Garvee Issues on the Rise," *Innovative Finance* 12:1 (Fall 2006), online at http://www.fhwa.dot.gov/innovativefinance/ifq-fall06.htm.

Chapter Eleven

1. Federal Highway Administration, "Highway Statistics 1994," October 1995, iv-22.

2. Congressional Budget Office, "Study," January 1998, 5–6.

3. Federal Highway Administration, "Financing Federal Aid Highways," May 1992, 12–14.

4. Congressional Budget Office, "Study," 7.

5. Ibid., 9.

6. Ibid., 14.

7. Conversation with Mark Foster, finance director, North Carolina Department of Transportation, May 8, 2008.

8. Congressional Budget Office, "Study," 8.

9. Ibid., 18–20.

10. Federal Highway Administration, "Evaluation of the U.S. DOT State Infrastructure Bank Pilot Program," June 1997, online at http://www.fhwa.dot.gov/innovativeFinance/contoc.htm.

11. Congressional Budget Office, "Study," 23.

12. Federal Highway Administration, *Innovative Finance* 12:1, 1–9.

13. Brookings Institution. Federal Transportation Reform. http://www.brookings.edu/metro/TransportationSeries/TransportationReform.aspx.

14. Ibid., 2.

15. Ibid., 2–3.

16. The Federal Highway Administration approves only the project, not the bond issue. Federal Highway Administration, "Garvee Bond Guidance," March 2004, online at http://www.fhwa.dot.gov/innovativeFinance/garguid1.htm.

17. Brookings Institution. Federal Transportation Reform. http://www.brookings.edu/metro/TransportationSeries/TransportationReform.aspx. Maryland General Assembly. "Transportation Infrastructure Financing Policy — Limitations on GARVEE Bonds" (Senate Bill 75), 2005 session.

18. Federal Highway Administration, "Garvee Bond Guidance," 1–2; Brookings, 10.

19. Brookings, 13–15.

Chapter Twelve

1. *The Herald* (Mercer County, Penn.), Nov. 24, 2006, 1.

2. Federal Highway Administration, "Focus on Congestion Relief," n.d., 1–2.

3. "Congestion Management Solutions: Researchers Look to Improve North American Trade," *Texas Transportation Researcher* 43:4 (2007), online at http://tti.tamu.edu/publications/researcher/newsletter.htm?vol=43&issue=4&article=3&year=2007.

4. Federal Highway Administration, "Public Roads," July-August 2007, 4.

5. Ibid., 5.

6. Ibid., 9.

7. Ibid.

8. Texas Transportation Institute as quoted in *Metro,* 2006, 1.

9. U.S. Department of Transportation, "Fact Sheet," n.d., 1–7.

10. *Public Roads,* July/August 2007, 16–17.

11. Federal Highway Administration, "Urban Partnerships," online at http://www.upa.dot.gov/.

12. Christopher Sheil, "Public-Private Partnerships," Evatt Foundation paper, Sept. 5, 2006, online at http://evatt.org.au/publications/papers/150.html.

13. *Public Roads,* July/August 2007, 23–24.

14. Ibid., 25–26.

15. Ibid., 27.

16. Ibid., 28–46.

17. Federal Highway Administration, *Congestion Pricing — A Primer: Overview.* October 2008, online at http://ops.fhwa.dot.gov/publications/fhwahop08039/cp_prim1_00.htm.

18. University of California, Institute of Transportation Studies, 2003, 2–4. The annual costs of congestion can run as high as $6 billion in the New York area and $10 billion in Los Angeles/Long Beach. *Public Roads,* July/August 2007, 4 .

19. Anthony Downs, *Still Stuck in Traffic* (Washington, D.C.: Brookings, 2004), 152–176.

Chapter Thirteen

1. U.S. Government Accountability Office, "Highways and Transit: Private Sector Sponsorship of and Investment in Major Projects Has Been Limited," March 25, 2004, online at http://www.gao.gov/products/GAO-04-419.
2. Ibid.
3. Ibid.
4. U.S. Department of Transportation, "Design," 1.
5. U.S. Government Accountability Office, "Highways."
6. Federal Highway Administration, "Infrastructure," 1987, 1. This is the only highway bill vetoed in the twentieth century.
7. Brach, Anne. "Surface Transportation Reauthorization Arrives: What Are the Outcomes and the Prospects for Research?" *Transportation News* 240 (September/October 2005), 1–2.
8. By a big margin, the Senate refused to reduce any earmarks for the benefit of Katrina victims. Sen. Don Young said they "could kiss my ear." *The Washington Post*, Oct. 21, 2005.
9. U.S. Government Accountability Office, "Highways," 13.
10. Ibid., 11–12.
11. Ibid., 15.
12. Steven Malanga, "The New Privatization," (New York) *City Journal*, Summer 2007, online at http://www.city-journal.org/html/17_3_privatization.html. pp. 2–3.
13. U.S. Government Accountability Office, "Highways," 18–20.
14. Ibid., 22–25.
15. Leonard Gilroy, Robert W. Poole, Jr., Peter Samuel and Geoffrey Segal, "Building New Roads through Public-Private Partnerships: Frequently Asked Questions," Reason Foundation policy brief 58, March 1, 2007, online at http://reason.org/news/show/1002866.html.
16. Wright Reports (http://wrightreports.ecnext.com/), "MacQuarrie Company Profile;" *Indianapolis Star*, Nov. 15, 2006.

17. Hoover's Reports, (www.hoovers.com/), "Zachry Construction Corporation;" Zachry information sheet, n.d., 1.
18. U.S. Department of Transportation, "D.C., USDOT Sign Agreement With Contractor To Preserve, Enhance City's Major Roads and Bridges," press release, June 19, 2000, Online at http://www.fhwa.dot.gov/pressroom/fhwa0043.htm; Goliath Business Knowledge on Demand, "VMS, Inc.," online at http://goliath.ecnext.com/coms2/product-compint-0000927956-page.html; VMS information sheet, n.d., "Welcome to VMS, Inc.," 1–4.
19. Transurban Company brochures, 2005, 2007; *Atlanta Business Chronicle*, March 31, 2008.
20. Grupo Ferrovial pamphlet, 2008, 1–2.
21. Cintra/Zachry Team Fact Sheet, 1–2; *The Washington Post*, March 20, 2006, 1–4; *Corridor Watch*, Feb. 7, 2007, 1–2; Reed Construction Data, "Cintra Zachry," June 2006, 1–2.
22. Poole, Robert W., Jr. "Three Lessons in Highway Privatization." *Budget and Tax News*, March, 1, 2005.
23. BNET Research Center, "Privatizing our Highways," 2007, 1–3.
24. Peter Samuel, "Highway Aggravation: The Case for Privatizing the Highways," Cato Institute Policy Analysis 231, June 27, 1995, online at http://www.cato.org/pubs/pas/pa-231.html.
25. Ibid., 7–8.
26. Ibid., 12.
27. Ibid., 35.
28. Daniel Schulman, and James Ridgeway, "The Highwaymen," *Mother Jones*, January/February 2007, 1–7, online at http://www.motherjones.com/politics/2007/01/highwaymen.
29. Ibid.; Reuters, GAO Report, June 3, 2008, 1.
30. *Indianapolis Star*, Feb. 10, 2007, 1–2; *Pittsburgh Post Gazette*, Dec. 12, 2006, 1–2.
31. Eduardo M. Engel, Ronald D. Fischer and Alexander Galetovic, "Privatizing Highways in Latin America: Is it Possible to Fix What Went Wrong?" *IDEAS*, July 28 2004, online at http://ideas.repec.org/p/ysm/somwrk/ysm417.html.
32. Federal Highway Administration, "Chicago Skyway," n.d., 1; *South Bend Tri-*

bune, March 22, 2006; Letter, Indiana Economic Development Corporation to legal counsel Indiana Department of Transportation, Feb. 10, 2006; *USA Today*, Oct. 16, 2006.

Chapter Fourteen

1. *Americana Annual* (New York: Grolier, 1993), 224; *Facts on File*, Nov. 11, 1993, 849; *Christian Science Monitor*, May 3, 1994, 3.

2. John G. Mitchell, "Thirty Years on Ike's Autobahns," *Audubon* 88 (November 1986) 73.

3. Helen Leavitt, *Superhighway-Superhoax* (Garden City, N.Y: Doubleday, 1970); *Austin American Statesman*, May 28, 1992; A1; *Austin American Statesman,* July 15, 1993, A8; Anthony Orum, *Power, Money and the People: The Making of Modern Austin* (Austin: Texas Monthly Press, 1987).

4. Ronald Buell, *Dead End. The Automobile in Mass Transportation.* (Englewood Cliffs, N.J.: Prentice Hall, 1972).

5. Bruce Seely, *Building the American Highway System: Engineers as Policy Makers* (Philadelphia: Temple University Press, 1987).

6. Mark H. Rose, *Interstate: Express Highway Politics* (Knoxville: University of Tennessee Press, 1990).

7. Anthony Downs, *Stuck in Traffic* (Washington, D.C.: Brookings, 1992).

8. *Worcester Telegram*, Oct. 8, 2006.

9. *Boston Globe*, Nov. 23, 2006 and Feb. 2, 2007; Commissioner William F. Callahan, "Master Highway Plan for Boston Metropolitan Area," Massachusetts Department of Public Works, 1948, online at http://www.bostonroads.com/history/1948-plan/; *CBS Evening News*, Dec. 24, 2006.

10. *Berkshire Eagle*, Sept 18, 2006.

11. *Boston Globe*, March 2, 2007.

12. *ASU Insight*, Sept. 9, 1994, 1.

13. Wolfgang Zuckerman quoted in *Congressional Quarterly Researcher*, May 6, 1994, 389.

14. PBS program, June 19, 1994.

15. *Congressional Quarterly Researcher,* May 6, 1994, 396.

16. Kenneth Small, Clifford Winton, and Carol A. Evans, *Roadwork* (Washington, D.C.: Brookings, 1983); *The Christian Science Monitor*, April 13, 1994, 7.

17. Federal Highway Administration, *The National Highway System* (n.d.), 1.

18. Gary Toth. "Back to Basics in Transportation Planning: Rediscovering Our Roots Can Solve 21st Century Traffic Woes," Project for Public Spaces Web site, online at http://www.pps.org/info/bulletin/back_to_basics_in_transportation.

19. Rodney Slater. "The National Highway System: A Commitment to America's Future," *Public Roads On-line*, Spring 1996, online at http://www.tfhrc.gov/pubrds/spring96/p96sp2.htm.

20. Federal Highway Administration, "Public Roads," (n.d.)

21. Ibid., 7.

22. Ibid., 8–9.

23. Ibid., 10–11.

24. AARoads, "Future Interstates and Potential Interstate Corridors," http://www.interstate-guide.com/future.html.

25. Robert Dunphy, "What Comes after the Interstate?" Urban Land Institute, March 2006, online at https://commerce.uli.org/AM/Template.cfm?Section=Home&CONTENTID=78457&TEMPLATE=/CM/ContentDisplay.cfm.

26. All of the items are from Leigh Ferrara, "Who's Buying Your Commute?" *Mother Jones*, Jan. 1, 2007, online at http://www.motherjones.com/politics/2007/01/whos-buying-your-commute.

27. *Tuscaloosa News*, Dec. 3, 2006.

28. *Pine Bluff Commercial*, Nov. 20, 2006.

29. *Sacramento Bee*, Dec. 25, 2006.

30. *Evansville Courier and Press*, Oct. 11, 2006.

31. *Shreveport Times*, Jan. 8, 2007; Shreveport radio KTBS, Dec. 17, 2006.

32. *Mankato Free Press*, Dec, 27, 2006.

33. *Daily Record* (Morris County, N.J.), Nov. 22, 2006.

34. *Raleigh Chronicle*, Nov. 10, 2006.

35. *Oklahoman*, (Oklahoma City), Dec. 2, 2006.

36. *Pittsburgh Post Gazette*, Jan. 28, 2007; *Sunbury Daily Item*, Nov. 19, 2006.

37. *Austin American Statesman*, March 1, 2007.

38. *Public Roads*, January/February 2008, 38.

Bibliography

Articles

"Along the Road." *Public Roads* 71 (January/February 2008). Online at http://www.tfhrc.gov/pubrds/08jan/along road.htm.

American Scientist (September/October 2006).

ASU Insight (Sept. 9, 1994).

Business Week (Feb. 21, 2005).

Basso, Jack. "The Future of the Highway Trust Fund." Presented to the Institute of Transportation Engineers, Aug. 8, 2006. Online at http://www.transportation.org/sites/aashto/docs/Basso-2006-08-08.pdf

Baum-Snow, Nathaniel. "Did Highways Cause Suburbanization?" *Quarterly Journal of Economics* 122:2 (May 2007): 775–805.

_____. "Reply to Cox, Gordon, and Redfearn's Comment on 'Did Highways Cause Suburbanization?'" *Econ Journal Watch* 5 (January 2008), 46–50.

Brach, Anne. "Surface Transportation Reauthorization Arrives: What Are the Outcomes and the Prospects for Research?" *Transportation News* 240 (September/October 2005): 39–42.

Burress, David. "The Impacts of Highway Bypasses on Kansas Towns." *Institute for Public Policy and Business Research.* Research report prepared for the Kansas Department of Transportation. Ames, Iowa. October 1966.

Callahan, Commissioner William F. "Master Highway Plan for Boston Metropolitan Area." Massachusetts Department of Public Works, 1948. Online at http://www.bostonroads.com/history/1948-plan/.

Clapp, Tara. "Sustainability and the Highway 20 Environmental Corridor." Unpublished thesis, Iowa State University, 2007.

Comer, Jonathan C. "Socioeconomic Impacts of Highway Bypasses in Oklahoma." Applied Geography Conference, Colorado Springs, Colo., 2000.

"Congestion Management Solutions: Researchers Look to Improve North American Trade." *Texas Transportation Researcher* 43:4 (2007). Online at http://tti.tamu.edu/publications/researcher/newsletter.htm?vol=43&issue=4&article=3&year=2007.

Congressional Digest. 1955.

Congressional Quarterly, Feb.1, 1992.

Congressional Quarterly Researcher, May 6, 1994.

Copeland, Larry. "U.S. Interstate System Marks 50 Years Today." *RedOrbit*, June 29, 2006. Online at http://www.redorbit.com/news/business/554109/us_interstate_system_marks_50_years_today/index.html.

Cox, Wendell, Peter Gordon, and Christian Redfearn. "Highway Penetration of Central Cities: Not a Major Cause of Suburbanization." *Econ Journal Watch* 5 (January 2008): 32–45.

Douglas, Paul H. "The Development of a System of Federal Grants-in-Aid." *Political Science Quarterly,* March 1920.

Duncan, David. "Horatio's Drive." *Texas Journey* (September/October 2003).

Dunphy, Robert. "What Comes after the Interstate?" Urban Land Institute, March

2006. Online at https://commerce.uli. org/AM/Template.cfm?Section=Home& CONTENTID=78457&TEMPLATE=/ CM/ContentDisplay.cfm.

Forbes, Oct. 25, 2005.

Forbes, March 23, 2006.

Engel, Eduardo M., Ronald D. Fischer and Alexander Galetovic. "Privatizing Highways in Latin America: Is it Possible to Fix What Went Wrong?" *IDEAS,* July 28 2004. Online at http://ideas.repec.org/ p/ysm/somwrk/ysm417.html.

Federal Highway Administration. "Evaluation of the U.S. DOT State Infrastructure Bank Pilot Program." June 1997. Online at http://www.fhwa.dot.gov/in novativeFinance/contoc.htm.

_____. "The Finer Points of Garvees." *Innovative Finance* 12:1 (Fall 2006). Online at http://www.fhwa.dot.gov/innovativefinance/ifqfall06.htm.

_____. "Garvee Issues on the Rise." *Innovative Finance* 12:1 (Fall 2006). Online at http://www.fhwa.dot.gov/innovative finance/ifqfall06.htm.

_____. "Garvee Roundup." *Innovative Finance* 12:1 (Fall 2006). Online at http:// www.fhwa.dot.gov/innovativefinance/ ifqfall06.htm.

_____. *The National Highway System* (n.d.).

_____. "SIB Highlights." *Innovative Finance* 12:1 (Fall 2006). Online at http:// www.fhwa.dot.gov/innovativefinance/ ifqfall06.htm.

_____. "Special Federal-Aid Funding." June 26, 2008. Online at http://www. fhwa.dot.gov/specialfunding/.

_____. "Thomas H. MacDonald on Toll Roads." Online at http://www.fhwa.dot. gov/infrastructure/mcdonaldtoll.cfm.

_____. "Urban Partnerships." Online at http://www.upa.dot.gov/.

Ferrara, Leigh. "Who's Buying Your Commute?" *Mother Jones,* Jan. 1, 2007. Online at http://www.motherjones.com/poli tics/2007/01/whos-buying-your-com mute.

Gilroy, Leonard, Robert W. Poole Jr., Peter Samuel and Geoffrey Segal. "Building New Roads through Public-Private Partnerships: Frequently Asked Questions." Reason Foundation policy brief 58, March 1, 2007. Online at http://reason. org/news/show/1002866.html.

Good Roads. *Bulletin.* February 1920, July 1920, September 1920, and October 1920.

Graf, Lt. Col. William S. "The Great Overland March." *Soldiers* (October 1975): 47–50.

Harrison, Pat. "The Road to Riches." *Illinois Issues* 2 (February 1996): 28–29.

Hataway, Marsha P. "The Development of the Mississippi State Highway System, 1916–1932." *Journal of Mississippi History* 28 (November 1966): 286–295.

"Highway Finance Information." *Public Roads* (2006–7).

Howell, Alice. "The Lincoln Highway." In *Buffalo Tales.* Kearney, Neb: Buffalo County Historical Society, 1983.

Human Events, Oct. 31 and Nov. 6, 2006.

Innovative Finance Quarterly (Fall 2006).

Inside Business, Oct.16, 2005.

Land, J.L. "Alabama Highway Department History," *The Alabama Roadbuilder* 2 (March 1958): 10–29.

Landline Magazine, Aug. 22, 2006.

Malanga, Steven. "The New Privatization." (New York) *City Journal,* Summer 2007. Online at http://www.city-journal.org/ html/17_3_privatization.html.

McClure, Major Charles. "Long Distance Motor Convoy Operation." *Quartermaster Motor Transportation,* April 1992, 1–13.

Meyers, Harry. "Displacement Effect of Federal Highway Grants." *National Tax Journal* 40 (June 1987): 221–235.

Miller, Edward, "The Economics of Matching Grants: The ABC Highway Program." *National Tax Journal* 27 (June 1974): 221–229.

Mitchell, John G. "Thirty Years on Ike's Autobahns." *Audubon* 88 (November 1986).

Motor Trend, December 1967.

The Nation, Nov. 29, 2004.

"National Highway Bill." *Outlook* 124 (March 31, 1920).

Northeast Midwest Institute. "What Is the Highway Trust Fund?" Online at http:// www.nemw.org/HWtrustfund.htm.

O'Toole, Randal. "The Interstate Highway System: What Works, What Doesn't." Posted at NewsWithViews.com, July 19, 2006. Online at http://www.newswith-views.com/O'Toole/randal1.htm.

PB Consult Inc. "The Economic Impact of the Interstate Highway System" (technical memorandum prepared as part of the Transportation Research Board's National Cooperative Highway Research Program Project 20–24(52), *Future Options for the National System of Interstate and Defense Highways*), June 13, 2006. Online at http://74.125.95.132/search? q=cache:B-QN7iVxKC8J:www.inter state50th.org/docs/techmemo2.pdf+P.B. +Consult,+%E2%80%9CEconomic+Im pact+of+the+Interstate+Highway+Sys tem.&cd=1&hl=en&ct=clnk&gl=us.

Perry, Gov. Rick. "Gov. Perry Signs New Law Protecting Property Rights." Press release, Texas governor's office, Aug. 31, 2005. Online at http://governor.state.tx. us/news/press-release/3239/.

Peters, Mary. "The Now and Future Interstate System." *Better Roads,* May 2006. Online at http://www.betterroads.com/ content/Issue-Story.45.0.html?&no_ cache=1&tx_magissue_pi1[keyword]= Mary%20Peters&tx_magissue_pi1[point er]=2&tx_magissue_pi1[mode]=1&tx_ magissue_pi1[showUid]=197.

Poole, Robert W. Jr. "Three Lessons in Highway Privatization." *Budget and Tax News,* March, 1, 2005.

Pringle, Nelson. "U.S. Army Truck Test" *Translog,* March 1970, 17–20.

Quartermaster Review, July/August 1926.

Reuters, GAO, *Report,* June 3, 2008.

Roads and Bridges 44 (Dec. 11, 2006).

Rogers, C.I. and R. Marshment. "Measuring Highway Bypass Impacts on Small Town Business Districts." *Review of Urban and Regional Development* 12(3): 250–265.

Samuel, Peter. "Highway Aggravation: The Case for Privatizing the Highways." Cato Institute Policy Analysis 231, June 27, 1995. Online at http://www.cato.org/ pubs/pas/pa-231.html.

Scientific American, July/August 1907.

Schulman, Daniel and James Ridgeway. "The Highwaymen." *Mother Jones,* January/February 2007. Online at http:// www.motherjones.com/politics/2007/ 01/highwaymen.

Sheil, Christopher. "Public-Private Partnerships." Evatt Foundation paper, Sept. 5, 2006. Online at http://evatt.org.au/pub lications/papers/150.html.

Slater, Rodney. "The National Highway System: A Commitment to America's Future." *Public Roads On-line,* Spring 1996. Online at http://www.tfhrc.gov/ pubrds/spring96/p96sp2.htm.

Smith, Captain Edward K. "Road Development for National Defense." *Alabama Highways* 1 (September 1927): 3–8.

Southwest Farm Express, Dec.6, 2006.

This Money Magazine, June 7, 2006.

"Toll regulation on the Chicago Skyway." *Tollroads News,* Nov. 23, 2004. Online at http://www.tollroadsnews.com/node/92 3.

Toll Roads News, June 24, 2007.

Toth, Gary. "Back to Basics in Transportation Planning: Rediscovering Our Roots Can Solve 21st Century Traffic Woes." Project for Public Spaces Web site. Online at http://www.pps.org/info/bul letin/back_to_basics_in_transportation.

U.S. Census Bureau News. "New York Has Longest Commute to Work in Nation, American Community Survey Finds." Feb. 25, 2004. Online at http://www. census.gov/Press-Release/www/releases/ archives/american_community_survey_ acs/001695.html.

U.S. Census Bureau News. "Americans Spend More Than 100 Hours Commuting to Work Each Year, Census Bureau Reports." March 30, 2005. Online at http://www.census.gov/Press-Release/ www/releases/archives/american_com munity_survey_acs/004489.html.

U.S. Census Bureau News. "Most of Us Still Drive to Work — Alone: Public Transportation Commuters Concentrated in a Handful of Large Cities." June 13, 2007. Online at http://www. census.gov/Press-Release/www/releases/ archives/american_community_survey_ acs/010230.html.

U.S. Department of Transportation. "D.C., USDOT Sign Agreement With Contractor To Preserve, Enhance City's Major Roads and Bridges." Press release, June 19, 2000. Online at http://www.fhwa. dot.gov/pressroom/fhwa0043.htm.

U.S. Government Accountability Office. "Highways and Transit: Private Sector Sponsorship of and Investment in Major Projects Has Been Limited." March 25, 2004. Online at http://www.gao.gov/ products/GAO-04-419.

University of California, Institute of Transportation Studies. 2005.

Weingroff, Richard F. "Federal-Aid Highway Act of 1956: Creating the Interstate System." Online at http://www.fhwa.dot.gov/infrastructure/rw96e.cfm.

_____. "Federal Aid Road Act of 1916: Building the Foundation, Sidebars." Summer 1996. Online at http://www.fhwa.dot.gov/infrastructure/rw96b.cfm.

_____. "The Genie in the Bottle: The Interstate System and Urban Problems, 1939–1957." *Public Roads* 64 (September/October 2000). Online at http://www.tfhrc.gov/pubrds/septoct00/urban.htm.

_____. "The Lincoln Highway." 2007. Online at http://www.fhwa.dot.gov/infrastructure/lincoln.cfm.

_____. "Edward M. Bassett: The Man Who Gave Us 'Freeway.'" Online at http://www.fhwa.dot.gov/infrastructure/freeway.cfm.

World Net Daily, Jan.10, 2007.

Younger, Maud. "Alone Across the Continent." *Sunset,* May/June 1924.

Books

Ambrose, Stephen. *Eisenhower 2: The President.* New York: Simon & Schuster, 1984.

Bliss, Carey. *Autos Across America: A Bibliography of Transcontinental Automobile Travel, 1903–1940.* Austin: Jenkins & Reese, 1982.

Buell, Ronald A. *Dead End: The Automobile in Mass Transportation.* Englewood Cliffs, N.J.: Prentice Hall, 1972.

Braddy, Haldeen. *Pershing's Mission in Mexico.* El Paso: Texas Western Press, 1966.

Brandon, Dorothy, *Mamie Dowd Eisenhower: A Portrait of a First Lady.* New York: Scribner's, 1954.

Cray, Ed. *Chrome Colossus,* New York: McGraw-Hill, 1980.

Cronon, E. David, ed. *The Cabinet Diaries of Josephus Daniels, 1913–1921.* Lincoln: University of Nebraska, 1963.

Dearing, Charles. *American Highway Policy.* New York: Arno, 1978.

Downs, Anthony. *Still Stuck in Traffic.* Washington, D.C.: Brookings, 2004.

_____. *Stuck in Traffic.* Washington, D.C.: Brookings, 1992.

Eisenhower, Dwight D. *Mandate for Change, 1953–1956.* Garden City, N.Y.: Doubleday, 1963.

General Motors, the First 75 Years of Transportation Products. Princeton: Automobile Quarterly Publications, 1983.

Gould, Lewis F. *Lady Bird Johnson and the Environment.* Lawrence: University of Kansas, 1988.

Hart, Virginia. *The Story of American Roads.* New York: William Sloane, 1950.

Hindley, Geoffrey. *A History of Roads.* Seacaucus, N.J.: Citadel, 1972.

Holbrook, Stewart. *The Old Post Road.* New York: McGraw-Hill, 1962.

Karnes, Thomas L. *William Gilpin, Western Nationalist.* Austin: University of Texas, 1961.

Kaszynski, William. *The American Highway.* Jefferson, N.C.: McFarland, 2000.

Laxalt, Robert. *Nevada, a Bicentennial History.* New York: Norton, 1977.

Leavitt, Helen. *Superhighway—Superhoax.* Garden City, N.Y.: Doubleday, 1970.

Lewis, Sinclair. *Free Air.* New York: Harcourt, Brace and Howe, 1919.

Lewis, Tom. *Divided Highways.* New York: Viking, 1997.

Lief, Alfred. *The Firestone Story.* New York: McGraw-Hill, 1951.

Lincoln Highway Association. *The Lincoln Highway.* New York: Dodd, Mead, 1935.

Long, J.C. *Roy D. Chapin: The Man behind the Hudson Motor Company.* Detroit: Wayne State University Press, 2004.

Noble, Warrum, Charles W. Moss and W. Brown Ewing. *Utah since Statehood,* Salt Lake City: S.J. Clark Publishing, 1919.

Orum, Anthony. *Power, Money and the People: The Making of Modern Austin.* Austin: Texas Monthly Press, 1987.

Post, Emily. *By Motor to the Golden Gate.* New York and London: Appleton, 1915; republished, Jefferson, NC: McFarland 2004.

Rae, John B. *The American Automobile Industry.* Boston: Twayne, 1984.

Ramsey, Alice. *Veil, Duster, and Tire Iron.* Covina, Calif.: Castle Press, 1961.

Rose, Mark H. *Interstate: Express Highway Politics.* Knoxville: University of Tennessee Press, 1990.

Scott, Michael. *Packard.* Blue Ridge Summit, Pa.: Tab Books, 1985.

Seely, Bruce. *Building the American Highway System: Engineers as Policy Makers.*

Philadelphia: Temple University Press, 1987.

Small, Kenneth, Clifford Winton, and Carol Evans. *Roadwork*. Washington, D.C.: Brookings, 1983.

U.S. Department of Transportation. *America's Highways, 1776–1976*. Washington, D.C.: Federal Highway Administration, 1976.

U.S. War Department. Report of the Adjutant General. *Annual Report of the War Department 1920*. Washington, D.C.: Government Printing Office, 1921.

Williams, T. Harry, Richard N. Current and Frank Freidel, *The Essentials of American History*. New York: Knopf, 1972.

Dissertations

Cary, Norman Jr., "The Use of the Motor Vehicle in the U.S. Army, 1899–1939." PhD diss., University of Georgia, 1980.

Encyclopedias

Americana Annual. New York: Grolier, 1989–1995.

Encyclopaedia Britannica. Chicago: Encyclopaedia Britannica, 1995.

Facts on File.

Morris, Richard B., ed. *Encyclopedia of American History*. New York: Harper and Row, 1976.

Flyers, Broadsides, Pamphlets

American Trucking Association. "Tolls on the Interstate." n.d.

BNET Research Center. "Privatizing our Highways." 2007.

Cintra. "Chicago Skyway." June 2008.

Cintra. "Fact Sheet."

Cintra. "Cintra Reports."

Cintra Zachry. "Team Fact Sheet." n.d.

Corridor Watch. Jan. 18, 2005 and Feb.7, 2007.

Dixie Manufacturer, 1903–6.

"Ferrovial Fact Sheet." 2005.

German Way. "The Autobahn." n.d.

Grupo Ferrovial. Pamphlet. n.d.

Lincoln Highway Association. "First Transcontinental Motor Convoy" (album). Bentley Library, University of Michigan, Ann Arbor.

Lincoln Highway Association Museum Publications. "Choosing a Route."

_____. "Hoosier Tour."

Scrapbook VC-5, Alabama Archives.

Transurban brochures 2005, 2007.

Transurban flyer, May 3. 2006.

VMS flyer, Dec.23, 2006.

VMS information sheet, n.d.

Zachry information sheet, n.d.

Public Documents

Federal Highway Administration. "Chicago Skyway," n.d.

Federal Highway Administration. *Congressional Biographies*. Edward M. Bassett, May 2, 2005.

_____. "Financing Federal Aid Highways." May 1992.

_____. "Focus on Congestion Relief." n.d.

_____. "Highway Statistics." October 1995.

_____. "Infrastructure." 1987.

_____. "National Highway System." n.d.

_____. "Public Roads." November/December, 2005 and July/August 2007.

_____. "Study." Dec.29, 2006.

_____. "Design, Dwight David Eisenhower National System of Interstate and Defense Highways," 2002.

_____. "Garvee Bond Guidance." March 2004. Online at http://www.fhwa.dot.gov/innovativeFinance/garguid1.htm.

_____. "A Guide for Hot Lane Development." March 2003. Online at http://www.its.dot.gov/JPODOCS/REPTS_TE/13668.html.

_____. "Portrait of a General: General Roy Stone." Online at http://www.fhwa.dot.gov/infrastructure/stonetoc.cfm.

_____. *Congestion Pricing—A Primer: Overview*. October 2008. Online at http://ops.fhwa.dot.gov/publications/fhwahop08039/cp_prim1_00.htm.

Federal Highway Administration Office of Transportation Policy Studies. "Highways and the Economy." Online at http://www.fhwa.dot.gov/policy/otps/highways.htm.

Jackson, 1st Lt. E.R. "Report on First Transcontinental Motor Convoy." October 31, 1919. U.S. Army, Transport Corps, Transcontinental Convoy: Records, 1919, Box 1. Online at http://www.eisenhower. archives.gov/Research/Digital_Docu ments/1919Convoy/1919documents.html.

Maryland General Assembly. "Transportation Infrastructure Financing Policy — Limitations on GARVEE Bonds" (Senate Bill 75), 2005 session.

Massachusetts Turnpike Authority. Brochure. n.d.

U.S. Bureau of Transportation Statistics. June 2006.

U.S. Congress, Congressional Budget Office. "Study." January 1998.

_____. *Congressional Record.* Nov. 19, 1993.

U.S. Congress, Joint Economic Committee. "Testimony on Congestion Pricing for Highways." May 6, 2003. Online at http://www.cbo.gov/doc.cfm?index=419 7&type=0.

U.S. Department of Transportation. "Design." n.d.

_____. "Fact Sheet." n.d.

U.S. Office of Safety. "Report." Oct. 18, 2005.

Manuscripts

Bankhead family papers. Alabama Archives. Birmingham.

Bankhead Highway Association papers. Alabama Archives. Birmingham.

Bankhead scrapbook. Alabama Archives. Birmingham.

Carl Hayden papers. Arizona State University. Tempe.

Chapin files. Bentley Library. Ann Arbor, Mich.

Diary of O.E. Forsling, sheriff, Kimball Co. (Neb.), 1919.

Joy papers., Bentley Library. Ann Arbor, Mich.

Newspapers

Alliance Review, July 12 and 14, 1919.
Arizona Republican, 1920.
Atlanta Business Chronicle, 2008.
Atlanta Constitution, 1920.
Aurora Beacon News, July 20, 1919.
Austin American Statesman, 1992 and March 1, 2007.
Austin Chronicle, Oct. 6, 2006.
Bedford Gazette, July 4 and 18, 1919.
Berkshire Eagle, Sept. 18, 2006.
Birmingham Argus, 1920.
Bisbee Daily Review, 1920.
Boston Globe, Nov. 23, 2006, and March 2, 2007.
Chambersburg Public Opinion, July 7 and 9, 1919.
Chappell Register, Aug. 7, 1919.
Christian Science Monitor, December 1984; April and May, 1994; and Feb. 16, 2006.
Clinton Herald, June 28 and July 8, 12, 18, 21, 22, and 23, 1919.
Columbus Telegram, Aug. 1, 1919.
Daily Non-Pareil (Council Bluffs), July 25, 1919.
Daily Record (Morristown, N.J.), Nov. 22, 2006.
Daily Texarkana, 1920.
Dallas News, Sept. 28, 2006.
DeKalb Daily Chronicle, July 14 and 21, 1919.
Denison Review, July 23 and 30, 1919.
Delphos Herald, July 14, 15 and 17, 1919.
Deseret Evening News, Aug. 12–16, 19 and 20, 1919.
Dixon Evening Telegraph, July 22, 1919.
El Paso Morning Times, 1920.
Evansville Courier and Press, Oct. 11, 2006.
Ft. Wayne Journal Gazette, July 18, 1919.
Ft. Wayne News and Sentinel, July 17, 1919.
Fremont Evening Tribune, July 30, 1919.
Gothenberg Times, Aug. 6, 1919.
Grand Island Daily Independent, July 31, 1919.
Greensboro (N.C.) *Daily News,*1920.
Greensburg Daily Tribune, July 9 and 11, 1919.
Green River Star, Aug. 15, 1919.
Houston Chronicle, Nov. 8, 2006.
Imperial Valley Press (El Centro), 1920.
Indianapolis Star, Nov. 15, 2006, Feb. 10, 2007.
Joliet Evening Herald News, July 21, 1919.
Keith County News (Ogallala), Aug. 7, 1919.
La Porte Daily Argus, July 19, 1919.
Laramie Boomerang, Aug. 9, 1919.
Lexington Clipper Citizen, Aug. 7, 1919.
Los Angeles Daily Times, 1920.
Lonoke (Arkansas) *Democrat,* 1920.
Mankato (Minnesota) *Free Press,* Dec. 27, 2006.
The New York Times, 1903–2008.
North Platte Evening Telegram, Aug. 1, 1919.
Oakland Enquirer, Sept. 5, 1919.

Ogden Standard, Aug. 12, 15, 16, 17, 18, 19 and 20, 1919.
Oklahoman (Oklahoma City), Dec. 2, 2006.
Omaha World Herald, July 25, 28, 29, and 30, 1919.
Peoria Star, 1916.
Pine Bluff (Arkansas) *Commercial,* Nov. 20, 2006.
Pittsburgh Post, July 11 and 12, 1919.
Pittsburgh Post Gazette, Dec. 2, 12 and 23, 2006; and Jan. 28, 2007.
Pittsburgh Sun, July 11, 1919.
Raleigh Chronicle, Nov. 10, 2006.
Raleigh News and Observer, 1920.
Rawlins Republican, Aug. 14, 1919.
Red Orbit (Aruba), 2006.
Reno Evening Gazette, Aug. 25, 1919.
Sacramento Bee, Dec. 25, 2006.
Salt Lake Tribune, Aug. 15, 17, 20 and 22, 1919.
San Francisco Chronicle, Aug. 25 and Sept. 4, 1919.
Sewickley Herald, July 19, 1919.
Shreveport Times, Jan. 8, 2007.
Sidney Morning Herald, Dec. 28, 2006.
Sidney Telegraph, Aug. 8, 1919.
South Bend Tribune, July 17, 1919, and March 22, 2006.
Stockton Daily Evening Record, Sept. 3–5, 1919.
Sunbury (Massachusetts) *Daily Item,* Nov. 19, 2006.
The Daily Leader (East Palestine), July 9, 10, 12 and 14, 1919.
The Firestone Non-Skid (Akron), July 18, 1919.
The Herald (Mercer County, Pa.), 2006.
The South Reporter (Holly Springs, Miss.), 1920.
Texarkana State Press, 1920.

Tucson Citizen, 1920.
Tuscaloosa News, Dec. 3, 2006.
Valparaiso Daily Messenger, July 8, 17, and 19, 1919.
Walker County (Alabama) *Mountain Eagle, 1922.*
The Washington Post, March 20, 2006.
Western Nebraska Observer (Kimball), Aug. 7 and 14, 1919.
Wooster (Ohio) *Daily News,* July 14, 15 and 16, 1919.
Wooster Daily Republican, July 11, 12 and 15, 1919.
Worcester Telegram, Oct.8, 2006.
Wyoming State Tribune (Cheyenne), Aug. 7, 1919.
Yuma Sun, 1920.

Web Sites

AARoads. "Future Interstates and Potential Interstate Corridors." http://www.inter state-guide.com/future.html.
Brookings Institution. Federal Transportation Reform. http://www.brookings.edu/metro/TransportationSeries/Trans portationReform.aspx.
Hoover's Reports. www.hoovers.com/.
Investopedia. www.investopedia.com/.
Justia.com. U.S. Supreme Court Center, Wilson v. Shaw, 204 U.S. 24 (1907).
Meteorlogix. http://www.dtnmeteorlogix.com/.
Reed Construction Data. "Cintra Zachry." 2006. http://www.reedconstructiondata.com/.
Texas Department of Transportation. http://www.txdot.gov/.
Wright Reports. http://wrightreports.ec next.com/.

Index

Numbers in *bold italics* indicate pages with photographs.

213